W9-AGY-431

LIKE NO OTHER TIME

LIKE NO OTHER TIME

The 107th Congress and the Two Years that Changed America Forever

SENATOR TOM DASCHLE

WITH MICHAEL D'ORSO

CROWN PUBLISHERS / NEW YORK

Published by Crown Publishers, New York, New York.
Member of the Crown Publishing Group, a division of Random House, Inc.

www.randomhouse.com

CROWN is a trademark and the Crown colophon is a registered trademark
of Random House, Inc.

Printed in the United States of America

DESIGN BY LEONARD HENDERSON

Library of Congress Cataloging-in-Publication Data
Daschle, Thomas.
Like no other time : the 107th Congress and the two years that changed
America forever / Senator Tom Daschle, with Michael D'Orso.—1st ed.
1. United States. Congress (107th : 2001–2002) 2. United States—
Politics and government—2001– I. D'Orso, Michael. II. Title.
JK1059107th.D38   2003
328.73'09'0511—dc22   2003016191

ISBN 1-4000-4955-5

10 9 8 7 6 5 4 3 2 1

First Edition

*To my wife, Linda, my mother, my children, and my grandchildren,
without whom none of this would be possible*

IV

Contents

LIKE NO OTHER TIME

Introduction

T HE WIND WAS BLOWING HARD the night of November 5, 2002—election
night—hard and cold, as it tends to do that time of year in South
Dakota. It was late, nearly 2:00 A.M. The cavernous main hall of the
Sheraton Sioux Falls Hotel and Convention Center looked like a morgue.
Eight hours earlier, the room had been filled wall to wall with hundreds of
men, women, and children bursting with excitement and hope, with
visions of victory for our own man from South Dakota, my colleague Tim
Johnson, and of celebration for the Democratic Party across the whole
nation.

Now those hopes lay in ruins. A few dozen faithful lingered around the
auditorium's TV sets, fatigued and in shock, watching the final bad news
trickle in from the West Coast. We still didn't know if Tim might hold
on to his Senate seat, but almost everywhere else—Georgia, Minnesota, Missouri, North Carolina, Texas, South Carolina, Colorado, New
Hampshire—lay a landscape of loss. Flags and banners and a few sad,
sorry balloons dangled limply from the main hall's ceiling. A battery of a
dozen or so TV cameras and light towers arrayed on a platform at the rear
of the room stood dark and untended, their crews off in the hospitality
suites picking at leftover trays of crackers and cold cuts. The Eagles' "One
of These Nights" drifted out from the stage-mounted speakers.

I was up in our sixth-floor suite—my wife Linda's and mine—standing
at the window, looking down at the streetlights of Sioux Falls and out at
the black, flat blankness of the prairie beyond. I was devastated. Numb. I'd
done my best to put on a game face several hours before, when the network anchors—Tom Brokaw, Peter Jennings, Dan Rather, Aaron Brown—
had moved toward the conclusion of their election evening coverage by
each asking me, as I sat miked in a makeshift studio down in one of the
convention center's back rooms, to react to this "sweeping victory" for the
Republicans.

What could I say? How could I begin to describe the heartache I felt for my colleagues who had fallen that day, most of all my dear friend Max Cleland? Max didn't deserve this fate, purely and simply. It was gut-wrenching to watch a war hero victimized by a campaign that questioned his patriotism—this man of such courage and honor, who lost an arm and both legs to a grenade in Vietnam, linked to Saddam Hussein and Osama bin Laden by Republican television ads that questioned his commitment to our nation's security.

All politics *is*, in one way or another, personal, and that night I felt Max Cleland's loss in a deeply personal way. I felt responsible, as the leader of our party, for what had happened to Max. And to Jean Carnahan in Missouri. And to Erskine Bowles in North Carolina. And to Jeanne Shaheen in New Hampshire. And to Tom Strickland in Colorado. And to Walter Mondale in Minnesota.

Minnesota. How to even begin sorting out the swirl of thoughts and emotions about what had transpired there? The shock of Paul Wellstone's death less than two weeks before had not yet faded for any of us—sweet, unyielding Paul, his wife, Sheila, their daughter Marcia, and the five others who lost their lives in that terrible plane crash in the freezing October rain of that gray Minnesota morning.

Had any of us been able to truly and completely grieve that loss? The clock had been ticking toward an election, and it would not slow down, not even for death. A new candidate had to be found. Walter Mondale stepped forward, and under very difficult circumstances, he did his states-manlike best. But it wasn't enough.

For me, this was the end of two of the most grueling years of my life— and the end of two of the most eventful, tragic, and historic years in the life of the United States Senate, if not of the United States itself.

It might seem strange to begin a book about hope and the future with an image of failure and defeat. But I think that's exactly where this book ought to begin. Why? Because we have come to a point in our nation's history where—as individuals and as a society—the spaces that lie between hope and despair, between triumph and disaster, between vision and blindness, or between candor and deceit have never been so minuscule. We have arrived at a time in our culture where the alignment of politics, of power, of ideologies, and of beliefs is arrayed so incredibly evenly that, while the visions and views of one group or another may be a universe apart, only the narrowest of margins separates them.

The result is an unprecedented sense of precariousness. The very parity that we pursue in a society based on a desire for diversity and inclusion has created a climate of instability like never before, a sense that the way things seem at one moment can be turned completely upside down the next.

Look at the last presidential election, with winners and losers stepping forward and then back, in a tense, unprecedented dance that was ultimately ended not by voters, but by judges.

Look at the Senate, split straight down the middle by that same election, for the first time in history, fifty lawmakers on one side and fifty on the other, as fragile and contentious a context for guiding our nation as could possibly be created.

Think of how that structure became rearranged, first by one man changing his mind (Jim Jeffords), then by another man speaking it (Trent Lott).

Think of the heartaching brilliance of a cloudless blue September morning, shattered forever by the televised sight of two silver aircraft plunging soundlessly into those defenseless towers and plunging us all into a new way of seeing ourselves and the world.

Think of it—the wafer-thin shadings that have come to separate those we call friends from those we call foes, the slightest of factors that determine the difference between those who will lead and those who must follow.

The first three years of this new century have been marked by a head-spinning succession of critical turning points for America, one after the other, crucible moments balanced on the edge of a razor, where the slightest shift in the winds of circumstance can alter the course of an entire nation, and one unthinkable blow can transform the fate of the entire planet.

Forty-eight hours after election day 2000, as America was confronting the first contested presidential results in more than a century, I found myself flying to speak in Austin, Texas. I didn't know who the next president would be. With two Senate races still too close to call, I also didn't know whether we Democrats might actually retake the Senate—a possibility almost no one had predicted. I didn't know if I was still the minority leader of the United States Senate or the majority leader.

All I knew for sure as the plane touched down that Thursday evening was that, even with my many close friends who live there, Austin, Texas, was the last place on earth I wanted to be. But there I was, at the Lyndon Johnson Library, speaking to a packed auditorium about the challenges LBJ had faced as the Senate Democratic leader in a situation as tenuous in its own way as the one we were facing at that moment. During the course of the 84th Congress, from 1955 through 1956—a Congress in which Johnson served as a Democratic leader—nine of his Senate colleagues passed away. *Nine!* I was stunned to discover that figure. I was also strangely comforted, which I told the audience in Austin that day. We might be in an unstable situation, I said, but no matter what crises the next Senate may have to weather, there was no way we were going to lose nine senators. Incomprehensible.

What I didn't realize—what none of us could have imagined—was that the events that actually came to pass would be even harder to comprehend.

It was ten months after that address in Austin that I stood at my office window in the U.S. Capitol, looking west past the Washington Monument, across the Potomac, as smoke rose from the Pentagon, blackening the sky over Arlington Cemetery. At that same moment, two hundred miles northwest, a hijacked airliner that many now believe was intended to destroy the building in which I stood crashed in a field near Shanksville, Pennsylvania. Meanwhile, both towers of the World Trade Center in New York were aflame, billowing black smoke, soon to collapse, filled with trapped human souls.

A month after that, in mid-October of 2001, my own Senate office became the site of the largest bioterrorism attack ever on United States soil, when an intern opened a letter that exposed twenty members of my staff to what we would later learn was up to three thousand times the lethal dose of anthrax. The amount of anthrax in that single envelope could have killed every person in the Hart Senate Office Building, which houses the offices of half the U.S. Senate and their staffs.

All of this lay ahead as I stood there in Austin. Two years later, as I stood in that hotel room in Sioux Falls looking out at that bleak, cold night, it all lay behind. And I was consumed by a question: Had the world around us changed so drastically in these monumental two years that the very practice of politics as we had come to know it was altered?

As for this particular election, had I done enough? What might have been done differently? What *should* have been done differently? Had we as the Democratic Party, and I as one of its leaders, lost our way, our vision, our very identity?

Each of these questions would resound for some time to come, and rightfully so. They still resound and are at the heart of the pages that follow. But the question that matters the most, and that tore at me as I stood at that hotel window, is: How, in the wake of this loss, with the Senate now aligned with the Republican House and presidency, could we as Democrats pull together to help lead our nation through the gathering storm of forces propelling our nation toward crises of potentially unimaginable consequences?

This was—and *is*—the question that matters most to America. Because those crises continue to swell, both domestically and abroad, and they will likely have grown even larger by the time these words are published.

Among them are the following:

- A war against terrorism that began with the world community on our side but then, in the ensuing eighteen months, turned much of that community against us, an unclear, unfinished war that began in Afghanistan, then moved to Iraq, and now, as I write these words, could possibly spread to Syria, Iran, or North Korea.

- A plunging American economy, already reeling before the shock of September 11, devastated by that day's horrific events, crippled further by the subsequent revelations of massive corporate corruption, and now set to spiral further downward with a sweepingly dangerous administration tax policy that asks Americans, in the face of an exploding national debt, to believe that rewarding the rich by giving them tax breaks will reverse this economy's downward spiral and better the lot and the lives of the rest of our nation.

- A federal judicial system poised now to be aggressively packed, up through the level of the United States Supreme Court, with men and women whose personal ideologies and agendas are aimed directly at reversing two generations of decisions affecting the freedoms of each and every American, from women's rights to workers' rights to civil rights.

- A fragile environment facing assaults on all fronts with new threats to the quality of our air, water, and land.

During the two years of the 107th Congress—from the presidential election of 2000 to the midterm election of 2002—I led the Democratic Party in the United States Senate as we became the last line of defense against the forces that have pushed these crises forward.

What I firmly believed that night last November, and what I have come to believe even more as time has passed, is that our country is once again at a critical and historic crossroads. Both nationally and internationally, the ramifications could not be greater. Our choices will affect our future in profound ways. And the first choice lies with what kind of representation and leadership we want in government. It is a choice between a political party with a core philosophical belief in the power of our collective will to confront these challenges through its government and one dominated by a group of people who don't like and don't believe in government.

This is what I want to explore in the pages that follow — the incredibly volatile sequence of events that have led, one after another, from the presidential election of 2000 to the present moment, with nothing less than the fate of our nation and that of the entire world now hanging in the balance.

This is like no other time for America. We Americans have always found it within ourselves during such periods of challenge and change to summon the leadership, common sense, and vision to lead our country to new heights, new achievements, and a better life for the generations that follow. More often than not, at such times Americans have found that direction with the help of the vision, values, and policies that come with Democratic leadership. I am confident those values and ideas will continue to help guide us.

As we have done throughout our nation's rich history, we can control and determine the direction in which we are headed, both at home and abroad, but only if we understand how we came to choose that direction to begin with. The past three years, since the election of 2000, have seen an incredible shift in that direction. I've been fortunate to be near the center of that process, to witness that shift.

Let me share what I saw and learned during that time, a time that was truly like no other.

— End of Intro —

– chpt. 1 –

CHAPTER ONE ⟩ *goes to pg. 26 = 20 pgs.*

chpt. 1

Setting the Stage

IT IS HARD TO OVERSTATE the disappointment and, yes, the despair that we—my Democratic colleagues and I—felt the morning after that 2002 election. Never mind the fact that of the seventy-seven million ballots cast across the nation that Tuesday, a scant forty-one thousand (nineteen thousand in New Hampshire and twenty-two thousand in Missouri)—less than ⁵⁄₁₀₀ of 1 percent of the entire vote—determined the difference between our party retaining control of the Senate and the Republicans seizing it. Perception, as they say, is reality, and the perception of this defeat, reflected in newspaper and magazine headlines across the country in the days that followed, was of an unmitigated disaster. The headlines arrayed on that week's newsstands echoed the theme:

IT'S HALLELUJAH TIME IN THE WHITE HOUSE

FOR BUSH AND GOP: A MANDATE

DEMORALIZED DEMS

A NEW LEADER IS NEEDED

The term "shellacked" was used more than once in these reports, and despite the narrowness of the results, that's just how we felt. I knew when I went to bed that election night that I'd awake to a barrage of blame and recrimination that was going to continue for some time, both from outsiders and, more consequentially, from my colleagues within the Democratic Party. And understandably so. I knew we were in for a period of soul-searching and self-flagellation the likes of which few of us had ever experienced. I had doubts and questions myself. As the saying goes,

"Success has a thousand parents; failure is an orphan." The morning after that election, I felt pretty alone.

How had this happened? That question kicked at us all in the wake of this defeat. Everyone, of course—the press, the pundits on radio and television, my colleagues, our opponents—had their own answers and were eager to share them:

- We Democrats "had no message." We "ran without new ideas." This was a "*Seinfeld* election"—it was about nothing.
- We offered "no difference between 'us' and 'them.'" We had become victims of "centrist caution." In the name of political expediency, we had "compromised our party's identity" and become nothing more than "Republican Lite."
- We had "pandered to the Republicans." We had "surrendered on issues of defense and foreign policy." We had "attacked the President's economic policies but offered no real alternative."
- Our campaigns had been marked by "caution, vagueness, niche issues, and sloganeering."
- We had lost our "soul."
- We were "leaderless."

I knew that we needed not to panic. But neither could we deny that the consequences of this defeat, as narrow as it might have been, *were* disastrous, not just for the Democratic Party, but for the American people in terms of where they might now be led. House Democratic Leader Dick Gephardt shared my deep frustration and was shaken by what had transpired.

As Congress returned to Washington in December following the elections, Dick came to visit my personal office in the Hart Building, and we had a good long talk. First, we met with staff to discuss the aftermath of the election and the legislative schedule for the final weeks of the 107th Congress, that period of time traditionally known as a "lame duck" session. Then, at the end of the meeting, Dick asked if staff could be excused so that he and I could talk privately. As we sat alone, we talked again about our disappointment with the election and our need to regroup and move forward. Dick then said that he had come to the conclusion that for him the way to move forward was to move on—and, hopefully, up. He told me he intended to give up his House leadership role and run for president.

I knew how frustrated Dick was with the way things had gone in the House, and I felt terrible for him. He was a terrific partner during our years guiding the Democratic leadership in Congress. Our offices occasionally acted as rivals, but each legislative challenge and each passing year cemented the friendship that Dick and I had built. He worked incredibly hard yet never got the gratitude and appreciation he deserved, largely because he had to lead the House Democrats from under the heavy thumb of the House Republicans during his entire time as leader. I hope history will recognize Dick's service more than many of his colleagues in Washington did.

As for seeking the presidency, I told him that I, too, was weighing that same decision. If the political challenge we faced as Democrats was to truly help the people who we felt were being left out and left behind by this administration, the question was which would be the more effective role . . . that of caucus leader or presidential candidate. I told him that I would make my decision within the next few weeks.

We talked for a few more minutes, and then there was a long pause, nothing but silence as we sat across from each other in the quiet confines of my office, with its high ceilings and Native American art, the winter sun shining through the tall windows. For the first time, we were confronting the possibility that we could soon find ourselves adversaries—a prospect neither of us would relish.

Dick broke the silence. "Whatever you decide," he said, "you will always be my friend."

I looked back at him and replied, "We've been through a lot together. You'll always be my friend, too."

We gave each other a big hug. Then he turned without another word and left the room.

I knew that I had to make my own decision soon—certainly within the following few weeks. And losing the majority complicated things significantly. Had we strengthened, or even just held on to, the majority, I would have felt more confident about turning over the reins of responsibility. But now I had to make the decision about running for president with a caucus in the same minority position in which I found it when I became leader in 1994.

For the first week or two after the election, Republicans and the conservative press pointed gleefully to the results as evidence of my failure as a leader. More editorials than I can count were written that blamed my "obstructionist" tactics for our defeat. Whatever path my future would take, I felt strongly that as a party we needed to bounce back quickly. Yet while my mind was resolved about what had to be done, my body language apparently exposed a deeper disappointment than I realized—at least according to some of my friends and staff.

Some said it was even reflected occasionally in my wardrobe. That fact provided a moment of comic relief in one of the first press conferences I held after I returned to Washington. In the months leading up to the election, Linda and I had become grandparents—twice. There really is no experience in life quite as miraculous and gratifying as becoming a grandparent. The joy of seeing your children so happy, of watching a new person enter the world as an extension of your flesh and blood, is truly one of the great blessings of life. And we were blessed not once, but twice in the same year. On this particular December morning, with the press conference scheduled for that day, Linda and I went to an early morning family photo session at a local studio to show off the two new grandbabies. The photographer told me to wear contrasting colors for the shoot, so I brought a black shirt and a white one. While taking the pictures, our three-week-old granddaughter, Ava, relieved herself on my white shirt. Just before the press conference, I changed into the black—dark mourning black. As I entered the room, the first question from one of the reporters seated around the conference table was, "What are you trying to tell us with that shirt?" That got a good laugh.

Subconsciously or not, that shirt did reflect my mood, so you can imagine the gratitude I felt when Robert Byrd, a former Democratic leader himself, who had served as both minority and majority leader during his more than half a century in Congress, stood up in our first caucus meeting after the election and asked unanimous consent that I be reelected leader by acclamation. The response was a standing ovation. Harry Reid, our assistant Democratic leader, then asked, "What about *me*?" Everyone laughed. I said that was the shortest nominating speech on record. Harry was then reelected the same way, as was Barbara Mikulski, our caucus secretary, and then our entire leadership team.

Gratifying as that display of support was, it did not alter the fact that within our caucus a heated debate had begun that was echoed by pundits across the nation—namely, whether it was time for our Democratic Party to move back to the "Left," to reclaim the liberal roots from which we had steadily drifted away over the course of the past three decades, or whether we needed to move even more toward the "center" to break the partisan gridlock in Washington that so much of the American public rightfully detests.

On the one side—the liberal, progressive side—were voices urging that it was time to "stop accommodating," to "take a stand," to "reclaim our identity," to become "an opposition party worthy of the name." Dick Durbin, one of the most articulate members of our caucus, argued that we needed to define ourselves more effectively and forcefully with a stronger message and more aggressive legislative strategy. Paul Wellstone's name and the memory of his firebrand liberalism were intoned more than once in these discussions.

On the other side—the moderate side—were the voices warning that we must "face reality," that with so many tightly contested elections in a contemporary political landscape as evenly divided as we now face in America, where victory or defeat depends on a tiny percentage of "swing" voters, we can't afford to alienate those precious few voters by taking "extreme" positions. Proponents of this argument—Evan Bayh, Tom Carper, Ben Nelson—urged that we needed to try even harder to compete with the administration for the swing voters by striving more effectively for bipartisan compromise with the administration.

I had my own thoughts even then about this argument. But it wasn't time for me to speak—not yet. In these first meetings after the election, my job was to listen to what those around me had to say. And to think hard about how we had come to this critical juncture. This meant analyzing, scrutinizing, and trying hard to understand the tumultuous events of the preceding two years. Beyond that, it meant examining the path that our national politics has traveled over the course of the past *thirty* years, since the time I first entered politics in 1972—a year that many, including me, consider a watershed in modern American politics, the year the Democratic Party began seeking a new identity.

It was this search for identity that has been the subject of so much internal debate within our party these past three decades. It has had a profound effect on our decisions on both leadership and issues. That has, in turn, affected my own leadership role and the issues we have faced. And it all began in 1972.

That was the year my dear friend George McGovern ran for president. For the Democratic Party, that election was a painful loss. An outspoken champion of liberalism and progressive politics, George was defeated by Richard Nixon in a Republican landslide that was considered by some to be a definitive verdict against the aggressive 1960s liberalism of John F. Kennedy's New Frontier and Lyndon Johnson's Great Society.

I worked as one of George's volunteers on that campaign—my first involvement in national politics. At the time, I was an Air Force intelligence officer stationed at Offutt Air Force Base in Nebraska. By night, I volunteered to help run the Omaha office of the McGovern campaign. It was a combination that gave me a window into two worlds.

As that election unfolded, I could see what was happening. We could all see. The sense of excitement, hope, and optimism that had swept up so many of us in the wave of social movements and their legislative manifestations that washed over America in the early to mid-1960s—the Civil Rights Act, the Voting Rights Act, the War on Poverty, Medicaid, Medicare, the Clean Air Act, the Peace Corps, and so many more—had, by the end of that decade, given way to the anguish and confusion of the war in Vietnam, chaos on college campuses, the assassinations of Martin Luther King Jr. and Bobby Kennedy, race riots in our cities, the lunacy of the 1968 Democratic Convention in Chicago.

The center, as the poem by W. B. Yeats puts it, was not holding. Anyone who was not there at that time in America and did not experience this social tumult directly can't appreciate how very real it all was, how alarmingly close our society seemed to be to coming apart at the seams, especially to conservatives, who blamed the social chaos on the Democrats, the liberals, and the anarchic energy unleashed by all those federally supported movements.

So Nixon and an emerging core of right-wing Republicans stepped in to stop the bleeding. "Law and order" was their battle cry, and a frightened, roiling nation responded. They labeled the Democrats as the party of high taxes and anti-Americanism, and the label stuck. "Never again," these conservatives said, drawing a line in the sand to separate themselves from the forces that had, in their view, nearly brought down our society. This was a historical moment. Because from that point forward, "liberal" became a dirty word, one even most Democrats came to avoid.

It hadn't, of course, always been so. The Roosevelts—both Theodore and Franklin—had drawn their own lines in the sand back in the 1920s and 1930s, aggressively creating government programs and institutions to respond in an unprecedented way to the needs of the American people. In the process, they established "liberalism" as a near religion. Teddy Roosevelt—a Republican—did it in the name of our land, creating the network of national parks that today still protects our most treasured public lands. FDR, of course, stepped in with the New Deal, the sweeping range of federal programs that helped lift America out of the depths of the Great Depression and carried us through World War II and beyond. In a 1941 speech, Franklin Roosevelt offered as succinct a definition of the difference between liberals and conservatives as I've ever seen—a definition that is as accurate today as it was at that time.

Liberals, he said, believe that "as new conditions and problems arise beyond the power of men and women to meet as individuals, it becomes the duty of government itself to find new remedies with which to meet them."

Conservatives, he continued, believe that "there is no necessity for the government to step in."

From FDR in the 1930s straight through to LBJ in the 1960s—with the brief exception of the somnolent Eisenhower administration—liberalism guided the way in Washington and "conservative" was the term that most politicians, even Republicans, avoided. Barry Goldwater, in his 1964 campaign for the presidency, with the civil rights movement cresting in the South and with the Vietnam War protest movement just around the corner, became the first Republican in modern times to stand on a national stage and proudly wave the conservative label with defiance. Goldwater didn't win, but he inspired a new generation of Republican warriors to carry that banner forward, including a young Ronald Reagan, who brought down the house at the 1964 Republican convention with his fiery nominating speech for Goldwater—the same basic speech, more or less, on which Reagan built his career for the next twenty years.

Government, Reagan liked to say, is the problem, not the solution. That, even more precisely than FDR's definition, sums up the difference between the Republican and Democratic ideologies that have evolved in the past thirty years, the schism that separates two divergent views in American politics.

On one side, the Republican side, is the belief that government should stay out of people's lives as much as possible. The individual, they say, should be empowered to make the decisions that guide his own life, not government agencies or judicial bodies. Paramount among those decisions, the argument goes, should be the individual's freedom to decide how his (or her) own money is spent. This is how the Republicans justify the tax cuts they so zealously pursue. "It's your money," they say, which is a fine proposition on the face of it. If only it were that simple.

Democrats, too, believe that it's "your money." But they also believe in community, in collective as well as individual strength, in the idea of people pitching in together to help one another, with the united faith that a rising tide lifts all boats. The vehicle that most efficiently allows us to collectively help one another, Democrats believe, is the government.

There's a wonderful film called *The Straight Story*, directed by David Lynch, that contains a perfect metaphor for the difference I'm talking about. Lynch, of course, is best known for his somewhat surreal, off-center work, such as *Twin Peaks* and *Blue Velvet*. *The Straight Story* is a departure for him, a beautiful true story about an elderly man coming to terms with the end of his life by making a pilgrimage on a riding lawn mower to visit his estranged brother two states away.

During the journey, the man encounters a young woman who emerges from the woods and joins him by his campfire. She's on a pilgrimage, too, trying to figure out what her own life's about. At one point in their conversation, the old man picks up a stick and breaks it in two. "That's a person on their own, by themselves," he tells her. Then he picks up a bundle of sticks and asks her to try breaking them. She can't. "That's family," he says.

That's what Democrats believe. We are stronger together than alone. I like that parable because it so clearly illustrates something that, growing up in South Dakota, I came to feel intuitively. South Dakota was settled as a result of the Homestead Act. That act was our government's bold experiment to trade public lands for hard work and the promise of opportunity. Many South Dakotans are grandchildren and great-grandchildren of homesteaders. My own grandparents were German farmers who immigrated to South Dakota because of the promise of free land. My grandparents and those who undertook the journey with them worked hard. It is no exaggeration to say that they were some of the most self-reliant people in the world. But they also understood that no matter how hard they worked, there were some essential things they couldn't do by themselves. It took neighbors working together to raise the barns, clear the land, and plant the crops. It took communities to build schools and hire teachers. It took everyone in small towns, working together, to weather storms and clean up after floods. Their politics were dictated by one thing—the desire to harvest a living and build a future on the harsh plains. So they came to believe deeply in the principles underlying the Homestead Act's social bargain—the same principles at the core of the Democratic Party—that collective action is sometimes a necessary complement to individual effort.

Put another way, by gathering our "sticks," by pooling our resources in the form of taxes, Democrats believe that we can and we should, through the wise and efficient administration of government, provide *all* Americans, not just those who can afford it, with quality education, decent health care, the sense of security that comes from well-trained, well-funded, and wisely directed police and military forces, and a host of other government-directed community services aimed at enabling every American man, woman, and child to fulfill his or her individual potential as he or she pursues that blessed trinity of the American dream: life, liberty, and the pursuit of happiness.

I don't want this to sound like a boilerplate political speech. But there is no other way to describe the rift that has come to separate these two views of government, these two views of *America*. The philosophy of the Republican leadership in Washington, as it has sharpened itself over the past thirty years, has become a form of social Darwinism, survival of the fittest. In the name of empowering the individual, the Republicans' purpose is to consolidate power in the hands of the few who already have it while disassembling the one institution that protects and pursues the interests of *all* Americans, including the powerless.

That institution, of course, is the government.

It's more than ironic that Richard Nixon, who launched the modern conservative backlash against the "liberal welfare" state with his opposition to taxes, government spending, government regulation, and government enforcement of civil rights, unintentionally deepened the public's mistrust and suspicion of government even further with his involvement in the Watergate scandal and his subsequent resignation from office. By the end of the 1970s, a new generation of conservative soldiers, under their own "commander in chief," Ronald Reagan, had taken the Republican stage. In the early 1980s a group of House members that included Dick Cheney, Trent Lott, Tom DeLay, Dick Armey, and Newt Gingrich formed a caucus with a revealing title: the Conservative Opportunity Society.

Opportunistic indeed. Seizing on the growing anxieties and fears aroused by the cold war, coupled with the now decade-old anti–"big government" backlash still running strong through American society, Gingrich tossed aside all remaining restraint and declared open warfare against the Democrats. Up to that point, even with the strong feelings that divided the two sides of the political arena in America, a sense of decency and decorum still ruled the public debate. But no more. The tactics of these Gingrich-led "new" Republicans were to confront and to demonize. Our differences, according to them, were no longer political. They were *moral.* We Democrats were not only wrong or misguided, now we were "evil." The crass, stigmatizing language used by Newt Gingrich and his lieutenants in their public discourse was unprecedented in American politics. Democrats were, according to Gingrich, "corrupt," "loony," "stupid," and "traitors." We were, according to him, "the party of total hedonism, total exhibitionism, total bizarreness, total weirdness."

Does this kind of language sound familiar? It's no coincidence that the ascent of Rush Limbaugh and his combative brand of right-wing "talk radio" programming coincided with the rise of Newt Gingrich and this new strain of Republicanism. Gingrich's strategy of vicious, bombastic demonizing was taken directly to the airwaves by Limbaugh, whose diatribes against "Commie libs," "feminazis," and "environmental wackos" gained him, by the end of the 1980s, a national audience.

Conflict sells—at least for a while. Gingrich realized this. Limbaugh did, too. Their reaction to the very real, very understandable, and very justifiable anxieties and confusion that gripped and divided our nation in the wake of the upheavals of the 1960s, coupled with the fears created by the shifting cold war international landscape of the 1980s, was to *exploit* those fears for their own gain. In Gingrich's case, there was the political power that he and his party could gather. For Limbaugh, there was the audience, the advertising (how many serious political commentators shamelessly hawk their sponsors' products during commercial breaks?), and the personal profit he could accrue.

There was, during this same period, a Democratic response as well to the climate of the times, an effort to address the cultural gap that had come to divide America right and left. Rather than exploit this gap, however, many in our party chose to try bridging it.

That bridge was a "third way," as it was called. Not right. Not left. But something else, a third position that was often also described as "center-out." Rather than to move from the Left or the Right to obtain the necessary majority, the idea was to start in the center and move in both directions in search of a majority and common ground.

Many of the national leaders of the eighties and nineties began their careers as leaders of the Democratic Leadership Council (DLC). Al Gore was one of the founding members, and Dick Gephardt was its first chairman. Bill Clinton followed shortly thereafter. So did Joe Lieberman.

There was a brief attempt among the more liberal arm of our party, led by Howard Metzenbaum, to create a "countergroup," as it were—the Coalition for Democratic Values. But that effort withered away almost immediately, and by the turn of the 1990s, the "centrist" DLC philosophy had become the dominant ethos of our party. Bill Clinton's presidential victory in 1992 came in no small part from his ability to avoid the "liberal" label while maintaining the Democratic Party belief in the active role of government to better the lives of Americans.

Gingrich and his crowd hated Clinton. There is no other term for it. They detested him politically. They detested him personally. And to them, there was no difference between the two. I'm not the first person to observe that Gingrich's 1994 Contract with America, which swept him and his Republican colleagues into control of the House and the Senate, turned out to be little more than a "Contract on Clinton." Given control of Congress, the Republican leadership chose politics over policy. Rather than constructing effective responses to the needs of the American people, they directed almost all of their energy and resources toward attacking Bill Clinton. These attacks reached their climax with the 1999 impeachment and trial of the President.

As minority leader of the Senate during that trial, I realized, as did the majority leader at that time, Trent Lott, that the very fabric of our nation might be torn beyond repair if the Senate proceedings degenerated into the same spectacle seen in the House. The well-being of our society, Trent and I both agreed, was far more important than a political victory for one side or the other.

But the "war" did not end with Clinton's acquittal. Far from it. In fact, the battle lines became drawn even more sharply, with both armies, as it were, gathering on each side of the nation's political divide, facing each other in almost identical size—virtually a "fifty-fifty" America.

There were the American voters themselves, divided so evenly among the loyal Republican and the loyal Democrat "bases" that elections could now well be expected to ride on a single percentage point or two—on the thin sliver of "swing" votes that remained among the few voters who hadn't quite made up their minds.

As the election of 2000 approached, the presidential race between Al Gore and George W. Bush sized up as just that—an extremely close contest, with perhaps no more than a point or two deciding the difference at the end.

That contest turned out, of course, to be even closer than that. But what no one foresaw, and what set the stage for the unprecedented events of the following two years, were the results of that same fall's United States Senate elections.

No one imagined, no one was even really paying attention to, before that election, the possibility that the advantage the Republican Senate enjoyed going into that November—fifty-five to forty-five seats—might be erased. Among those forty-five seats we did hold, three were vacated by the retirement of three of our most distinguished members—Pat Moynihan,

Bob Kerrey, and Frank Lautenberg. So things did not look good for us, to say the least.

By the end of that election night, however, we had shocked everyone, including ourselves, with seven challengers winning seats (Hillary Clinton, Tom Carper, Jon Corzine, Bill Nelson, Ben Nelson, Mark Dayton, and Jean Carnahan) and two more challengers (Debbie Stabenow in Michigan and Maria Cantwell in Washington) locked in "too close to call" races. Recounts lay ahead for both Stabenow and Cantwell. If both were to win, the Senate would be split fifty-fifty for the first time in history. As much as election night 2002 would be fraught with a definitive loss and the disappointment that came with it, election night 2000 was filled with confusion and hope. As returns continued to trickle in, and the prospect of an evenly divided Senate came into focus, a member of my staff turned to me and said, "It looks like *you* might be the big winner tonight."

At that point, with just the *possibility* that this historic face-off might occur, we—our Democratic leadership—began playing out the scenarios. If the presidential election was pushed to a recount (as, of course, it eventually was), there was a likelihood that the decision might ultimately have to be resolved in Congress—which, if things wound up in an evenly divided Senate, would create a very interesting situation indeed.

Some observers began immediately wringing their hands at the possibility of the presidential election being decided by Congress, calling such a resolution of a contested election a "constitutional crisis"—which it was not. It would be an extremely unusual situation, no doubt, but like almost everything else our government is faced with, if you look back through history, you'll find that we've faced it before.

In this case, it had happened twice, first in 1800, then again in 1876.

The 1800 presidential election between Thomas Jefferson and Aaron Burr ended with both men receiving seventy-three electoral votes (there was no popular vote at that time). That left it to the House of Representatives to choose one man or the other. On the second floor of the Capitol today, across from the old Senate chamber, is the original House chamber. A plaque on the wall outside that room tells the story:

For over three months after that election, the nation teetered on the verge of this crisis, not knowing who would be president. The House convened on February 11, 1801, and over the next six days, they voted twenty-five times. Every vote ended in a tie. Finally, on the thirty-sixth ballot, the tie was broken and Jefferson was named the third president of the United States. In the end, there was no lasting damage to anyone except Alexander Hamilton. While the House was casting all those ballots, Hamilton worked feverishly behind the scenes to persuade his fellow Federalists to support Jefferson, whom Hamilton didn't particularly care for but whom he preferred to Burr (whom he abhorred). Four years later, in their legendary duel, Burr shot and killed Hamilton, whose campaigning during those House votes on that 1800 decision certainly hadn't helped their relationship.

That was America's first experience with a contested presidential election. Seventy-six years later, another disputed presidential contest posed an even greater risk to the nation. The candidates in this case were Samuel Tilden and Rutherford Hayes. On election night, the *New York Tribune*'s special edition banner headline declared Tilden the winner. He *had* won the popular vote. But neither candidate had enough electoral votes to claim the White House. The problem lay in the returns from three southern states: Louisiana, South Carolina, and Florida. All three states had conflicting sets of ballots, one certified by their state governments, which were still sympathetic to the Confederacy (this was roughly a decade after the end of the Civil War), and the other certified by the Reconstructionist governments set up in each of these states by Washington. When Congress convened in December, it faced a crisis: Which sets of ballots should they count? Republicans chose the Reconstructionist sets; Democrats insisted on the others.

The argument continued until February, when the Louisiana and South Carolina results were finally settled. But Florida (yes, *Florida*) remained unresolved. Unable to work out which sets of ballots to count, the parties created a bipartisan commission composed of selected House and Senate members along with five Supreme Court justices (yes, here too we had the Supreme Court weighing in on the final decision) to settle the issue. The Republican-majority commission chose Hayes, which enraged Tilden's Democrats, who refused to accept the decision. They called for a one-hundred-thousand-person protest march on Washington. Their Speaker of the House drafted—but never introduced—a bill to make the secretary of state president until another election could be held. Tensions were so high, there was genuine concern that another Civil War might erupt.

21,

It wasn't until several weeks later that a settlement was finally reached. Democrats agreed to accept Hayes as president if he would order the withdrawal of federal troops from these three contested southern states and provide federal economic aid to help them rebuild from the ruins of the war. The Republicans agreed, and Hayes was declared president.

Believe me, we pored over the details of those two elections in the wake of the 2000 returns, preparing for the possibility that we might be put in the position of deciding the Gore-Bush decision ourselves. Beyond that, the ramifications for our newly balanced Senate—if it did indeed wind up fifty-fifty—would be immediate if Gore was declared the winner. That would make Joe Lieberman the vice president, requiring Lieberman to step down from his Connecticut Senate seat, which would then be filled by an appointee of Connecticut's governor—who happened to be a Republican. In other words, a win by Gore would tip the scales of the Senate back to the Republicans, fifty-one to forty-nine.

It was a problem that would have paled in comparison with the one we face now . . . a Bush presidency.

I have to say I didn't know much about George Bush personally at that time. I was certainly going to get to know him in the years to come, but at that point I hadn't seen much more of him than had most Americans— mostly on television. I'd seen Bush make speeches, I'd watched the debates, and in one sense I was amazed that we'd even reached this point—Al Gore's breadth and depth of knowledge, his experience, his grasp of the issues were clearly superior. But people *liked* Bush. At a time when the economy was going gangbusters and terror had not become a part of the national consciousness, people had the luxury of voting for someone they liked. Even with that, the American voters wound up choosing Al Gore's ideas over George Bush's personality by a margin of half a million popular votes.

It was fascinating to watch the nation fixate on this historic presidential deadlock while the fate of the Senate, which hung in the same kind of limbo, went largely unnoticed by most of the American public. We took to calling it a "shadow" election, flying under the radar of the nation's attention. When Debbie Stabenow was declared the winner in Michigan on November 8, that left Maria Cantwell's still undecided recount against

Slade Gorton in Washington as the last step of our unlikely climb toward fifty Senate seats.

While the country was focused day after day on the Bush-Gore developments, we were zeroed in on Maria. Several times each day, we checked in with our people on the ground in Washington State, getting reports from each precinct on the progress of the recounts, which, like the presidential recount in Florida, shifted up or down by the hour. Several times it looked as though it were over, as though we'd lost. At one point Maria was behind by 14,916 votes, a huge number in these circumstances, but my political staff ran their computer models on the precincts that had not yet reported their recounts—largely Native American precincts—and those numbers indicated that Maria could still possibly pull off a win.

That Maria was even in position to win was, quite frankly, remarkable. She was running against a strong incumbent in Gorton. But Gorton made a serious mistake by underestimating the importance of the Native American vote, and that wound up costing him his Senate seat.

I know something about Native American politics, having spent my life in South Dakota and having spent my political career working with and learning to understand the lives and cultures of the tribes in our state—the Lakota, Nakota, and Dakota Sioux. There has been a significant surge in recent years in political engagement and involvement among these tribes at all levels—local, state, and federal—that has been both heartening and riveting to witness. It's also something no politician can afford to ignore, because it's not just happening in South Dakota—it's happening all over America.

Maria Cantwell understood these dynamics. I don't think Slade Gorton did. He was openly scornful of many of the Native Americans' concerns and stands on several key issues in Washington State. In the end, that cost him his seat in the Senate. When that race's recount was finally finished on December 1, Maria came out the winner, as my political staff had predicted . . . by 2,229 votes. And, as those predictions had indicated, the votes that put Maria over the top turned out to be largely Native American.

The day the Cantwell victory was announced, Harry Reid, noticing the absence of reporters and camera crews, said to me, "This was a victory as significant as it was quiet." And he was so right. "Nobody saw this coming," he added. Including, it turned out, Trent Lott.

Linda and I often go to her parents' home in Oklahoma for Thanksgiving, which is where I was when I finally got Trent on the phone following Maria's win in Washington. Trent had, of course, been following that race as closely as I. But where my days had been driven by excitement and hope, Trent had been living in trepidation. Now, with the results final, he couldn't accept it.

When I first managed to reach him after the Senate officially became fifty-fifty, Trent could hardly finish a sentence. He was in shock. It was simply too soon for him to accept the fact that his world—his position as Senate majority leader—had just been turned upside down.

It would turn out to be several weeks before Trent finally acknowledged what had occurred. Meanwhile, we continued to have conversations—in person, by telephone, by fax—about the historic situation we were now facing. I tried gently to introduce him to the reality that, like it or not, this was going to have to be a partnership. The phrase "power sharing" was hard for Trent to even utter. But that's what we were confronted with as we moved toward the end of that year. Several times over the course of the ensuing weeks, Trent admitted privately what he and the Republican leadership were facing. "We're in denial," he told me.

"Well," I told him, "at some point you and I are going to have to figure out how we're going to deal with this."

Meanwhile, I was free to turn to the still unanswered question of who our next president would be.

From the beginning, many of us felt as if Al Gore had been cheated in Florida. We were shocked and dismayed by the circus atmosphere surrounding the recount. Watching the television coverage of what was happening in Florida deepened my determination to see that there was a fair count of the votes. I indicated to the Gore campaign that I would be available to come to Florida should they find any need.

It was a Sunday afternoon when I got a call from Al asking if I would be willing to go down there with Dick Gephardt to show that the Democratic leaders in Congress were united behind Al in this effort. I told him I would be happy to go. When would he need me? "Tomorrow," he answered.

I don't think I've ever seen anything that compares to the media frenzy we flew into that day in Tallahassee. It was incredible. There must have been a hundred television cameras not just from all across the country, but from all over the world.

One of the images the Gore people wanted was of Dick and me reporting from the scene in Florida to the Vice President, who was in Washington. Given the passion that surrounded the situation, it didn't feel quite right to me to have us sitting at a speakerphone, gamely telling Al Gore that the vote counts were incomplete and that we were going to make sure every vote was counted, which is what the Gore camp asked us to do. I was concerned that the whole thing looked and felt staged, and that fear was confirmed by virtually everybody who saw that conversation broadcast live on television. In the middle of a state simmering with anger and tension, at the end of a hotly contested election, it seemed worse than awkward to have two congressional leaders addressing the disembodied voices of Al Gore and Joe Lieberman. And it was.

After that unfortunate experience, we went to the Gore recount headquarters, where Dick and I made statements to the media and answered questions.

"This is not over with until the votes are counted," I told the roomful of reporters.

That was about as simple and clear as I could put it. It was the same message I carried with me wherever I went over the next two weeks, including an eye-opening, somewhat disturbing trip back home to South Dakota, where I had been invited by the Rapid City Chamber of Commerce to give a speech.

Understand that this was my home territory. The crowd was largely Republican, but I'm used to that. The majority of South Dakotans are conservatives. But in South Dakota, as in many states with smaller populations, people form their judgment of their elected leaders on a more personal basis. Most have met their representatives or candidates, or at least have been able to hear them speak in person. Many have directly asked for and received help. There is a truly personal connection, and as a result, philosophy or political labels have secondary importance. You can see that in the type of relationship I have with South Dakota's former governor and current congressman, Bill Janklow. He may be a staunch

Republican, but he and I are good friends and have always been able to work together.

This is one of the reasons, I think, that I've never faced much hostility when I go home, not even in the staunchest Republican strongholds. Which is why I was shocked by what I encountered in Rapid City that day. Outside the hotel where I was to speak, there was a massive anti-Gore and anti-*Daschle* demonstration. This was the first time in my life this had ever happened to me. People pushing in from all sides. Angry faces shouting and waving signs and placards. I realized this was not just something happening down in Florida. The intensity and emotions that had seized this election had swept into every nook and cranny of our nation—including South Dakota, where it had come home in a profound, palpable way. These people had seen my phone conversation with Al on television—and they didn't like it one bit.

It was such a surreal contrast to make my way through that crowd, then walk into the hotel and be greeted by warm smiles and a standing ovation from the audience I had come to address. That experience still resonated for me two weeks later, when Al Gore announced his decision to concede.

To this day there are many opinions and heated debates about whether Al Gore made the right decision. There are those who say he abandoned the people who had voted for him, the people he represented, the actual majority of the people who voted in that election. There are those who feel that he should have seen this fight through to the bitter end, in the name of those millions of Americans who had given him the popular vote victory.

But there was something else at stake here, something larger than the presidency itself, and it's something that brings us back to that fundamental difference between the Democratic and Republican belief systems. If this fight had been taken to its conclusion, whoever the victor, political chaos unlike anything we've ever seen would have ensued. This was not unlike the situation we faced with the impeachment of Bill Clinton. The very stability of our government and of the public's faith in that government was at stake here, and Al Gore understood that. The acrimony over this issue, which was mounting exponentially by mid-December—six weeks after the election—would only have gotten worse if that battle had continued. So Gore decided, in the better interests of the nation, to call an end to it.

Tom Friedman, one of my favorite columnists in the *New York Times,* wrote a column in the wake of this decision that I'll never forget. Friedman likened Al Gore's decision to taking a political bullet in order to save his country. And I think that's exactly what happened. Gore could have dragged this thing out, which, if the roles had been reversed, is exactly what Tom DeLay and his crowd would have advocated. They would have fought to the bitter end, using every tactic possible, with no concern for the damage it might do to our institutional framework.

Al Gore announced his decision on December 14. A week and a half later, on Christmas Eve day, a fax came over my machine at home. It was from Trent Lott. It simply said, "The election is over. It's time to go to work. Let's work this out soon. Have a Merry Christmas!"

I couldn't have asked for a nicer Christmas gift or a better bounce into the new year. We were now ready to begin the 107th Congress.

- Chpt. 2 -

CHAPTER TWO *goes to pg. 43 = 17 pgs.*

Chpt 2

Sharing Power

TWO OF THE FINER MEN I'VE MET during my years in the U.S. Senate are Dick Baker and Don Ritchie, who together run the Office of the Senate Historian. I've always had a fascination with history, and when I came to the Senate in 1986, I wanted to learn everything I could about its past. I still do, and whenever I have a question, I ask either Dick or Don, who invariably have, or can dig up, the answer.

The Senate, amazingly enough, had no historical office until 1975. When one was created that year, Dick and Don were hired as its first historian and associate historian, respectively. They still hold those positions today, a reassuring testament to permanence and continuity in an institution so filled with transformation and flux.

Don likes to refer to the Senate as a "club," and he's certainly right about that, at least when you compare it to the House of Representatives. The numerical differences alone—435 members in the House, who each face an election every two years, versus 100 members of the Senate, who run only once every six—is enough in itself to make it much more difficult in the House to develop the long-term relationships among members both within and between parties that one finds in the Senate.

But that said, I'm afraid the Senate is nowhere near the "club" it was when I joined it seventeen years ago. And even then it was a world away from what it was back in the Lyndon Johnson 1950s or the Mike Mansfield 1960s, when senators actually stayed in Washington over the weekends and socialized with one another rather than flying back to their home states or some other out-of-town location.

Today, those weekend travels are part of the job. They're necessary in order to keep in touch with the people we represent—a positive development—or to raise money for the enormous costs of modern campaigns—a negative one. Not only has the money chase become a significant factor in our lives (it's not uncommon for me to attend two or three political events in a single evening), but the polarization and partisanship that has grown between the parties has also taken its toll.

I'm not suggesting that there hasn't always been a degree of polarization, partisanship, and even open violence throughout the history of our "club." Look at the duel between Burr and Hamilton. Or the caning of Massachusetts's Charles Sumner on the floor of the Senate in 1856, a nasty bit of business aroused by the passions preceding the Civil War. Sumner was beaten so badly by South Carolina representative Preston Brooks—pounded bloody and senseless—that it took him three years to recover from his injuries and return to his Senate seat, and he never was the same man after that. "Bleeding Sumner" became a rallying cry for the northern abolitionists as the war clouds of the late 1850s gathered.

We haven't seen that kind of combat on the Senate floor in a long time, but there's more animosity and more distance between the parties today than I'd like to see—more distance, I mean, between the individuals not just as politicians, but as *people.*

Back in the 1950s, when Lyndon Baines Johnson was Senate majority leader, partisanship often took a backseat to collegiality, at least behind closed doors. At about four every afternoon, when the day's votes were winding up, senators from both sides of the aisle would drop by the leader's suite, grab a drink from a small bar set up in the corner of what is now my personal office, then sit around and play cards well into the evening. Arguments over everything from appropriations for home state projects to larger national issues made way for deal making and card dealing.

Even twenty years ago, cross-party friendships were much more common in Congress than they are today. When Tip O'Neill was Speaker in the 1980s, he and then House minority leader Bob Michel used to play golf together regularly. Michel was also close to Dan Rostenkowski, the powerful Democratic chairman of the House Ways and Means Committee. There's even a story that as young representatives in the 1960s, these two future congressional heavyweights would drive home to Chicago each weekend in a station wagon with a mattress in the back. One man would drive while the other slept.

Chpt. 2 (cont)

29

In the Senate today, there still are a few of these cross-party relationships. John Breaux and Trent Lott have had a personal friendship for years. So have Danny Inouye and Ted Stevens. But those kinds of friendships are not encouraged by the core leadership that runs the Republican Party—Tom DeLay and his colleagues. In fact, they're distinctly discouraged. Bob Michel was driven from his leadership position and into premature retirement by Newt Gingrich and his band of doctrinaire followers. Nearly a decade later, part of the undercurrent that eventually led to Trent Lott's downfall as Republican leader was the fact that he was seen by some of the more extreme elements in their leadership as being too "friendly" and too "accommodating" to me and some of the people on "our side."

This is one of several fundamental differences between our parties, at least here in Washington, these days. There is sometimes an element of coercion and fear used by certain Republican leadership that just doesn't exist on our side. It is often reported that House Majority Leader Tom DeLay possesses the power he does by taking such a heavy-handed approach to leadership. I wonder why the people around him don't just rise up and revolt. But then I recall what one Republican House member told me: "They rule by fear and intimidation, and punish those who disagree."

That is not the Democratic way. We've chosen to lead by consensus rather than fear, even if it's sometimes harder to build consensus than to issue a dictate.

These differences are significant, because they reflect an attitude that extends to the way we—the Democrats and the Republicans—view society and the legislation we promote. The Republican rigidity, the strict sense of hierarchical structure, and the insistence on conformity go straight back, I think, to the reaction against (and fear of) what they saw as the loss of order and the resultant chaos that occurred in the "anything goes" sixties. They grip the reins so tightly today, I think, largely because of their discomfort with, and insecurity about, what happens when the reins are too loose.

Call it a trust issue. Not only do we Democrats trust diversity, we also encourage and embrace it as a fundamental tenet of our society. We feel enriched and strengthened by the differences among ourselves that we believe deepen our culture as they broaden it. That's what we believe America has always been about—the enrichment that comes from diversity.

Most of the Republican hard core and their followers don't. When President Bush says, "You're either with us or against us," he's not just speaking to the world; he's articulating an attitude that permeates the Republicans' view of our own society, and, within their party's core leadership, of themselves.

The Republican Party's hierarchy doesn't often appear comfortable with diversity, not when it comes to people and certainly not when it comes to opinions. Within the inner circles of the Republicans' higher ranks, certainly within the leadership that controls Congress and the White House at the moment, they simply don't tolerate it.

There are advantages to that militaristic discipline, no question. When you've got a group in lockstep unison, they can at times act more efficiently and effectively than a group where more divergent and different voices, opinions, and styles are tolerated. Let me tell you, it's not easy being the captain of a team where diversity and independent voices are valued and encouraged. I've often compared the challenge of uniting our Senate Democratic caucus to "loading frogs into a wheelbarrow." Trying to move fifty United States Senators from various points on the political spectrum to a common position is a test, to say the least.

But I wouldn't have it any other way. We are a society founded on tolerance of and respect for differences—different opinions, different worldviews, different values, different religious beliefs, different ideologies. In a world filled with horrific repression and intolerance, worse than many of us can imagine, it is America's spirit of tolerance, I believe, much more than our wealth or our power, that continues to shine like a beacon to people all over the planet.

The current core Republican leadership, from George Bush on down, not only runs the internal affairs of its party, but would like to run the affairs of our nation with a "with us or against us" attitude. This attitude reflects not only a lack of respect for dissent, but the forceful imposition of one's ideas on another.

It disturbs me when I see this attitude guiding America's actions in the international arena as well as the efforts of too many of our lawmakers here at home. I don't think our Founding Fathers, whose spirit is so often invoked by the core Republicans to justify their political agenda, had anything like this attitude in mind when they framed our Constitution.

There is no better scholar of our Constitution and of the history of the United States Senate than my Democratic colleague Robert Byrd. He literally wrote the book on the Senate, a massive four-volume history published in 1988. All four volumes sit in my office, and I refer to them often for some insight or understanding about a particular problem that might be confronting us. There's an old adage about Congress that is underscored by every page in those books: "Congress was created by geniuses so it could be run by idiots."

It is simply incredible that this venerable institution of ours has endured the countless mistakes and missteps and outright attempts to change the framers' vision of the Senate by so many of its members throughout its history. And that its framework has been able to adapt to and meet challenges and situations confronting it in modern times that were unimaginable when it was created more than two and a quarter centuries ago. What a testament to the foresight and brilliance of our forefathers and to their deep understanding of the human spirit—of its dark sides as well as its brightness—that they were able to create such a resilient and adaptive system of government as the one under which we are lucky enough to exist.

Which brings us to the results of that 2000 election.

It had been more than a century since the United States had had an equal split between Republicans and Democrats, and never with fifty members of one political party aligned against fifty members of the other. With those 2000 results, we were faced with just that circumstance. When those results were finally acknowledged by Trent Lott and the Republicans, it was time to get down to the business of figuring out how to operate in this uncharted environment.

One of the major differences between the House and the Senate is that the House's rules and procedures are pretty strictly and precisely spelled out, while the Senate's rules are written more broadly, in a way that has allowed for much more interpretation, flexibility, latitude, and adaptation in response to circumstances and situations as they have arisen throughout the course of the Senate's history. The position of Senate majority leader, for example, which is such an important fulcrum of congressional power today, didn't even exist until it was created during Woodrow Wilson's presidency. And it meant very little in terms of real power until Lyndon Johnson grabbed hold of it in the 1950s and shaped it to his gargantuan political appetite and needs.

From the time I assumed the Democratic leadership in the Senate in 1994 until that election of 2000, the Republicans held the advantage, and first Bob Dole and then Trent Lott enjoyed the position of majority leader. This numerical edge also meant that Republicans controlled the ability to set the Senate's legislative agenda in each Senate committee and on the Senate floor. No one imagined that was going to change anytime soon, but it did that November. The fifty-fifty split created an intriguing institutional challenge—determining who would control the chamber and set its agenda in this evenly divided Senate.

While each party hopes to have the majority and the power that comes with it, the majority's advantages are not as great as some might imagine. The Senate's longstanding institutional checks on the majority make it easier for a minority to block initiatives than for a majority to pass them. A sixty-vote "supermajority" is needed to invoke "cloture"—limit debate and force a final vote on a bill—while only forty-one votes are needed to continue debate and delay a vote.

Right-wing activists have accused Democratic senators of subjecting legislation and nominees to "unconstitutional" filibusters, claiming the founders never envisioned a cloture requirement. The former allegation is both false and hypocritical—Republican senators turned the filibuster into an art form in the 1990s. The latter statement—that the founders never anticipated cloture—is correct, since the founders never provided *any* means to cut off debate. The cloture option—a recent addition to Senate rules—didn't make it easier to *block* Senate legislation; it made it easier to *pass* it. In fact, until 1917, there was no way for the majority to break a filibuster—even if ninety-nine senators wanted to do so. Any senator could block a bill single-handedly. The founders envisioned a Senate that would vigorously protect the rights of the minority against a reactionary majority.

The framers of our Constitution *did* anticipate that the House might become almost a lawmaking factory, bending to the will of popular passion and churning out bills with less apparent attention to their ramifications, which, certainly over the course of the past decade, it has done. The Senate's rules were constructed to discourage swift, impulsive decisions, to force compromise and concessions rather than allow those in power to force their will on a barely outnumbered minority.

There is a piece of Senate lore recorded by an early historian named Moncure Conway that is often invoked by Senate watchers to explain this deliberative aspect of our "club." Thomas Jefferson, upon his return from a trip to France in 1789, apparently met with George Washington over breakfast and confronted him with the question of why he had agreed to allow this second chamber of Congress—the Senate—to be created alongside the House of Representatives. Washington, according to Conway's account, pointed to Jefferson's coffee.

"Why," asked Washington, "did you pour that coffee into that saucer?"

"To cool it," answered Jefferson.

"Even so," said Washington, "we pour legislation into the senatorial saucer to cool it."

The rules that allow the Senate to cool the coffee that might arrive too hot from the House can certainly be used by the minority party to its advantage. Beyond that, there is also the minority's ability to hold the majority responsible, as the party in power, for whatever legislation does (or does not) emerge from the Senate.

That said, without question, both parties would prefer to be the party in power in the Senate. To begin with, all Senate legislation begins in the committees, whose memberships and chairmanships are controlled by the party in power. Each of the chairmen, within his own committee, wields enormous power in terms of controlling the committee's budget and deciding which hearings will be held and which legislation he will allow to be released to the Senate floor for a vote. Many a bill (or nomination) is kept locked "in committee" where it finally withers and dies on the vine.

Beyond the committees, the majority party has the advantage of its leader, who controls the all-important "calendar," with which he decides when and how a particular bill will be considered. By tradition and Senate rules, the leader is generally the one individual in the Senate who can call bills or nominations to the Senate floor. Or not. If a bill the leader doesn't like makes it out of committee, he can block it, or at least stymie it, through a host of procedures. If he likes it, he can push it toward a decision in ways no other senator can.

Both the majority and minority parties have their own weapons of parliamentary procedure, developed over the course of the Senate's history, to advance or defend their particular positions. The filibuster, of course, is the most powerful and visible tool of the minority. The cloture rule is the majority's most common answer, as Robert Byrd's book puts it, to "all but the most determined filibusters carried on by a sizable minority."

The host of tools and tactics employed by both sides in the Senate had evolved over the course of 106 Congresses by the time of that 2000 election. Now, with the start of the 107th, we were facing something the Senate had never faced in modern times, a situation in which neither party held the upper hand. Suddenly—wonderfully for us and nightmarishly for the Republicans—the phrase *power sharing* had entered our lexicon.

Early on, the Republicans couldn't bring themselves to even utter that phrase. Don Nickles, the Senate Republican whip, put it quite simply at the time. "It's difficult," he told a reporter, "for me to see how two people can drive a car at the same time."

Difficult, maybe. But Trent and I had done it before, during the Clinton impeachment trial. An image used often during that ordeal was of Trent and me as "copilots." It wasn't easy then, and it wouldn't be easy now. But the Republicans had no other choice, and Trent knew it.

One year after the September 11 terrorist attacks, Trent and I sat together at a Pentagon ceremony. At one point he leaned over and told me, "You know, we've been through a lot together, and while there have been times when I've attacked you and you've attacked me, and our relationship has been strained, we've gotten though all this *together*. People will never know what an accomplishment that really is."

I agree. To have kept open the lines of communication, in spite of the tense political climate, was not easy. Trent and I were forced to confront each other many times, occasionally in personal ways. I'm often asked how it's possible to square off with someone as intensely as Trent and I sometimes did and then be able to work with that person the next day. We're all asked that in Congress today, especially by people who watch Washington from a distance, on the TV news or talk shows, where our conflicts are highlighted—and, in the case of some of the talk shows, *encouraged*—while the hard, unglamorous, mundane hour-by-hour, day-by-day, week-by-week cooperation between us that is required to do the work of government goes unseen and ignored.

And that's the thing—this *is* our work, the work of government. It's our *job*. No matter how bitter the toe-to-toe fighting might sometimes become, you can never stop talking. Because if you don't talk, you can't govern. And that, in the end, is your obligation as a public servant—not to win elections, but to do the work of government once you *do* win. To

Trent's credit, he was sometimes able to resist forces within his own party who wanted to close off all lines of communication between us many times during the eight years we shared as our parties' leaders in the Senate.

I don't think any association I've had in my political career has been as complex and layered as my relationship with Trent Lott. For two people so completely different in ideology, politics, and even personality, we're actually quite alike in some ways. We both come from relatively small states. We both began our careers in the House. We were both elected to our party leadership positions by extremely close margins.

Trent actually began his career as a Democrat, working as an aide for Mississippi representative William Colmer, a staunch segregationist, back in the late 1960s. In 1972, the same year I began my career as a volunteer for George McGovern in Nebraska, Colmer retired and Trent switched to the GOP to run for that seat, which he won.

In 1994, I was elected Senate Democratic leader by one vote. Less than two years later, Trent was elected Republican leader by that same minimal margin. If several Republican moderates had not rallied behind Trent during that election, he wouldn't have won. One of those moderates was Jim Jeffords, which would turn out to be more than a little ironic, considering the events that were about to unfold during 2001.

Perhaps it was because of this complex relationship that I terribly misjudged the consequences of Trent's now infamous comment made in December 2002 at Strom Thurmond's one-hundreth birthday party. Trent offered that the country would have been much better off had Strom been elected president back in 1948, when Strom ran for the presidency on the segregationist "Dixiecrat" ticket.

Trent called me early the following Monday morning to explain the circumstances and to apologize. I was on my way to a news conference when the phone rang. By then, I had seen news accounts of Trent's comments, so I was familiar with what he had said.

"I screwed up," Trent told me. "I didn't intend for it to come out the way it did. I hope that you will pass along my apologies to anyone who took offense."

I told Trent I would. Then I left to go meet the press.

Our primary purpose for the press conference was to announce the new Democratic Senatorial Campaign Committee (DSCC) leadership team—Jon Corzine and Debbie Stabenow. After asking a number of questions about the team and our new minority status in the Senate, one of the reporters wanted to know my reaction to Trent's comments.

I said that Trent had just called me to apologize and that I accepted his apology. I added that there were many times when both Trent and I wished we had said something differently.

Hindsight, as they say, is twenty-twenty. I should have done more than just consider Trent's feelings. My immediate response to his call was to feel empathy for him and to believe the best, to believe that Trent would not have intentionally uttered a racist remark. But in my desire to be fair to Trent, I didn't fully appreciate the emotional anguish that his words caused for many, many people—especially members of the African American community. There is no excuse for not considering this, and neither is there any excuse for not considering more deeply how I felt about it. It doesn't matter that I took Trent's call just minutes before I left to meet the reporters. If I didn't have time to gauge my thoughts and feelings more fully, then I shouldn't have said anything at all—because there were already many people who *had* measured their own thoughts and feelings, and were outraged, and rightfully so, by Trent's comments. Now, because of my lack of criticism, they were also outraged at me.

The whirlwind that grew from this incident wound up sweeping Trent Lott out of his Senate leadership position. Once I was able to sit down and look at his history on this subject, including similar comments he made over the course of many years, and after a number of lengthy conversations with members of the Congressional Black Caucus leadership about these statements, I understood much more fully the significance of his comment at the party for Thurmond and the great pain that such statements both reflected and ignored. I had my own apologies to make.

But that all still lay far ahead as the year 2000 drew to a close. What concerned Trent and me at that time, once he'd conceded that we had to share power in the now evenly divided Senate, was how to begin hammering out a set of rules by which we would run the Senate's affairs. These rules, agreed upon at the beginning of each Congress, are codified in what is called an "organizing resolution." We now needed to draft such a document for this Congress, a set of rules that both sides could accept.

Naturally, the first thing we and our staffs looked for were precedents, of which there weren't many.

The only previously evenly divided Senate occurred during the 47th Congress, back in 1881. The 1880 election had given Republican James Garfield the presidency, and the Republicans had regained control of the House as well. The Senate, however, wound up split between thirty-seven Democrats and thirty-seven Republicans, with two independents whose leanings were Democratic. Those independents allowed the Democrats to claim the majority votes needed to organize that Senate.

One of those independents, however, was a Virginian named William Mahone, who belonged to an odd little breakaway faction from the Democratic Party that called themselves the "Readjusters." The name turned out to be perfect for what Mahone did to that situation in the Senate. Wooed by the Republican White House, which actually delivered a gift basket of flowers to Senator Mahone's desk, and by the Senate Republican leadership, which promised him the chairmanship of the Agriculture Committee, Mahone announced ten days into the session that he was joining the Republicans. This deadlocked the Senate and stalled the organizing resolution procedure, which the incensed Democrats drew out to eleven weeks before an agreement was finally forged.

Another interesting situation occurred in the 83rd Congress. The death of Robert Taft, a Republican, and the appointment of a Democrat to finish out his term had given Democrats a numerical advantage: 48–47–1. (The one independent was Wayne Morse of Oregon, who had left the Republican Party out of disgust with Eisenhower's campaign and pro-business policies.) LBJ, then the Democratic floor leader, decided against pushing for a formal reorganization of the Senate, leading to a classic exchange between Johnson and his Republican counterpart, William Knowland. After listening to Senator Knowland complain at great length about how difficult it was to have the title and responsibilities of the majority leader but a minority of votes, LBJ replied: "If anyone has more problems than a majority leader with a minority, it is a minority leader with a majority!"

I often wondered why LBJ didn't push for a formal reorganization of the Senate when he could have. Part of the reason, I learned, is that LBJ feared his party's advantage would be short-lived, given the advanced age of many senators. He didn't want to turn the Senate upside down if doing so might come back to haunt him within a few months. It turns out it was a wise decision. This was, as I mentioned earlier, the Congress during which nine senators died.

Unlike LBJ, who had a choice whether to take the majority or stay where he was, Trent and I *had* to reorganize the Congress because we were at the beginning of a session. And unlike the situation in 1881, we weren't about to take eleven weeks. Although we had nowhere to look for a power-sharing precedent in modern congressional history, we were able to find several interesting solutions at the state level of government. In fact, we discovered that in just the preceding thirty years alone, *thirty-one* state legislatures had been faced with evenly divided chambers.

Some of their solutions were pretty creative. In 1988, for example, the Indiana House was forced to deal with a stalemate. Their answer was to split their committees evenly and have the House Speakers alternate every other day, from Republican to Democrat and back again. That plan worked out so well that a plaque now hangs in the Indiana statehouse, commemorating that success. In 1992, the Florida Senate chose to have a Republican president for its first year and a Democratic president for the second. That worked out well, too.

Some of my colleagues liked that Florida idea—have Trent serve as majority leader for the year 2001 and me serve as leader for 2002. But Trent would have none of it—or, more precisely, his colleagues wouldn't stand for it. The fact was, most of Trent's caucus wasn't ready to stand for any kind of compromise at all. While Trent had come around from his state of denial, many of the Republicans were still refusing to accept this reality and were ready to fight any kind of compromise to the bitter end.

Trent and I talked every day that month, often several times a day. He was really in a tough spot, really going through hell with his people. Each of our caucuses always has a one- or two-day retreat in January, when we gather together to welcome new members and assess the coming year. We held our retreat that January in the Library of Congress, in a breathtakingly ornate room called the Hall of Congress. Our mood was positively euphoric.

We were making history, and the fifty-fifty split was only the beginning. The demographics of the Senate were changing as well, unquestionably for the better as far as we were concerned. Out of the 1,864 senators who had served in all of U.S. history up to that point, only 31 had been women. With the 2000 election, 13 women were serving now, more than had ever served at the same time in the Senate before. Two of them—Jean Carnahan, whose husband, Mel, had been governor of Missouri, and Hillary Clinton, whose husband . . . well, we all know who he is—were former First Ladies, another first for the Senate.

The room was filled with optimism at our January retreat as we congratulated one another. Even President-elect Bush asked if he could stop by. Meanwhile, Trent was facing a gathering of gloom, anger, and recrimination. His caucus had been primed to roll forward as part of a powerful Bush machine, only to see that power slip from their grasp. Trent reported back to me how angry everyone was over there, how there was finger-pointing and people saying, "I don't want to hear about resolutions and power sharing. . . . We're just going to defy all this. . . . We're not going to let them do that. . . . We're going to *hold.*"

It was against their self-interest, however, to hold out too long. The Bush administration needed to begin confirming its cabinet appointments, and that process couldn't begin until we hammered out an organizing resolution. The longer this took, the longer the administration would have to wait, a predicament their side wanted to avoid.

Meanwhile, we were pretty clear about what we wanted. We wanted equal committee membership, to replace the one-member advantage the Republicans had enjoyed as the majority party. We wanted the budgets for each committee—which are a very important issue, largely ignored by the public—to be divided evenly between both parties rather than split two-thirds to the majority and one-third to the minority, as was traditionally done. There was a lot of discussion as well about insisting on co-chairmen for each committee.

But co-chairmanships weren't as important to me as the issues of membership and budgets. In fact, the more we discussed it, the more I believed it was to our advantage to let the Republicans keep the committee chairmanships and to let Trent keep the role of majority leader as well. The Republicans maintained that Trent deserved that position since, in a fifty-fifty Senate, all tie votes would be broken by the Vice President, who would be Dick Cheney, a Republican. We had no problem with that argument, just as we were willing to allow the Republicans to keep the committee chairmanships. If the money and memberships were evenly divided, the chairmanships would be hardly more than a cosmetic difference.

Finally, there were two other things on which we insisted. The first was that in my capacity as Democratic leader, I would have the power to call bills to the floor. The second turned out to be more prophetic. We said that should anything change in the makeup of the Senate, the new organizing resolution we were creating would become void.

In the public eye, the Republicans would remain in charge, which was fine with us. With a far right president and a far right House poised to take our nation in a direction we didn't want it to go, the more we could hold the Republicans responsible for what they were doing, the better. We were intent on contrasting our agenda for the country with that of the far right, but meanwhile it wouldn't hurt, if they *did* get their way, to have the onus be on Republican-chaired committees and a Republican majority leader.

Another motivation for the Republicans to get this agreement done, besides the President's need to begin filling his cabinet, was that until we rewrote the resolution, the previous Congress's resolution would still stand, and the fact that the Republicans had lost nine senators in the 2000 election meant that they were now a minority on most of those committees. Replacements could not be appointed until a new resolution was adopted.

So Trent and his group were really stuck. They had to move forward. They had to bite the bullet, and finally they did.

The agreement we ultimately reached was called Senate Resolution 8. We wound up getting exactly what we sought, and Trent wound up taking a lot of heat from his troops. Phil Gramm wondered aloud, publicly, whether Trent wasn't "giving away the store." Paul Weyrich, the head of the right-wing Free Congress Foundation, told a reporter, "I don't think anybody has disappointed me more in public life."

Trent was already, at this point, losing favor both with the hard-liners within his party and with the White House. He would have to continue to deal with those people, as difficult as that might be. For our part, we had to be ready to begin dealing with them, too.

That new organizing resolution was passed on January 5, 2001. The new President and Vice President would be sworn in on January 20. That meant, during those two intervening weeks, while Al Gore was still Vice President, I would serve as the Senate majority leader. I made quite a few quips during that time about this brief taste of that role, but the fact was there was important business to attend to immediately. Our nation, after enduring the exhausting suspense of the drawn-out presidential election, was ready for us to get back to work.

The first order of business, which began during those two weeks, was the confirmation process for President Bush's cabinet appointments. Few final votes would be taken during that time, but there would be hearings held, arguments made, and positions taken.

We had no real problems with most of the nominees: Colin Powell, Donald Rumsfeld, Paul O'Neill, Don Evans, and the rest. We were ready to move on those rather quickly. But John Ashcroft, that was another matter.

Ashcroft had lost his Senate seat from Missouri in that fall's election to Jean Carnahan's husband, Mel, who died in a tragic plane crash just three weeks before election day—circumstances eerily similar to Paul Wellstone's death two years later. Under very sad circumstances, Jean Carnahan promised Missouri voters she would come to Washington in her husband's place if they elected him. And they did. It was the first time in history that a deceased candidate for the United States Senate actually defeated an incumbent U.S. senator. One more of the historic firsts in the 107th Congress.

Now, two months later, John Ashcroft was back, this time as George Bush's nominee for U.S. attorney general.

At that point in my career, I had voted on thirty-six cabinet nominations, two-thirds of those submitted by Republican presidents. On only one of those nominations did I vote no. That was against Ronald Reagan's nomination of John Tower for secretary of defense. In every other case I voted yes, because I believe strongly in a president's right to choose cabinet secretaries with whom he is philosophically comfortable.

The position of attorney general, however, is the one that always gives me the most pause, because it is the one cabinet position that must be kept most free of ideological partisanship. The attorney general is more than just the "president's lawyer." He or she is the guardian of the constitutional rights of all Americans, the protector of our fundamental freedoms. The attorney general of the United States has enormous power, and he must, in the interest of the very justice he is beholden to represent, administer that power impartially.

Nearly a century ago, Teddy Roosevelt—a Republican president, by the way—heard rumors that some district attorneys and marshals were about to be ordered to replace their deputies for political reasons. Roosevelt immediately sent a letter to his attorney general, a man named William Moody, demanding that these orders be stopped. As Roosevelt put it, "Of all the officers of the Government, those of the Department of Justice should be kept free from any suspicion of improper action on partisan and factional grounds."

John Ashcroft's entire political career had been built on partisan, factional grounds. I had strong reservations about his fitness to serve as attorney general at the time of his nomination, and his performance in office has only confirmed my deep doubts and suspicions.

During the six years he served with me in the Senate and during the nearly two decades he spent in Missouri before that—first as Missouri's attorney general and then as its governor—Ashcroft openly and defiantly used the power of his positions to advance his right-wing ideology.

As a senator, he once proclaimed that there are only "two things you find in the middle of the road: a moderate and a dead skunk." He also said, "There are voices in the Republican Party today who preach pragmatism, who champion conciliation, who counsel compromise. I stand here today to reject those deceptions. If ever there was a time to unfurl the banner of unabashed conservatism, it is now."

Since its creation more than two centuries ago, the U.S. Constitution has been amended only twenty-seven times—including the ten amendments of the Bill of Rights. During his *one term* in the Senate, John Ashcroft introduced or co-sponsored seven constitutional amendments, almost all involving one aspect or another of abortion or birth control. His record in the Senate demonstrated what the *New York Times* called "a radical propensity for offering constitutional amendments that would bring that document into alignment with his religious views."

During his sixteen-year political career in Missouri, Ashcroft also fought fiercely against the federal courts' efforts to end segregation in public schools in that state, battling those efforts all the way to the Supreme Court, where he lost three times without winning once. As a U.S. senator, he blocked one Justice Department nomination because the nominee's views on affirmative action differed from his. He blocked two nominations for surgeon general because both men supported a woman's right to choose. He blocked a nomination for an ambassadorship because the nominee had, as Ashcroft put it, "been a leader in promoting a lifestyle"— in other words, this person was gay.

Ashcroft's reprehensible treatment of Missouri Supreme Court Justice Ronnie White, an African American and the first nominee to the federal district court to be rejected on the floor of the Senate in fifty years, is well documented. His defiant refusal to distance himself from Bob Jones University, a cauldron of intolerance that has described Mormons and Catholics as "cults which call themselves Christian" and which awarded Ashcroft an honorary degree in 1999, was more than disturbing to those of us debating his fitness to become the "country's top law enforcement officer."

I had no question about it—not then and not now. John Ashcroft's opinions on civil rights, on women's rights, on workers' rights, and on the separation of church and state put him far to the right of most Americans, which would be fine if he were just another citizen or even if he were just another senator. But putting a man like this, with an ideological agenda like his, in a position that is supposed to *protect* the freedoms of Americans, not *impinge* on them, was, in my opinion, unwise.

That's how I felt. That's how I voted.

We considered mounting a filibuster as a last resort. We had the forty-one opposing votes necessary to do that. But out of respect for the fact that, like it or not, John Ashcroft *had* been one of our colleagues, we decided to allow his nomination to move to the floor, where he was finally confirmed by a margin of 58–42.

That was our first battle of the 107th Congress.

There were many more to come.

End of Chpt. 2

Chpt. 3

CHAPTER THREE) goes to pg. 72 = 28/29

One Man's Move

G EORGE W. BUSH AND I NEVER really met before he was elected presi-dent. Our paths had crossed once or twice—I remember speaking briefly with him at the funeral of Georgia Senator Paul Coverdell in July 2000—but we had not had a substantive conversation until he called a week before his inauguration and asked if he could come see me at my Senate office.

My opinion of Bush at that point had been shaped, as I've said, from a distance. Unlike many people who were both alarmed and amused by his frequent malapropisms, I did not think all those "Bushisms" necessarily reflected his intellect. For all of the gaffes, the fact is that George Bush is an undeniably effective communicator, not unlike Ronald Reagan. He gets his message across, and he gets it across in a way that is convincing to a large number of people. That skill has very little to do with vocabulary or sentence structure.

I think Bush benefited a great deal from low expectations during his campaign against Gore. People underestimated his intellect as well as his *political* intelligence. He may not have Bill Clinton's encyclopedic grasp of the details and complexities of every possible issue, but Bush knows where he stands and is smart enough to understand what he needs to do in order to frame and express his stance on a particular subject. Not only was he not out of his league in his debates with Gore, as many thought he would be, but the consensus after the fact was that he won every one of them.

One area in which George Bush *is* absolutely Clintonesque is in his capacity to build relationships, to work one-on-one with people, individually or in small groups. His personal style, especially in more intimate settings, is very disarming. He's good at making people feel comfortable, putting them at ease. He doesn't put on airs. He's very good at this—as good, in fact, as any president I've personally witnessed.

With Ronald Reagan, for example, as personable as he was, there was always a certain distance about him, a larger-than-life presence that worked against the kind of connection Bush is able to make with people. Maybe some of that came from Reagan's movie star background, I don't know. But there's an *ease* about President Bush—and Bill Clinton has this, too—a way of making people relax, of throwing a little humor into the conversation, of tagging people with nicknames when he begins to get to know them, that is very effective and very useful in the day-to-day, nitty-gritty, often one-on-one work that politics in Washington entails.

Personality matters, and however you feel about his politics and policies, there's no denying that George Bush has a very effective, very likable personality. I could see that even before we got to know each other. There were other things I could see as well, though, several of which gave me reason to pause.

One was his background. There's little question that George Bush wouldn't be where he is today if he hadn't come from the family he did, with the father he had. I think even he would admit that had his name been George W. Smith, he would not be president of the United States.

There are people who know him who say George W. Bush never had any real presidential ambitions, that he was perfectly content being governor of Texas and turned toward the White House only after he was pushed in that direction by circumstances, by the people around him, and by his family. He has made no secret of how hard it was to watch his father's presidency falter in the wake of the Gulf War, then fall at the hands of Bill Clinton.

Which is all understandable. But what troubled me about the Bush family tree was where it is rooted—ideologically and politically. I'm talking about Texas, but a very different Texas from the one that produced, say, Lyndon Johnson. President Johnson's quest for power and his political acumen were second to no one's—not even George W. Bush's. Johnson's path to the White House was paved with as many Machiavellian power plays and backroom deals as can be found in American history.

But what Johnson did once he *got* to the presidency was framed by a vision of government that he inherited from his father, who had been a populist legislator in the hardscrabble "Hill Country" of rural Texas, where Johnson grew up in the early part of the last century. LBJ's father taught him that the government's purpose was to help people who were, as he put it, "caught in the tentacles of circumstance." It's a short leap from those roots to the slew of 1960s federal aid programs that flowed out of LBJ's Great Society White House.

George Bush's Texas—a thin but powerful sliver of that immensely large and multilayered state—is a quite different place from the Texas that produced LBJ, and indeed from the Texas that produces most Texans. George Bush's Texas is a place of insular privilege and conservative politics, of a tightly knit network of families and fortunes built on wealth accumulated largely by oil, of a commitment to ensuring that that wealth and its consequent power be kept among themselves, and of a deeply parochial vision of government that views Washington, D.C., and the federal judiciary as the enemy.

This is how George W. Bush saw Washington—as the enemy. This was the message of his campaign against Gore, that if he was elected, he would "give back the government to the people." This wasn't the Jacksonian mantra of "trust the people"—a principle that lies at the heart of the Democratic Party. It was a thinly transparent code for the right-wing Republican agenda of dismantling the government, an agenda highlighted by regressive tax cuts that reward the people who already have wealth and power (including that circle of friends back in George Bush's Texas), the relaxation of federal regulations, environmental and otherwise, that impede the "freedom" of industry to do business (including the oil industry back in George Bush's Texas), and the restoration of "family" and religious "values" to our culture (including the religious fundamentalists who occupy the inner circles of political power in George Bush's Texas).

This religious fervor of Bush's public persona made me more than a little uneasy, in the same way that John Ashcroft's fundamentalist faith did. Faith has its place in all of our lives, and that place should be central, whatever our beliefs. But we must be careful about how we introduce faith into government. Our Founding Fathers were certainly concerned about this, as evidenced by their separation of church and state. They recognized and respected the fact that one man's "God" is not necessarily another's, and they took great pains to ensure the freedom of every American to worship (or not) in whatever way he or she chooses.

George Bush made no bones about his "born again" Christianity during the presidential campaign, which was fine. But how far those beliefs, and the extremely aggressive political reach of the fundamentalist Christian movement, would extend into the White House and its policies concerned me.

It was hard to see how the religious fervor of people like John Ashcroft and others in the President's inner circle could not directly affect the policy decisions they made. The morning of his first day as President-elect, Bush attended a prayer service at a church in suburban Austin during which the minister announced from the pulpit, "You were chosen by God, as was Moses, to lead the people." A Bush spokesperson stated later that day that the President-elect did not believe he was "chosen by God." But I had to wonder.

I had to wonder as well about the White House "team" Bush had assembled, a group that appeared to have been chosen to continue—or to complete—his father's legacy, as well as to bring the "culture war" we'd been fighting for the past thirty years back to the White House. Bush's incoming advisers included several "generals" who had been fighting that war since its inception.

There was the Vice President–elect, Dick Cheney, who had been President Gerald Ford's chief of staff in the 1970s, then had risen to the position of Republican whip in the House in the 1980s and, of course, at the turn of the 1990s, had served as secretary of defense to the elder Bush during the Persian Gulf War.

There was Paul Wolfowitz, who had been a chief adviser to Cheney during the first Gulf War and had been obsessed ever since with what he considered its unfinished business. Iraq and Saddam Hussein had never moved off the center of Wolfowitz's radar screen, and now, as Bush's new deputy secretary of defense, he was in position to do something about it.

And of course there was Wolfowitz's boss, Donald Rumsfeld, the new secretary of defense, whose Republican roots went even farther back than Cheney's, beginning as a rising star of the party as a thirtysomething congressman in the 1960s and proceeding to the Nixon cabinet post in 1969. Rumsfeld moved on from the Nixon White House to become President Ford's chief of staff and later defense secretary, where no small amount of friction developed between him and Ford's CIA director, George H. W. Bush Sr. In fact, Donald Rumsfeld now holds the interesting distinction of being both the youngest and oldest secretary of defense in United States history.

People may have questioned whether George W. Bush was ready to be president the day he took the oath of office, but no one doubted the punching power of the heavyweights who settled in with him, not just his closest advisers, but also an army of seasoned right-wing lawyer-warriors, battle hardened from the previous eight years.

Many of these attorneys were members of an ultraconservative organization called the Federalist Society, one of whose founders, Spencer Abraham—the senator from Michigan who had been defeated by Debbie Stabenow in the 2000 election—was now poised to become Bush's secretary of energy. Some had worked in Ken Starr's office. Larry Thompson, who had been Clarence Thomas's chief adviser during his Supreme Court nomination battle, was now Bush's choice for deputy attorney general. It was as if an entire regime had returned from exile.

That, in and of itself, wasn't surprising. Any president is naturally going to surround himself with like-minded and experienced advisers. But it was the rabidly fierce ideology of this group, the particulars of their intransigent beliefs, their crusader-like zeal to transform those beliefs into law, and their relentless pursuit of the power to allow them to do that that frankly alarmed me.

Of all Bush's advisers, however, the one who perhaps concerned me the most was Bush's senior adviser Karl Rove. Rove's roots, like so many of Bush's "team," stretched all the way back to the beginning of the "culture war." As a young college Republican in the early 1970s, Rove, who shares Bush's contempt for the liberal legacy of the 1960s, got involved in politics and befriended a young Lee Atwater, who went on to trailblaze the school of hardball politics as a GOP operative in the 1980s. It was Atwater who, as George Bush Sr.'s chief strategist during the 1988 presidential campaign, orchestrated the brutal attacks on Michael Dukakis's patriotism and masterminded the racially tinged Willie Horton TV ad, which exploited Dukakis's support for a program under which a convicted black rapist had been furloughed.

While Atwater was making his mark in Washington, Rove was building a career down in Texas, where he spent the better part of two decades as a Republican consultant for virtually every major GOP candidate seeking office in that state. Rove's tactics, straight out of the Lee Atwater scorched-earth campaign playbook, included a combination of behind-the-scenes rumormongering, innuendo, outright lies, and "whisper campaigns" that questioned everything from an opponent's sexuality to his or her sobriety.

Rove, according to journalists who covered the campaigns he worked on, was always careful to keep himself at least one step away from such questionable tactics, and he was even more careful to keep his candidate *two* steps away, so his client could plausibly deny any knowledge of these maneuvers, should they be questioned.

Rove was enormously successful in Texas, which led to his hookup with the Bush dynasty and, ultimately, to his orchestration of George Bush's 2000 presidential campaign—a blueprint of political brilliance, no question. Rove's role in that campaign brought him national attention, which he really didn't want. People began calling him "Bush's brain," an image that I think is too simplistic, because it misses what I consider the most troubling aspect of the relationship between these two men—that is, their shared obsession with, and complete absorption in, the political ramifications of every move they make. A more accurate image would be that their two brains are *one*, they think so much alike.

Bush, who promised during his campaign that he would never use polls, liked to joke—and still does—that he doesn't *need* to look at polls because he has Karl Rove to do it for him. Rove did it for him during the 2000 campaign, and now he was ready to move into the White House to do it for him as president.

This is what worried me most—the ascension of a consultant like Karl Rove to the White House's inner decision-making circle. Even George Bush's father, who allowed Lee Atwater to use his ends-justify-the-means guerrilla warfare to help get him the White House, set Atwater to the side once he was elected. George Bush Sr. made no secret of the fact that while he relished the business of government and policy, he didn't care much for politics and campaigning. The bare-knuckled fighting that modern elections entail was seen by the elder Bush as a necessary evil, something he had to tolerate to get him into the White House, but something to be left outside once he got there. I admired him for that.

George W. Bush brought a completely different view of the relationship between politics and policy to the White House. In his world, politics often takes precedence over policy. You could see Bush following this equation before he even made it to Washington. You could see it in the way he— and Rove—ran his campaign. He loves playing this game, and he's good at it. If there are people who question George Bush's intelligence, there is no one who has any doubts about his tactical, political brilliance. It was clear before he even assumed the presidency that everything he said, everything he did, had an underlying political purpose. And that purpose was always paramount, in both Karl Rove's and George Bush's minds. Which is why it alarmed me to see Bush bring Rove so deeply into the actual machinery of governing.

Less than a year after Bush assumed office, John DiIulio, a brilliant political scientist and scholar who had joined Bush's administration as director of the White House Office of Faith-Based and Community Initiatives, was pushed out of that position by Christian conservatives unhappy with his efforts, and he wound up telling a writer for *Esquire* magazine what he had witnessed during his year inside the Bush circle.

DiIulio talked most specifically about how influential Karl Rove had become. He described Rove as "enormously powerful, maybe the single most powerful person in the modern, post-Hoover era ever to occupy a political-adviser post near the Oval Office. . . .

"There is no precedent in any modern White House for what is going on in this one: a complete lack of a policy apparatus," DiIulio continued. "What you've got is everything, and I mean everything, being run by the political arm. It's the reign of the Mayberry Machiavellis."

But this all remained to be seen in January of 2001. When President-elect Bush called and asked to come see me that week before the inauguration, I welcomed him enthusiastically. With all the reservations I felt about him and his incoming administration, he had preached the gospel of "changing the tone in Washington" throughout the campaign, and if he wanted to follow through on that commitment, he would find in me a willing partner.

On that gray, overcast January morning, the President-elect and his entourage of Secret Service and personal staff entered my office on the second floor of the Capitol. While Bush's adviser Karen Hughes and his chief of staff, Andy Card, lingered in the reception area just inside the door, Bush began shaking hands with each member of my staff as he worked his way back toward my personal office.

Until then, I'd never noticed his Texas swagger. Perhaps it was the fact that in order to enter my suite in the Capitol, you actually need to pass through a set of swinging saloon-style doors. The combination of Bush's confident strut, his self-assured manner, and those saloon doors swinging shut behind him all combined to create an image of a new sheriff in town. Which, in essence, he was.

From the theatrical informality of that entrance, we moved into the formality of my personal office. With its high, vaulted ceilings, chandeliers, fireplaces, and breathtaking view of the Washington Monument, the suite of offices that belongs to the Democratic leader of the Senate is certainly every bit the legislative equivalent of the executive suite that Bush would soon occupy.

We sat alone in two blue wingback chairs on either side of my office's fireplace. I had stoked a strong fire, and its warmth fended off the damp chill that often permeates the more than two-hundred-year-old Capitol in the winter. The President-elect looked rested. In demeanor he was not as assertive as the candidate I had witnessed so many times on television.

"I just wanted to come by and tell you I hope we can have a good relationship," he said. He spoke of his fondness for the lieutenant governor of Texas, Bob Bullock, a Democrat who had served as one of the most powerful political figures in Texas during the 1990s. Bullock had been a loyal and dependable friend and ally to Bush during the years Bush served as governor of Texas.

"We got to be very close," he said.

He paused, then went on.

"I'd like to see if we could do that, too."

Another pause.

"I hope you'll never lie to me."

That statement caught me up short. What an unusual concern to express in such a meeting. Why was the issue of dishonesty, of "lying," on his mind at all? I wondered what reference he could have been making, even obliquely, that would prompt him to address this subject. I've often wondered since then what George Bush might have been told about me that would make him begin this conversation, this *relationship*, from an implied position of mistrust.

"Well," I answered, caught a little off guard, "I hope you'll never lie to *me.*"

We went on to talk, in a very general way, about several issues, including the subject of alternative energy, which touched off a trigger for him.

"You know, I've been around this business a long time," he said, referring to the oil industry. "I know how some feel about alternative energy, and I respect their opinions. But I have to tell you, alternative energy is something long into the future. There's nothing we can do with it that helps us much now.

"People have got to understand that energy independence means more oil," he said. "And that means we've got to drill."

I wouldn't say Bush's attitude was outright confrontational, but it was a lot more edgy, a lot more adamant, than I had expected. We went on to briefly discuss several other subjects. He talked about "compassionate conservatism" and about his intention to change the political tone here in Washington, to steer it back toward true bipartisanship, and I took him at his word.

As we were finishing up, he said, "I know there's been a lot of talk out there about who's in charge around here. There's not ever going to be any *question* about who's in charge. Decisions are going to come to my desk, and I'm going to be the one making them."

Again, I was surprised by his need to make this assertion at all. I certainly understood why he might have a measure of defensiveness, maybe even some insecurity, about moving into this position, with so many critics questioning not just the legitimacy of his election, but also his personal capabilities to serve as president. Still, it was surprising to see him directly addressing those doubts—addressing them to *me.*

Still, despite those few awkward and perhaps pugnacious moments, I was impressed by the meeting. As I thought about it, about the nature of campaigns and how confrontational and draining they can become, how they can leave your nerves raw, I understood how Bush might have felt in this immediate aftermath of that grueling experience. He had just emerged from the most contentious, drawn-out presidential contest in American history, so I didn't make too much of the adversarial edge that had crept into some of the things he had said.

After we shook hands and he left, I felt reasonably impressed overall and hopeful about what lay ahead.

* * *

Not long after that meeting with President-elect Bush, in my first address to our new Senate, I made a few jokes about the two weeks I would be serving as majority leader while the Senate was fifty-fifty and Al Gore remained the tie-breaking Vice President. Then I got to the business of laying out our party's agenda for the coming two years. I noted that the list might sound familiar. We'd been trying to pass some of this legislation, I said, for some time now. Looking back on that list today, three years later, I can *still* say it's familiar, as it should be, because our plans and proposals are sound, and little has changed on the domestic front except for the fact that President Bush has had his way with the economy, which has, as we warned it would, suffered terribly.

One of our priorities at the turn of 2001—and it's still a priority today—was cutting taxes for middle-class working families, for the people who need and deserve tax relief the most. I pointed out that we were inheriting from President Clinton, after eight years of the longest, strongest economic expansion in our nation's history, the largest surplus our federal government had ever enjoyed.

Economists predicted that the surplus would exceed $5 trillion over the next ten years and that virtually all of the national debt could be eliminated. In fact, there were arguments that there may be some economic danger in paying off the debt *too soon*. This was a remarkable turnaround merely a dozen years after facing the largest *deficit* America had ever known, at the end of the Reagan/Bush era, one that is unfortunately even larger today.

It was, of course, the elder Bush himself who, before becoming Reagan's vice president, had ridiculed Reagan's belief in the "trickle down" effect of supply-side theory as "voodoo economics." I remember sitting with Dick Gephardt in the House chamber back in 1981, when I was a congressman, listening to the newly inaugurated Reagan promise that by giving huge tax cuts to the wealthiest Americans, deficits would disappear and the economy would flourish. Congress—including me—unfortunately supported that experiment, and it turned out to be a disaster. Deficits skyrocketed. The national debt quadrupled. By 2001, the younger Bush's incoming Treasury secretary, Paul O'Neill, admitted that Reagan's approach put America "in a ditch that was horrendous."

Bill of Rights; creating the prescription drug benefit I mentioned before; strengthening our public education system; raising the minimum wage to keep up with inflation; protecting our environment and ensuring that polluters, not taxpayers, pay to clean up toxic waste sites; passing real campaign finance reforms; and helping preserve and strengthen family farms and rural communities. This last issue is especially critical for states like South Dakota, where so many family farmers never shared in the same economic prosperity that the rest of our nation experienced during the Clinton years.

So this was our Democratic agenda. As for the Republicans, their goals were spelled out quite clearly in a plan released by a newly formed group called the Issues Management Center, whose members included most of the same Republicans who had shaped Newt Gingrich's Contract with America. This group's publicly stated goal was not only to "support" the President as he pursued his agenda, but to prevent him from "selling out," as they put it, to this evenly divided Senate. Their succinct, five-point plan included tax cuts, school vouchers, a "choice-based" prescription drug plan, a military buildup, and Social Security privatization.

The fault lines couldn't be more clear. And sure enough, when President Bush announced his budget plan before the joint session of Congress that February—a plan that would virtually drain the federal surplus in one fell swoop and that, as Bush outlined it, would actually wind up with a price tag beyond $2 trillion—even some Republicans had to step forward and say this was simply too much.

It is times like this when political extremists make some members of the Republican Party uneasy. And it is such uneasiness that triggers what we call "missionary" work, to nurture and encourage the possibility that some "centrist" or "moderate" members of the Republican Party might be lured to our side. It doesn't happen often, but when it does, on either side of the political fence, it's no surprise to people who follow politics.

Or it shouldn't be.

Which is why, when Jim Jeffords jumped ship that March, the Republicans' outrage and shock seemed so disingenuous to me.

But then again, considering how hard it had been for their core leadership to stomach having to face us on even terms, I could understand the Republicans' dismay at losing even that position and becoming the *minority.*

I echoed O'Neill's acknowledgment, pointing out that it had
years of hard work and struggle on our Democratic side to get *out o*
ditch. But we had done it. And now that we were out, I said in tha
Senate speech of the 107th Congress, we had to be careful not to re
the mistakes of the past. Already President Bush was shaping a massiv
cut plan, which he intended to propose when he addressed his first
session of Congress in about a month.

We needed, I said, to approach any discussion of tax cuts within
broader context of the entire federal budget. Before considering a r
sive tax cut that would flow disproportionately to the wealthy, as the B
plan would have it—we had to keep in mind what that surplus gove
ment money was *needed* for, needs such as safeguarding the security of p
grams like Medicare and Social Security, providing a prescription dr
benefit for the elderly under Medicare, improving the quality of pub
education, helping families with the high cost of college for their ch
dren, and a reserve fund, should we face any unforeseen challenges.

We also needed to remember, I warned, that the sunny economic c
mate the Bush administration was inheriting—the lowest interest rates
years, record high job creation, record low unemployment—could eith
be strengthened or squandered, depending on the choices we were t
make.

The Bush administration's rush to slash taxes right out of the box was
in my opinion, irresponsible. But if we were going to talk about taxes here
I said—and I'm still saying it today—we needed to be sure to put the bulk
of that tax relief where it really belongs, in the pockets of middle-class
working families.

It would be not only shameful, I said, but also shortsighted, to give the
affluent the bulk of whatever tax cuts we decided upon, as the President
proposed. Forty percent of his $1.6 trillion tax cut would go to the wealth-
iest 1 percent of Americans. And as we've regrettably learned in the three
years since then—from the Enron, WorldCom, Adelphia, and Tyco experiences and more—there are a lot of people among that 1 percent who
don't want wealth to trickle down, trickle out, or trickle anywhere but
into their own pockets, to be used for their own (and not America's)
benefit.

That was—and still is—my take on tax cuts. From there, I also listed
other goals in that first speech to the 107th Senate: passing a real Patients'

And so soon after the election.

But that's exactly what happened.

The President and his people pushed hard throughout that spring for his budget plan. A dozen or so members of our caucus were inclined to support it. Zell Miller, Max Baucus, Ben Nelson, Evan Bayh, and John Breaux were wooed directly by Bush, who is very adept at the personal courtship all presidents use to persuade members of Congress to vote their way on a particular issue.

The power of a personal phone call from, or a meeting with, the president can't be underestimated. It's never a plea when the president calls—the president of the United States never pleads. Rather, it's a patriotic invitation to do something for the good of the country, coupled with the implicit fact that there are many things a president can do for you in your home state if he so chooses. He can, of course, discourage those same things if he desires.

I remember when my first boss in Congress, Jim Abourezk, on whose Senate staff I worked in the late 1970s, was holding out on the vote to turn over the Panama Canal. One night, very late, Jim had gotten up to use the bathroom when his home phone rang. It was the president, Jimmy Carter, on the line.

"I'm sorry to wake you, Jim," the President said.

Jim let the President know that nature's call had already done that, so he needn't feel guilty.

They had a short discussion, and Jim wound up voting for the bill.

Bill Clinton, of course, is famous for his late night calls. It's almost as if he gets the bulk of his work done between midnight and sunrise. As Senate Democratic leader, I got more than my share of those calls from him, usually when we were just launching a bill and he and his key people and my staff and I were shaping our strategy.

The president, whoever he might be, is typically involved like that early on with his own party, when a piece of legislation is being prepared. He'll continue to weigh in as the bill makes its way toward a vote. Finally, when things come to a head and the time for a vote has come, that's when the president will get personally involved and really start pushing—calling senators on both sides who are holding out or undecided, inviting them over to the Oval Office for a meeting, or even bringing them up to the White House's residential area, perhaps for a meal.

This activity can get pretty intense. Some presidents enjoy it more than others. Lyndon Johnson was born for this kind of work. The recently released White House audiotapes of his conversations with the political leaders of his day are as entertaining as they are enlightening. They give a firsthand sense of how calls like these are made and how successful these efforts can be. During his presidency from 1988 through 1992, I had the impression that George Herbert Walker Bush was not as comfortable as Johnson with this part of the job. The elder Bush seemed to prefer delegating this chore to members of his senior staff or cabinet. His son, on the other hand, is quite effective at personal lobbying. In the spring of 2001, President Bush managed to pick off many of our moderates, one at a time, persuading twelve of them to line up behind his budget plan.

But there were some fence-sitters on the Republican side as well, some members of the GOP caucus who not only had problems with the President's proposed budget, but had problems with the entire direction of this new administration and its party's core leadership. While the President was wooing some of the people on our side, we were talking to some of the people on his, at first just about the budget and then, unexpectedly, about much, much more.

The "missionary work" I referred to earlier is not an ongoing activity. It depends, for both sides, on whether there are any potential targets across the aisle. It also depends on the Senate's alignment, how close the parties are in terms of the number of seats they hold. If one party's clearly in control, there won't be much interest in switching sides. But when there's doubt about which way things are going to break, if the two sides are separated by only a couple of seats or so, that's when the activity can really pick up. And there are always people who are moving away from their party or feel that their party is moving away from them.

It's not hard to imagine how intense the cross-party probing became on both sides with a fifty-fifty Senate. A single member—whoever that member might be—could dramatically alter Washington, D.C.'s entire political landscape simply by standing up from his or her seat and walking across the aisle. Both parties were hunting for that person even before the 107th Congress convened.

There is, as I've said, nothing new about this. The very process of reaching out in this way builds relationships across party lines that are beneficial even if the person doesn't switch sides. In a setting as closely divided and partisan as the one we have in Congress today, you still have to find allies on the other side for support on one bill or another. It's always in the back of your mind that you might hit the jackpot and discover a person who's ready to move, but that's rarely the case, and it's rarely the primary reason you're reaching out. Sometimes, however, it happens. The planets align, the set and setting are just right, and someone decides to make a move.

It happened most recently in 1994, just before that year's midterm election. President Clinton had suffered through the defeat of his health care plan, and there was a lot of dissension in our Democratic ranks, especially among our members from the South and the West. We were becoming much more polarized within our party, with many conservative Democrats at the state level switching parties. As a result, control of many state legislatures was turning from Democratic to Republican.

In the Senate, one of those conservative Democrats was Dick Shelby of Alabama, who had joined the Senate in 1986, the same year I did. Dick and I had always been friendly. I can vividly recall talking to him that fall about supporting me for leader. We met in the beautiful marble room just off the Senate floor. Dick didn't tip his hand about his own intentions, but I had an uneasy feeling after that conversation. We had heard rumors, secondhand reports, that the Republicans were courting Dick and that they were also going after my friend Ben Nighthorse Campbell from Colorado. Sure enough, the day after the election, Dick announced he was switching parties.

As for Ben, he and I have had a great friendship during all the years we have served together. He and his wife, Linda, have traveled abroad with us, as part of congressional delegation trips—what we call CODELs. Prior to that election of 1994, Ben and I talked frequently about his discomfort with the Democratic Party in Colorado and his disagreements with the Clinton administration over western environmental policies. Shortly after my election that fall as leader, Ben announced his switch, too. It didn't change our friendship, but losing Ben was a significant personal disappointment for me.

That was the last time a sitting senator had switched parties before that spring of 2001, but as I said, there's almost always something brewing.

Even as I write these words, the Republican leadership is pushing pretty hard at two of the more conservative members of the House Democratic caucus—Ralph Hall of Texas and Bud Cramer of Alabama—to switch parties, and also they're urging Zell Miller of Georgia, here in the Senate, to do the same.

Zell has actually been number one on the Republicans' wish list virtually since the day he joined the Senate back in July 2000. He's never made any bones to our caucus about his conservative leanings on many issues or about his proclivity to vote with the Republicans. We've come to accept Zell's position by now, but it isn't really what we expected when he came out of retirement to accept an appointment to fill out the term of Paul Coverdell, who died of an aneurysm in July 2000. At that time, on the face of it, Zell was a good match for us. He had delivered one of three keynote addresses at the 1992 Democratic National Convention and had chaired the Democratic Platform Committee in 1996. He had been a very popular Democratic governor in Georgia, a champion of education. President Clinton incorporated some of Zell's innovative ideas on scholarships into the White House's education plan.

When Senator Coverdell died, Max Cleland immediately suggested we call Zell to urge him to accept the appointment of that Senate seat. At first, he refused. He told us he was enjoying retirement, relaxing at his home up in the Georgia mountains. But Georgia's governor, Roy Barnes, and Max persuaded Zell to accept the appointment for four months and then to consider a campaign to serve out the balance of the term—which he did in November of that year.

Both Bill Clinton and Max Cleland had been very complimentary about Zell. Each expected him to be a great asset to our caucus. And given the fact that he had been such a progressive governor, there was every reason to expect Zell would feel like an important part of the team when he got here.

That's why it was so surprising to see him arrive and announce, as his first decision, that he was going to keep many members of Paul Coverdell's staff. This was a little disconcerting, given that Paul Coverdell had been a member of the Republican leadership. That move, coupled with the first speech Zell gave on the Senate floor, in which he announced, "I'm not going to be a Democrat; I'm not going to be a Republican; I'm going to be a Georgian, and I'm going to speak my mind independently," were our first indications that Zell Miller would not be quite the Senator some had expected.

The Republicans were aware of all this and wasted no time moving in. I noticed immediately that Trent Lott and Phil Gramm were spending a lot of time with Zell on the Senate floor, sitting and talking with him and, in very short order, inviting him to join them for dinner and social events. It didn't surprise me when, right off the bat, Zell was invited by Phil Gramm and some of the other Republicans on the Banking Committee to join them on a trip to Mexico in January 2001. The Republicans made no secret of the fact that they were wooing Zell. He and Gramm, in particular, became very close friends. The two of them wound up partnering on many legislative projects, including President Bush's first tax cut and, eventually, the Republicans' version of the homeland security bill.

Naturally, seeing all this, we were worried about Zell early on, afraid that he might actually switch parties. Many of us talked to him and a few of his friends, people like Ed Jenkins, a former congressman from Georgia. They assured me that they were pretty certain Zell was not likely to leave the Democratic Party. He might vote with the other side at times, they said, but I didn't need to worry about him actually switching.

Still, the Republicans continued to come after Zell and Ben Nelson from Nebraska—and their pursuit really heated up with the new reality of our fifty-fifty Senate situation. For our part, there were three people on the Republican side on whom we had our sights set—John McCain, Lincoln Chafee, and Jim Jeffords.

The roster of centrist, moderate Republicans—the "Mod Squad," as some pundits call them—included Olympia Snowe, Susan Collins, and Arlen Specter as well, but none of them indicated any inclination at all to become Democrats or even independents. McCain, Chafee, and Jeffords, however, had at various times seemed to us to be open at least to an invitation.

In John McCain's case, we felt that he'd been treated poorly after he ran against Bush for the Republican presidential nomination. He was angry, I think, at the vicious smear campaign the Bush people ran against him and his family in the South Carolina primary and at the way they then slighted him when Bush took office. Very few, if any, of John's people made it into the administration. John didn't think that was right, that his staff should be penalized like that.

In addition, John was working very closely with us on campaign finance reform and several other issues on which we shared the same views. Over the years, he and I have become friends and talk frequently. We had a common agenda on many of the higher-profile issues, which naturally prompted speculation, both inside our caucus and among onlookers in the press and among the Republican membership, that John might switch sides.

As for Lincoln Chafee, he was perhaps the most consistent vote for us among the Republicans. He is far more progressive than most of his fellow Republicans, and he is from Rhode Island, a traditionally Democratic state. He has never had a problem with, or fear of, being the only Republican voice joining ours on an issue. On tax policy and budget, environmental, and education issues, he shares the same values as we do and votes accordingly.

Linc's father, John, who was elected as a Republican senator in 1976, had been someone we admired greatly and thought might consider switching parties. John actually had conversations about this with a number of Democratic senators over the years, but nothing ever came of those discussions. When John passed away in 1999, it was Lincoln who took his place.

So those two—McCain and Chafee—seemed like real possibilities. The third, Jim Jeffords, quite honestly seemed less likely a prospect until a series of circumstances, a combination of happenstance and events, transpired to push him to the center of our attention—and to push us to the center of his.

Jim Jeffords and I became friends when we served together in the House. It was clear even then that Jim was a rarity in Congress, a representative who would just as soon stay out of the limelight as long as he's allowed to get his job done. He's not bombastic. He's not self-aggrandizing. He's been variously described by the press as "quiet," "laconic," "effective," and "proud."

Throughout Jim's congressional career, which began with his 1974 election to Vermont's single seat in the House of Representatives, he made it clear that his primary responsibility was to the constituency that elected him, the people of Vermont. That state's spirit of independence is carried on today by Bernie Sanders, who is currently the lone independent in the House of Representatives.

By the time Jim Jeffords joined the Senate in 1988, he was known as a Republican who did not necessarily march to the beat of the leadership's drum. He voted against Ronald Reagan's 1981 tax cut. He voted against Clarence Thomas's Supreme Court nomination. During Bill Clinton's presidency, he voted for health care reform, minimum wage increases, and increased funding for the National Endowment for the Arts—all anathema to most Republicans.

Trent Lott and his colleagues knew they were dealing with a wild card in Jim. It didn't help matters that he endured countless snubs, cold shoulders, and petty slights from his fellow Republicans over the years for his ideological "transgressions." When Dick Shelby made his party switch in 1994, for instance, one of Jim's more conservative colleagues, Phil Gramm, suggested that Jim be traded for Shelby, so the Republicans "could be rid of him."

By the time of the 2000 election, what Jim himself called his "growing discontent" with the "Republican orthodoxy" was nearing a breaking point. His discomfort with the extremism of his party's right-wing leadership was amplified in the wake of that election by a series of discourtesies and strong-arm tactics by his colleagues, some of them just "petty grammar school stuff," as Jim called it. Others were more significant than that, but in the end their cumulative effect led to a decision that would BLOW UP WASHINGTON (as *Newsweek* magazine's cover headline put it) like a ONE-MAN EARTHQUAKE (as *Time*'s lead story was headlined).

The snubs started that winter, innocuously enough, with the Singing Senators, the Republicans' performing quartet, of which Jim was a charter member. He, Trent Lott, John Ashcroft, and Idaho's Larry Craig had formed the group in late 1995. They'd gotten plenty of fanfare since that time, and they deserved it. These guys were actually pretty good.

But the quartet took a blow when Ashcroft lost his Senate seat in that 2000 election. A month later, Larry Craig asked Jim to support his bid for the chairmanship of the Republicans' Policy Committee. When Jim told Craig he was sorry but he was voting for Pete Domenici instead, that was the beginning of the end of Jim's career with the Singing Senators— although no one bothered to tell him at the time.

A month after that, at an inaugural event, the Singing Senators were invited by the Oak Ridge Boys to come up from the audience and join them for a song. While the "guest appearance" by the senators had been planned in advance, Jim hadn't been told a thing about it. In fact, it was only by chance that he happened to show up at the event. Realizing he hadn't been a part of the plan, Jim was stung. At the urging of his son and daughter-in-law, who were with him, Jim gamely climbed up on stage, and the group played it off as if Jim were just a late arrival, but I know Jim was hurt.

That slight was merely insulting, and a little embarrassing. But it was the Republicans' subsequent handling of the issue nearest and dearest to Jim Jeffords's heart—education—that would be their undoing.

Jim brought as much leadership to his position as chairman of the Health, Education, Labor and Pensions (HELP) Committee as any committee chairman in Congress. Education was his passion, especially education for people with disabilities. Despite all the differences he had with his party, despite his treatment as an outcast black sheep, Jim still treasured the opportunity he had in that position to significantly affect and improve the educational system for all of America's children. His hopes were raised by the election of George Bush. Jim believed Bush when he called himself a "new kind of Republican." He believed that the compassion of this "compassionate conservative" would guide the government to support issues of education and the disabled. Jim believed the new president's promise that "no child would be left behind." And he believed Bush when he vowed to "change the tone" in Washington. Jim took that promise to mean both the tone of partisan warfare between the parties and the tone of petty vindictiveness and infighting of which he had so often been a target within his own party.

It didn't take long, however, for Jim to discover not just that it was business as usual for the Republicans' right-wing leadership with Bush in the presidency, but that things were now worse than ever.

As that spring began, Jim found himself a marked man because of his initial opposition to the Bush administration's original tax cut proposal, which he feared, rightly, would make it impossible for the President to keep his commitment to education. He was also publicly opposed to Bush's pro-drilling energy policy, and his health care proposals. The White House responded to Jim's opposition by including no guarantees of funding for education for children with disabilities in its proposed budget. None.

Jim was upset. Late that March, on a Friday afternoon, with most of the Senate gone home for the weekend, he met with Chris Dodd, one of our two Democratic senators from Connecticut, in Chris's office. They were there to discuss an amendment on child care but wound up talking about Jim's friction with Bush and with the Republican leadership. At one point in the conversation, Jim wondered aloud if there was any room left for him in the Republican Party.

Chris could hardly stay in his seat. As soon as Jim left, Chris got on the phone and tracked me down in my office.

"I think there's something going on here," Chris said. "I think we really need to begin talking to him."

At that point, we were actually having serious discussions with members of both John McCain's and Lincoln Chafee's staffs about either or even both of them possibly leaving the Republican side. Some of these conversations were between members of our staffs and some included other people who were mutual friends of their staffers and ours—all very informal discussions but nonetheless very serious.

The reports I was getting by late March were that it looked as though something might happen with McCain or Chafee. There was very little going on with Jim Jeffords—until that meeting with Chris Dodd. But when Chris said he told Jim how welcome we would make him on our side, and that Jim's response was that he could never become a Democrat but could see himself as an independent, that was enough to push him to the center of our radar screen.

Now our focus was almost entirely on Jim Jeffords. Pat Leahy, Jim's fellow senator from Vermont and a leader in our Democratic caucus, had a good relationship with Jim. They spent a lot of time flying back and forth to Vermont together. There was plenty of opportunity there and elsewhere for Pat and other members of our caucus to keep in touch with Jim, but we all understood that there should be no pushing—Jim was getting enough of that from the Republican side. All we needed to make clear to him was that when and if he wanted to talk to us—*whenever* he wanted to talk—we would be ready and eager.

As the first week of April began, so did the Senate debate on the budget. And so did a series of meetings between Jim and the Republican leadership—Trent Lott, Don Nickles, Pete Domenici, and even Vice President Cheney. The votes on both sides were lining up almost dead even, so

Jim's was crucial. A few weeks earlier, with the President's proposed tax cut still at $1.6 trillion, Jim had asked Lott to earmark $200 billion for special education, and Lott had agreed—or so Jim thought.

By the end of the first day of debate, with the tax cut now whittled down to $1.4 trillion, Trent Lott told Jim that his share for special education had shrunk to $180 billion. That was a hard pill to swallow, but Jim accepted it. He could still get a lot done with $180 billion. What he didn't know then was that even that amount would wind up being scaled back further.

The week ended with the Senate passing a budget that included a $1.35 trillion tax cut—down from what Bush had wanted but still too much for me and many others. Far from celebrating a substantial victory, however, the White House considered that figure a defeat, and they kept a virtual scorecard of the people who had given them trouble along the way—including, quite prominently, Jim Jeffords.

The Bush White House and the Republican leadership are accomplished at the politics of vindictive retribution. While Democrats would experience it often during the coming two years, Jim Jeffords felt it right at the beginning.

No sooner was that budget passed than the White House began hinting that it might cut or even eliminate a milk-marketing program that was critical to Vermont's dairy farmers. Meanwhile, one of Jim's colleagues on the Health, Education, Labor and Pensions Committee, New Hampshire's Judd Gregg—a loyal soldier in the most conservative wing of the Republican Party—began undercutting Jim's authority as chairman by convening private gatherings of the committee's Republican members without inviting Jim or even letting him know they were meeting.

Late that April came the coup de grâce, the kind of petty but pointed slight that the White House has made a specialty.

The announcement of the annual National Teacher of the Year Award is always a big event at the White House. It's a chance to showcase a positive, bright side of our nation's educational system. The award has for years included a ceremony in the Rose Garden, where the president honors the recipient before an audience of friends, family, select members of Congress, and the press.

This particular year was no exception. The winner, for the first time in the competition's fifty-one-year history, was from Vermont—a high school history teacher named Michele Forman. The ceremony was a beautiful, inspiring event. Conspicuous by his absence, however, was the Republican senator from Vermont, the chairman of the Senate HELP Committee and a champion of education in America, Jim Jeffords, who had pointedly *not* been invited to the affair.

That snub got plenty of publicity, none of it good for the White House. Frankly, I thought it was a dumb thing for them to do.

Later that month, Bill Nelson, one of our Democratic senators from Florida, traveled on a CODEL to Portugal. Dick Shelby was on the same trip. At one point, Susan Brophy, formerly a congressional liaison in the Clinton White House, and now wife of the U.S. ambassador to Portugal, Gerald McGowan, apologized to Shelby for the way some in the Clinton administration had treated him. That triggered a lengthy conversation in which Shelby asserted that the treatment he had received from President Clinton had been a factor in his switching parties. Early in 1993, Shelby had indicated his displeasure with the Clinton economic package. Rather than try to woo him, the inexperienced White House decided to send a clear message to the Alabama Democrat. When the University of Alabama's NCAA football championship team visited the White House, Shelby received only one ticket to the event. Shortly thereafter, the administration announced that much of NASA's operations would be moved from Huntsville, Alabama, to another state. Even though the White House eventually reversed itself on that decision, those public slaps were fresh in Dick Shelby's mind when he switched parties after the 1994 elections.

Bill Nelson immediately thought of Jim Jeffords and the treatment he was getting from the Bush White House. As soon as he got back to Washington, Bill contacted Jim and asked if they could get together for a talk, which they did on the last day of April. That discussion prompted several conversations between my assistant Democratic leader, Harry Reid, Jim, and me. Harry and Jim are actually very much alike, both in temperament and bearing. At one point in our conversations, Harry said, "Jim, this is beyond you and me. This is for your country."

But there was no way to minimize the devastation such a decision would wreak in the lives of many, many people on the Republican side, including some of Jim Jeffords's closest friends. If the Republicans lost control of the Senate, Republican senators who had spent their entire careers working their way up to a committee chairmanship would have those positions taken away from them. Jim's own staff would suffer. Those costs, the *human* price of this decision, more so than the damage his decision might inflict on the Bush White House or on the Republican leadership, were what had Jim tied up in knots.

He held until the second week in May, when, during Senate debate on the President's education bill, which Jim was managing on the floor, Jim sat down with Budget Committee Chairman Pete Domenici and was informed that there was now nothing for special education in the still-evolving budget. Nothing. Domenici assured Jim that billions of dollars from surplus funds would be available in the coming years, but Jim wasn't even listening anymore. He was finished.

That's when I started making personal overtures, calling Jim, commiserating with him, and letting him know we were willing to talk whenever he was. He came by my office a couple of times for brief chats in person, but we were very careful about that. I never came near him on the Senate floor itself or, for that matter, in any location where the press or the Republican members might see us. Rumors were already starting to leak out, and I didn't want to fuel what was at that point mere speculation.

Finally, the evening of May 14, a Monday night, Harry came into my office to report that, based on a conversation he had just had with him on the Senate floor, Jim was very interested in talking about the switch.

"Are you sure?" I asked.

"We can meet with him tomorrow in his hideaway," replied Harry.

Jim had chosen to meet early in the morning because so few people would be around, and he asked that we come to his hideaway for the privacy it would afford.

There are about seventy-five "hideaways" scattered throughout the Capitol building, in various corners and crannies. They're simple one-room offices, given out on the basis of seniority. Most have an incredibly rich history. One is where Daniel Webster used to store his wine. Another, occupied by Ted Kennedy, is the same room each of his brothers used during their time in the Senate. Some hideaways are nothing more than former storage rooms with no windows, tucked in quiet hallways on the upper and lower floors of the Capitol. More junior senators generally occupy those. The one I had before becoming Democratic leader was little more than a large closet outfitted with a desk and chair.

Jim's hideaway is straight down in the bowels of the Capitol. It's a pretty labyrinthine trip—quite a few turns and quite a few small stairways—to get to it. It's not as nice as that of his senior counterpart from Vermont, Patrick Leahy, or as the beautiful and historic ones occupied by Chris Dodd, Paul Sarbanes, Ted Stevens, or John Warner, but Jim's is better than average.

It was 7:00 A.M. when Harry and I arrived at Jim's hideaway that Tuesday morning, and Jim got right down to business. He had three primary concerns, and they could be summarized as: cows, committees, and co-workers.

The "cows" referred to the government's dairy policy, the one the White House was threatening to eliminate. It was a very complicated arrangement whereby dairy farmers in the Northeast, including Vermont, were guaranteed a minimum price for their milk without regard to the price Midwest farmers received. Knowing that Midwestern Democrats were on the flip side of this issue, Jim wanted our assurance that we would work with him to come up with an agreement that would be fair to both sides. I told him we would (and we did, it turned out, to everyone's acceptance).

As for "committees," the issue here was that by leaving the Republicans, Jim would lose the committee positions he held through their caucus. Naturally, he wanted to know what committee positions we might be able to offer him. By giving Jim a position, of course, we would have to bump one of our people.

I thought for a minute about who would become chairmen of the two committees Jim was currently on—that would be Ted Kennedy on the Health, Education, and Labor and Pensions Committee and Max Baucus on the Finance Committee. I didn't imagine either of them would be too enthusiastic about giving up those chairmanships.

Then Harry mentioned his own committee—Environment and Public Works—of which he was the ranking Democratic member at that point. With Jim's move, Harry would become chairman of that committee, and he offered that position there on the spot to Jim Jeffords. Harry's logic was, "Well, look, as the new assistant majority leader, I'm going to have my hands full on the floor, and I'll have that new power to bring to bear for the people of Nevada."

Jim was blown away by the generosity of Harry's offer. As for his last concern—"co-workers"—that was no problem. I promised him he could bring over every one of his staff.

With that we shook hands, and the deal was done.

Which didn't mean I stopped worrying. By that Friday, all Washington was abuzz with rumors about Jim's defection. As I was pulling my things together to fly back to South Dakota for the weekend, I saw a CNN correspondent reporting the rumor, and I thought, Oh, it's over. I figured the game was up. Bush was surely going to swoop in and grab Jim for the weekend, bring him out to Camp David, and make him recant.

Beyond that, I knew that Jim's own family was not happy with this decision. It was reported to us that his wife, Liz, was initially against it and that his son said he would speak out in public against it if Jim made this move. Some of Jim's staff said they'd resign, that they would leave him if he left the Republican Party. There's really no way to describe what a remarkable test of political courage and personal character this was for Jim.

Frankly, I wasn't sure that he—or anyone—could withstand that much pressure. I didn't get much sleep that weekend.

Miraculously, Monday came and nothing had changed, except for the heat of the rumor mill. Late that day, Jim told Republican Senator Olympia Snowe, one of the so-called Mod Squad, that he was thinking seriously about leaving. Olympia immediately put through a very alarmed call to White House Chief of Staff Andy Card, but Card had already gone home. She left an urgent message but didn't hear back from Card until late Tuesday morning.

Now the White House knew, and the Republican caucus literally converged on Jim, one after the other approaching his desk on the Senate floor. Nickles asked him what kind of "funny water" he'd been drinking. Lott and Craig invited him back to rejoin the Singing Senators. Phil Gramm, who as a House member back in the 1980s had switched from the Democratic to the Republican Party, told Jeffords he understood such a move and asked him to please "just don't screw up the tax bill."

That afternoon, Jim met with Dick Cheney in the Vice President's ceremonial office just off the Senate floor, then he went to the White House for a meeting with the President. The tone was cordial on both sides, but Jim did warn Bush that the right wing of his party was taking control and if he didn't push it back toward the center, he'd be, as Jim put it, "a one-term president." They both left it at that.

I'd been watching the heat grow around Jim all week, but nothing I'd seen prepared me for that Wednesday's display on the floor of the Senate.

We were in the midst of the critical budget debate, but no one was paying attention to that.

All eyes were on Jim, who was besieged by wave after wave of the Republican guard. They kept leading him out of the room into the Vice President's room, where they really worked him over, really put on the pressure. They reminded him how much would be lost, how many people would be hurt. Some yelled in anger and disbelief. Some of them were close to tears. For many, it meant the loss of a chairmanship, a committee position. For everyone in the Republican caucus, it meant the loss of their ability to move their legislative agenda, both in committee and through the Senate.

This was hard on Jim. Every time he returned to the floor, he looked grayer. Just ashen. We—Harry and I—talked to him a couple of times early in the day, just a few words. By that afternoon, though, I felt that we—our caucus—needed to keep clear of Jim, to give him what little space he might have. At one point, however, Harry Reid did go over and ask how he was doing.

"Well," Jim said, and he paused. "I think I'm still going to be with you."

Think? This was nothing like the certainty Jim seemed to have felt a week earlier.

"I just need to listen," he told Harry. "I need to hear these guys out. They're friends of mine."

By this time, the whole Senate was watching this drama unfold right before their eyes. Rumors began flying right there in the chamber. One minute the word was "He's staying." The next, he was going to leave. The next, he was going to wait till the 2002 election, *then* leave.

Late that afternoon, the White House sent over an offer to Jim of more money for education. Trent Lott threw in a seat at the Republicans' leadership table. Trent also told Jim he could chair the Health, Education, Labor and Pensions Committee for as long as he wanted.

So all this was on the table. And it was by no means clear to any of us, on either side, what Jim's final decision would be. All we knew was that he'd be making it that night, because he'd already scheduled a flight home that Wednesday evening—which is a very unusual thing to do, flying home in midweek—and he had a press conference set up for the next morning in Montpelier.

My thought as Jim left the Senate floor that afternoon, headed home to

Vermont, was that one more family meeting might change his mind. This doesn't, I thought to myself, look good. I can't say I had a great night's sleep that evening, either. But when the phone rang the next morning and Jim told me, "Tom, I'm going to do this," I was ecstatic.

There'd never been a contingent of press in Montpelier like the one that packed the town that morning. Jim's announcement was broadcast live on national television. That's how important this was. Harry Reid, along with several of my staff and me gathered in the office of my chief of staff, Pete Rouse, to watch it. We stood stone cold silent as Jim started to speak. He described in quite wrenching terms how difficult this decision had been. We knew we were watching history unfold. No one in the room dared breathe.

When Jim reached the point in his speech where he said, "I will make this change and will caucus with the Democrats for organizational purposes . . . ," the room exploded with cheers. You could hear us out in the halls.

His decision would have a monumental impact on the business of the U.S. Senate for the balance of the 107th Congress. All that we would achieve and all the political balance we would provide would be due to him and his remarkable decision. Beyond that, I believe it will be recorded as one of the most profound acts of political courage in the Senate's history.

I called Jim as soon as he was finished and told him what a wonderful speech it had been.

"I'm glad you liked it," he said in his typically self-effacing manner. "I worked on it through the night."

Then, again in his sincere, understated way, he said, "Tom, I hope we can make a difference."

"Jim," I answered, "we're going to make a *big* difference because of what you've done."

That was a promise I was determined to keep.

End of chpt. 3

CHAPTER FOUR ∕ goes to pg. 103=31/pgs

Majority Leader

EVERY YEAR, WHEN CONGRESS ADJOURNS for its August recess, I go home to make a pilgrimage of sorts. South Dakota is a fairly small state, with a population of a little less than three-quarters of a million people— smaller than the city of Indianapolis. I like that, because it makes it possible to enjoy the human, person-to-person kind of contact that is so rare in our modern world of media-driven politics. There are sixty-six counties in South Dakota. Every year I visit each of them, and every August I take a road trip to visit as many of them as I can. I used to do it alone, in a 1971 Pontiac Ventura whose odometer was pushing 260,000 miles by the time I was done with it. I loved to work under the hood of that car, changing the oil and filters and spark plugs, but those days are over, and that car now sits in its final resting place in the Pioneer Auto Museum, in Murdo, South Dakota. With all that's transpired in the past two years, I now have a security detail with me as well, often around the clock, wherever I go. At first, it was a little tough to get used to, and at times comical. For example, the morning after I was assigned twenty-four-hour protection, in the wake of the September 11 attacks, I opened the door to get the newspaper, and there they were. Linda and I weren't quite sure what to do, so we brought coffee and doughnuts out to their car, kind of like the service in the old drive-in restaurants. The next day, we did it again. Finally, after about three weeks of this, Linda just looked at me and said, "Sweetheart, you're on your own."

Though I deeply appreciate the job the protective detail of the Capitol Police does and how very well they do it, I wish it didn't have to be that way. I prefer, for example, to take my daily early morning run by myself. But by now, the constant company is something I've learned to live with. And I haven't let it change my annual August ritual. I still make that trip, without a set schedule. I still stop along the way to watch the eagles and the buffalo, still pull in at garages and grain elevators and cafés where the doors open at 6:00 A.M. and the local guys come in for coffee and we roll dice to see who pays. I've learned a lot about politics on these trips and a lot about people. And I like to think they've learned something about me, too.

There's one reason, in a state where Republicans outnumber Democrats by 11 percent among registered voters, and where many of the registered independents lean Republican, that South Dakotans have chosen to send me to represent them in Washington for the past twenty-five years. The reason they've honored me with their trust, I have little doubt, is that I have actually crossed paths with most of them in one way or another over the years, giving them a chance to make a judgment on a scale that extends beyond TV sound bites, or Sunday morning talk show appearances, or what they might hear on talk radio. That kind of face-to-face contact is a luxury neither the politicians nor the voters in most of America have a chance to experience today.

And that interaction with South Dakotans has influenced my approach to the work I do in Washington. I've always believed in the politics of inclusion, of consensus, of coalition building, of connection. This approach requires, above all, the ability to listen, to consider someone else's viewpoint and try, as much as possible, to incorporate that viewpoint (and hopefully that person) into the process of shaping and implementing a particular piece of legislation. Listening—really listening—isn't as simple as some people think. As my great friend and colleague Pat Leahy puts it, "There's a difference between just being quiet and actually listening."

I'm still not as good a listener as I wish I were, but listening is also probably just part of my character. And part of that, I'm certain, stems from the shyness that plagued me when I was a boy growing up in the town of Aberdeen, in northeastern South Dakota. I remember being very anxious as a youngster that someone would start a conversation with me and I'd have nothing to say. I was so concerned about this that I'd lie awake in my bedroom in the basement of my house in Aberdeen—the house I now own and my mother still lives in—and I'd play both parts in an imagined conversation.

By the time I began high school, I'd gotten that fear under control, but I was still more interested in what other people had to say than what I might have to offer. Plus, quite frankly, I was a pretty awkward kid, not the smoothest character around. It didn't help things when I broke half of a front tooth going for a rebound during a junior high basketball game and the dentist insisted on putting a silver cap on it. That cap stayed on until well into high school, which made me even less eager to open my mouth.

My confidence came around—and that silver cap was removed—by the time I started college in 1965. In 1973, after I'd earned my degree (in political science) from South Dakota State University, served three years in the Air Force, and worked as a volunteer on George McGovern's 1972 presidential campaign, I decided that I wanted to make politics my career. I was hired to join the campaign staff of Jim Abourezk, who was running for the Senate in South Dakota that year, too. He won and asked me to come to Washington as one of his legislative aides.

Some time ago, Jim, who was the first Arab American ever elected to the Senate, was interviewed by a writer from *The New Yorker* magazine and shared an anecdote that took place that first year I worked for him. It is a little incident I only vaguely remember—and one that may have had the benefit of growing exaggeration with each telling over the years—but it illustrates in its own way the power of listening. As Jim recalled it: "I was getting my ass chewed out by a bunch of American Legionnaires about Vietnam and had to go to the Senate floor for a vote. So I had Tom talk to them while I was gone. When I came back, he had them eating out of his hand. I told him he should think about running for office."

Five years after that, I mounted my first political campaign, running for a seat in the U.S. House of Representatives against a former Vietnam prisoner of war named Leo Thorsness. After being behind on election night and even the following morning, I won by a grand total of 14 votes (a subsequent recount, which lasted a year and twenty-one days and went all the way to the state supreme court, put the final margin at 110).

In 1982, as a result of the 1980 census, South Dakota lost its second congressional district, and I had the opportunity to run for Congress statewide. My opponent was South Dakota's other congressman, Clint Roberts. If Clint looked like he came out of a Marlboro cigarette commercial, that's because he did. He actually *was* the Marlboro man in the company's ads. In a sense, I was running against an icon. That, too, was a relatively close race, which I won by about three percentage points.

Four years later, I ran for the Senate against the incumbent, Jim

Abdnor, and won by 9,484 votes. In 1994, after I was elected Senate Democratic leader by a single vote, one magazine writer picked up on the trend and called me "the master of winning by a nose."

I don't know about that, but I do know that close elections, like close athletic contests, are decided by preparation—preparation and paying attention. By "paying attention," I mean not only listening to people, which of course is essential, but also trying to understand them. Beyond merely listening, which can be hard for anyone at times, understanding requires the ability to empathize, the ability to put yourself in other people's shoes, to look out through their eyes, to get a sense of what it feels like to *be* them. Regardless of how you feel about another person, whether he or she is your friend or your foe, it is always in your best interest to empathize, in order to understand. Quite often, this process can inform and shift your opinion. Just as often, it can shift theirs. If politics, as some say, is the art of persuasion, there is no better way to persuade others than to show them you understand what *they* need, not just what *you* need.

When I was in the Air Force, my job was to study satellite surveillance photographs—primarily photos of missile sites in China and Russia. It was fascinating work, analyzing these three-dimensional, stereoscopic images. The analogy has been made more than once by some in Congress that to excel in politics one has to study people in much the same way that I studied those photographs. What they're talking about, I think, is something more than just paying attention; it's trying to understand not just *what* the other person says or believes, which can sometimes be hard enough, but *why* he or she says or believes it.

It is especially important in a place like the Senate. The Senate is nothing but a complex web of relationships—one hundred men and women with different experiences, different backgrounds, different strengths, different weaknesses, different beliefs, and different points of view. Some are extremely wealthy. Some have very little personal wealth. All are given six years to prove themselves and have been thrown together to make the laws of the land. Each of these individuals has his or her own obligations, not just to the nation as a whole, but to their individual states and myriad constituencies as well. They're pulled in many directions, and being the informed, opinionated, strong-willed

chpt. 4 (cont)

77.

people that most of them are, they often have pretty firm ideas about the way things should be done.

Often, individual senators feel that they should be the one leading the way. My friend George Mitchell, who preceded me as Senate Democratic leader, used to refer to the Senate as a collection of "independent contractors." Byron Dorgan, a very close friend and a senator from North Dakota, sometimes calls our group "one hundred bad habits." As I said, pulling together such disparate individuals is like loading frogs into a wheelbarrow. Mary McGrory, the esteemed longtime political columnist for the *Washington Post,* compares it to managing the Metropolitan Opera, a job that requires, as McGrory puts it, "juggling enormous and fragile egos." The standard analogy around Capitol Hill is to say it's about as easy as herding cats.

But that's what the Senate is all about—creating alliances. The only way you can make such a disparate collection of individuals come together in a way that brings about the majority vote on any given issue is to understand what makes them tick, to understand what motivates them, what angers them, what approach works with them, and ultimately what can convince them to join with you.

If they choose to line up against you, it's just as important to understand why they did that, because in the Senate, every debate, every vote, every political battle, is merely a prelude to the next one. An opponent in today's fight may well become an ally in tomorrow's, *if* you have shaped an understanding of that person over time that has enabled you to develop a relationship with him or her.

The political skills required to build such relationships in the Senate are quite different from those required by, say, the presidency. Of course, it's in the president's best interest to establish as many relationships as he can with the members of Congress, but his primary focus is divining the will of the nation as a whole. He is constantly taking the pulse of the vast American public.

We in the Senate must do the same, of course, but we need to do more than simply dictate a desired outcome. We have to divine the individual temperaments and wills of *one another.* This ability is at the root of building coalitions and achieving consensus.

* * *

I first began learning these lessons during my eight years as a member of the House of Representatives under the tutelage of the late Mo Udall of Arizona. No one had a greater impact on my early years in Congress than Mo. I vividly remember my first meeting with him in his office. I had just been given the "Landslide Award" as the congressman who had won his seat by the smallest margin. My new colleagues jokingly referred to me as "Landslide Daschle" or the "Almost Congressman." I had a very tenuous hold on my new seat.

Mo reminded me that I had won with thirteen votes more than I needed. He said that it doesn't matter how many you got last time, the goal is to get more the *next* time. To do that, he told me, you have to work hard, go home often, build your base of political support, and start to develop relationships with your colleagues. To do that last part, Mo suggested that I consider running for the regional whip position in the House Democratic caucus. Given his legendary sense of humor, I thought at first that he was joking.

The House Democratic caucus was divided at the time into a number of regional whip regions. The regional whips attended a weekly leadership meeting and asked to serve as the contact person for head counts on particular votes and as a conduit for messages between the leadership and members. I was a member of the Rocky Mountain region.

Mo insisted he was serious about my running for that position. He urged me to personally pay a call on each of the members in our region to inform them of my candidacy.

"And you can tell them I support you," he said.

I did just that. And I won. It was my first foray into caucus politics and leadership, and the headlines at home were big and blaring: DASCHLE WINS HOUSE LEADERSHIP POST.

Thanks to Mo Udall, I was on my way.

There were others, too, who were extremely helpful and who greatly influenced me in those early years as a member of Congress: Claude Pepper, Dan Rostenkowski, Jim Wright, Tip O'Neill. Each of these men played a role and gave me help in many incalculable ways.

When I moved from the House to the Senate in 1986, George Mitchell took me under his wing. It was extremely instructive to watch George, as Senate majority leader, go toe-to-toe against the first President Bush's administration and agenda. In the heat of the fiercest debate, George was able to maintain a moderate, reasonable, well-balanced tone, even as he doggedly pursued a different agenda.

In spite of his natural, reserved Maine demeanor, George has a wonderfully wide grin when he smiles and an equally warm sense of humor. He loves to tell stories, and he is known to tell a good one quite frequently. One of his favorites took place during his first few months in the Senate. He had just given up his federal judgeship to become an appointed senator from Maine to fill out the term of his friend and mentor Ed Muskie. George loved being a judge. Taking the Senate seat was not an easy decision for him. Shortly after his arrival, the Senate was engaged in an all-night filibuster. As George considered his new status, thinking of the more stable and less demanding schedule of a judge, he began to feel sorry for himself. As the debate wore on long into the night, he was shown his cot in a room off the Senate floor. Cots had been set up so senators could take naps but still be available for an unscheduled vote. As he walked past the ranks of these sleeping senators, he noticed John Warner lying on a cot close to his. Immediately, George said he felt better. John Warner could be home with his wife, Elizabeth Taylor, he thought to himself. So what have I got to complain about?

George looked, talked, and worked like the senator and leader he was—calm but firm, smart, articulate, and cunning. I think some on the other side were intimidated by him. And they certainly did not enjoy the effectiveness of his style. More than a few people say it was George Mitchell who personally cost Bush the reelection he sought in 1992 by blocking much of Bush's agenda, including, most notably, the capital-gains tax cut Bush was hailing as a way to reverse the downward plunge of the economy at that time.

When Mitchell announced his retirement from the Senate in early 1994, I decided to run for his job. My announcement raised a lot of eyebrows, among both the press and my colleagues in the caucus. First of all, I had served in the Senate for only eight years. Only one man in history had become majority leader with less time than that under his belt—Lyndon Johnson, who was elected majority leader in 1954, after just six years as a senator.

Beyond that, there were questions about whether I was tough enough to take on that job. I'd never chaired a committee, never had to lead the way in the kinds of behind-closed-doors battles that take place in those committee rooms. More than one reporter dismissed me as a "back-bencher." Another called me a "park ranger in a dark suit." A core of my more senior colleagues in the caucus, whom the press tagged the "old bulls," considered me too low-key, too understated, too soft-spoken to lead the kinds of fights we were in for against the Republican majority.

I could understand their skepticism. They wanted more of a "puncher," as one of them put it, more of a "pugilist," someone more seasoned and dynamic than me. Their preference was Jim Sasser, from Tennessee, who announced his candidacy that summer. Jim was the politically savvy, highly respected chairman of the Senate Budget Committee.

I wasn't surprised by any of the reservations people had about me. I think I've benefited my entire life from low expectations, from being underestimated. When I first announced my candidacy for the House back in 1978, there were people who laughed, who told me I looked as if I were about sixteen years old (I was thirty at the time). Once, as I was campaigning in South Dakota during those winter months, going door-to-door asking for support, I was actually mistaken for the paperboy.

I got that same kind of reaction when I first ran for the Senate, and while I had worked doggedly on issues important to South Dakotans, I hadn't made a lot of national headlines during the eight years I'd spent in the Senate up to 1994. But I had worked hard at building strong individual relationships as co-chairman of the Senate Democratic Policy Committee (DPC). Despite the doubts of the naysayers, I believed I was ready to become our caucus's leader.

First, though, we all had to readjust to that fall's midterm election results, which completely scrambled our situation. The "Gingrich revolution" had swept into Washington, and Democrats were no longer the majority in the House or the Senate. I was now running for *minority* leader. And my opponent was no longer Jim Sasser. He lost a close reelection bid that November to a Tennessee doctor named Bill Frist. Now my opponent for our caucus's leadership position was Chris Dodd of Connecticut, a close friend.

As the day of that vote drew near, Chris and I each had twenty-three votes. Or at least we thought we did. There were a few whose votes neither of us could count on for sure. In elections like this, one needs to reconfirm commitments in some cases with regularity. And even with reconfirmations, luck sometimes plays a big role.

Luck was on my side the day before that election. As I was leaving the Capitol that afternoon, I caught up with Ben Nighthorse Campbell in the parking lot as he was getting on his Harley motorcycle to leave for the day. Ben, as I mentioned earlier, was struggling at that time with the Clinton administration over several issues.

"Now, you're coming to caucus tomorrow, right?" I asked him.

"Oh," he answered, fiddling with the strap on his helmet. "I've got to be in Chicago tomorrow."

This was not what I wanted to hear.

"Well, tomorrow's the vote," I reminded him.

"I'm sorry," he said. "I just can't be there."

Not even knowing if proxy votes were allowed, I asked Ben if he would vote by proxy before he left town. He thought for a second and said, "Sure."

I immediately called my staff to find out if proxies were legal and, if so, how we should go about getting one for Ben. They quickly looked into the rules and learned that proxies were indeed legal. I called Ben to report the good news and drew up a proxy ballot for him to sign, which he did.

The next day, as we sat in the old Senate chamber, nominations for Chris and me were made and seconded. Each senator wrote his choice for leader on a small piece of white paper, brought it down to the desk, and inserted it into a small, wooden box.

When all the ballots were cast, two senators were appointed to draw them out, one by one, and read them aloud to the caucus. When all the votes of those present were counted, the election stood at a 23–23 tie.

Ben's proxy ballot, the final slip of paper, was then opened and counted. His vote broke the tie and I was announced the winner.

Two weeks after that, Ben Campbell switched parties.

Nothing could have better prepared me for the situation I faced in the summer of 2001, as I assumed the majority leader's position in the wake of Jim Jeffords's "defection," than my assuming the minority leader's seat in 1994. I had already learned a lot about the tools a majority leader has at his disposal by watching George Mitchell wield them against George H. W. Bush. When I succeeded George, I learned firsthand what the minority position is like, which prepared me, as it turned out, for the tactics Trent Lott was surely going to confront me with when he assumed that position after Jeffords's move.

I've already mentioned one of the primary advantages the Senate structure gives the minority—the sixty-vote supermajority requirement to break a filibuster. There are other advantages as well, beginning with the foxhole-like sense of unity that comes from being on the defensive. People tend to pull together when they're surrounded, and that's certainly true in the Senate. There's more of a unified sense of purpose and camaraderie when your primary mission is simply holding your ground against a steamrolling majority.

That said, however, we're still talking about the same collection of people and personalities I described earlier. Majority or minority, you're still talking about some proud, strong-willed individuals with their own ideas about which direction to go and how things should be run. As I've already noted, we Democrats are a more, shall we say, disparate group than the Republicans.

When I first took over the minority leader position, there were plenty of skeptics who understandably wondered if someone with my lack of seniority was up to the job. I remember Fritz Hollings sighing to a reporter after one of my first speeches as leader, "He looks like a choirboy." Sam Nunn joked to a *USA Today* reporter at the time that I'd "need an Army division and one Air Force wing to unite the Democrats."

My hope wasn't just to unite our party, however, but also to build some cross-party coalitions among the "centrists" on both sides of the aisle who might share common ground on some issues. I wasn't sure at the time what those issues might be, but I believed that if the relationships were formed, the other pieces would eventually fall into place.

And they did. The centrist caucus is a growing group of Democratic and Republican senators who regularly influence the outcome of critical pieces of legislation including tax policy, social policy, and foreign affairs. Led by John Breaux and Olympia Snowe, they have become a real force both politically and legislatively.

But any bonds with members of the other party had to start with unity among our own. Efforts to achieve that unity became a major focus of our leadership organization. We initiated weekly leadership meetings at which the issues, strategy, and other matters affecting our unity would be discussed. Such meetings had not been held for decades. We also reorganized and revitalized the committees within the Democratic caucus. We revamped the Democratic Policy Committee, led first by Harry Reid and now by Byron Dorgan. This committee is responsible for bringing us together every week for meetings and discussions of the most important issues of the day. Over the years, we have met with many of the country's greatest thinkers and leaders through lunches hosted by the DPC. We also gave the DPC responsibility for organizing our annual caucus meetings and retreats.

We also changed the name of the committee responsible for determining each senator's committee assignments. Until then, this group had been called the Democratic Steering Committee. We changed it to the Democratic Steering and Coordination Committee and charged it with initiating a dialogue with important constituent groups and working to inform and expand our base. John Kerry was its first chairman. Hillary Clinton chairs it now.

Another change was our creation of the Democratic Technology and Communications Committee, which began building a technological infrastructure for stronger media outreach. Through the work of this committee, under the leadership of Senator Jay Rockefeller, we now have our own Senate studios for radio, television, and Internet outreach to the nation.

We also created special task forces to involve more members in areas of particular interest. And we set up biweekly lunch meetings between ranking committee members and the White House's chief of staff, Leon Panetta. We developed a message team, whose responsibility it is to carry our caucus's message of the day or week to the Senate floor or to the media. While these efforts paled in comparison with the advocacy and attack infrastructure that Republicans were developing at the same time, they were long overdue, concrete first steps toward getting our caucus rowing together and toward bringing us closer to the people we serve.

In the interest of history *and* bonding, I invited Dick Baker to come over from the Office of the Senate Historian and meet with our caucus on a regular basis, both entertaining and enlightening us over lunch with a "History Minute"—a short talk on one aspect or another of Senate lore. Once every quarter, we have also made it a practice to get together for dinner, along with spouses and family members, in one of the beautiful build-ings housing our archives, museums, galleries, and libraries, all in the interest of strengthening our personal connections and our connections to the rich history of this city and this institution. We have potluck dinners, and twice a year we hold a one- or two-day conference to discuss issues and enjoy one another's company in a setting away from Capitol Hill.

I think all these efforts have had an enormous positive effect. The record shows that we have achieved a great deal of unity in many key leg-islative battles over these past eight years. Sometimes our unity has been the source of some frustration among our Republican colleagues. I will never forget a moment early in 1996 when it was critical to an ongoing fil-ibuster of one of the components of the Republican Contract with America. After holding our position through a couple of rounds of votes, Majority Leader Bob Dole expressed his frustration and exasperation with his inability to move the legislation forward. In a rather brash moment on the Senate floor, which I admit could have been handled more diplomat-ically, I said, "Welcome to the Senate, Senator Dole."

I could have said the same thing to Trent Lott after Jim Jeffords's decision in May 2001. Lott and the Republican leadership were absolutely furious, livid, as if they had somehow been "swindled." Never mind that in the past decade two Republican Senators—Shelby and Campbell—had switched from our side to theirs. Jeffords's was the first decision that actually shifted the balance of power, and for that, the Republicans decided, he would pay.

The fallout from Jim's decision began immediately, and in many instances it was viciously ugly. Conservative analysts referred to Jim as a "liberal squish" and a "faithless opportunist." While Senator Jeffords's col-league from Vermont, Pat Leahy, printed green bumper stickers that read, "Don't Mess with Vermont," Republican activists produced rolls of toilet paper with Jim's face printed on each sheet. The savage attacks he received on the talk radio airwaves from Rush Limbaugh and his ilk don't deserve repeating.

But those were predictable. What was not expected, and what was deeply disturbing, were the death threats Jim began receiving the very day of his announcement. The threats continued, prompting the assignment of a Vermont State Trooper and an FBI agent to protect him for several weeks—the same kind of beefed-up, around-the-clock security protection I would be assigned in the wake of September 11.

Reports began to circulate among the press that Karl Rove, from his office at the White House, was orchestrating the smear campaign against Jeffords. *Time* magazine called Rove's behavior "selfish and power hungry." An editorial in the *New York Observer* declared, "The spectacle of a scoundrel trying to damage the reputation of a decent man should disturb the conscience of every fair-minded Republican. And there was once a time when it would have."

It was amid such an uproar that I met with the press for the first time as the new majority leader—although the position would not become official for another twelve days, when the Senate would reconvene after our Memorial Day recess.

Quite a crowd was gathered in front of the Capitol's east front steps that last Thursday in May as I approached the bank of microphones and two dozen TV cameras arrayed around the lectern. Several tour groups stopped to watch. A couple of teenagers even climbed into a tree to get a better view. One reporter joked that this was quite a change from the single C-SPAN camera that typically showed up for one of my press conferences. She was right.

I had hoped I could set the proper tone. In fact, I told my staff that our office was to be a "gloat-free zone." We saw no purpose in gloating. Yes, I said, the Senate's tilt had now changed, but we were still the same hundred people, still facing the same close divisions of parties and philosophies, and still needing to work together to bridge those divisions in order to effectively respond to the needs of our nation. The balance of power was still fragile. There were still twenty or so centrist senators from both parties who could swing either way on a particular issue. The presidency and the House remained under Republican control. The only thing that had radically changed was who set the Senate's agenda.

"But what does not change with this new balance of power," I said, "is the need for principled compromise."

I shared the same attitude in a brief phone conversation with President Bush. I called him that week to say that as majority leader, I had every intention of working with him and that I hoped he would feel comfortable calling on me as the need arose. He congratulated me and said that he would do so. The tone of his comments was businesslike. Characteristically, he didn't reveal any of the sense of disappointment or anger that was so apparent among his Republican colleagues on Capitol Hill. But I knew he felt that same anger.

A few weeks after that, Linda and I were invited to join the President at the White House for dinner. Laura Bush had planned to be there as well, just the four of us. But at the last minute, she had decided to return home to Texas to be with one of their daughters.

Both the dinner—enchiladas—and the conversation with President Bush were pleasant, very relaxed. He talked at length about how lonely the White House can be, especially on weekends. He said sometimes it felt like a prison, not being able to go out at all without it becoming a spectacle. He described winding up essentially trapped in a place that, he said, can feel pretty cold at times.

"That's the reason I like to go back to Texas," he said.

We talked about our kids, about the pluses and minuses for a child growing up with a politician for a parent. The President, of course, could relate to that from both ends of the experience, having grown up as a political child himself.

Our children, Kelly, Nathan, and Lindsay, have each grown up in the Washington area. The President's reflections on his own childhood reminded me of the many sacrifices they endured as the children of a public figure. By far the greatest sacrifice is my time away from them. The soccer games missed, the weekends of travel, and the late nights tending to congressional business are very tough on political families. That is especially true in families of divorced parents like ours.

Our kids have survived the experience exceedingly well. Each has done very well in school and graduated from college. Nathan has graduated from law school and is now working at a law firm in Washington. Kelly is a producer for Associated Press Television and Lindsay works for the Elizabeth Glaser Pediatric AIDS Foundation. Kelly and Nathan both have wonderful spouses, Eric Chader and Jill Gimmel, with whom we feel very close, and have blessed us with two dear grandchildren, Ava and Henry.

On the flip side, we also agreed that the biggest plus for political kids is the access and exposure to people and places that most children never have the opportunity to experience.

In fact, there is a family story involving the first President Bush that I used to recount often years ago when I was in the House of Reprsentatives, and that we retold to the President during the dinner.

Long ago, during the mideighties, I occasionally took the kids to the House of Representatives indoor swimming pool on weekends when I was in Washington. Of course they were very young at the time.

On one particular Saturday, the telephone in the pool area rang. The kids rushed to answer it.

"It's George Bush," they excitedly announced to me.

I took the telephone and the Vice President greeted me and then indicated that he left his glasses somewhere on one of the locker benches and hoped that someone might look for them and then put them in his locker.

Nathan immediately piped up, "I can find them, George!"

Moments later, he loudly announced into the telephone, "George, I've found them!"

The Vice President was elated and thanked the kids for responding so quickly and successfully.

After we hung up, I, too, thanked them, but told them that they should always address the Vice President by his proper title. They should never call him "George."

I had mentioned this incident to my staff the following Monday. Word got around quickly and it soon appeared in a cute story in the "Style" section of the *Washington Post*.

Once it did, the Vice President kindly wrote the kids a note. He thanked them for finding his glasses and offered to see them sometime in his office. He signed the note: "George Bush, Vice President of the United States."

Then he added a P. S.: "But you can call me George."

I think the President enjoyed the personal account of his father and his kindness to a congressman's children. But the moral of the story was that, along with its many downsides, there were wonderfully rare opportunities for families in public life, too.

That was the kind of dinner it was. We didn't talk about politics or policy that evening until toward the very end.

After dinner, President Bush walked us to the elevator on his third-floor residence. There, he bade us good night, and that was it, a pleasant, very engaging evening. Linda and I talked about it while driving home, about how charming and disarming the President had been. I'd finally gotten a firsthand taste of George Bush at his best. I hoped at least some of that collegiality might carry on into what lay ahead of us.

But I knew I couldn't count on that.

Even as the President and I were discussing the importance of working together constructively, the Senate Republican leadership had already drafted a document they called a "Declaration of War," which found its way to my office toward the end of that week. Here is how it began:

June 2, 2001

MEMORANDUM TO: REPUBLICAN OPINION LEADERS
FROM: COMMUNICATIONS: SENATOR LOTT
RE: DELIVERING ON OUR MANDATE

Background:
The decision this past week by Senator Jim Jeffords to defect from the Republican Party will result, as of close of business on June 5, 2001, in a shift of control of the U.S. Senate to the Democrat Party. The decision by Senator Jeffords is particularly disturbing as it effectively subverts the will of the American people who voted to put the Republicans in control of both Congress and the White House. This coup of one puts at peril the agenda that Republicans were given a mandate by the American people to deliver.

As a result, it is absolutely critical that Republicans launch an aggressive offensive effort to ensure that we deliver on our promise of lower taxes, smaller and more effective government, and meaningful reform in education, Social Security and Medicare, and energy policy. We have a moral obligation to deliver the agenda we were elected to the majority to achieve. We cannot allow the impetuous decision of one man to undermine our democracy.

The first battle will be reorganizing the Senate. The Senate Republican Conference has selected a dream team of outstanding Republicans to negotiate the reorganization of the Senate. They represent the smartest, most disciplined, and toughest negotiators the GOP can field. They are: Senators Pete Domenici, Phil Gramm, Mitch McConnell, Orrin Hatch, and Arlen Specter.

My colleagues and I were quite amused by the memo. Our Republican colleagues were smarting, and they allowed their emotions to come through loudly and perhaps too clearly. They also unintentionally confirmed to us that they had felt outmaneuvered in the original power-sharing negotiations earlier that year. The Republicans' candor and blunt-spoken attack was all the warning we needed to be cautious and calculating with our strategy in response. We would try to be as reserved and even-tempered in our words and actions as they were outspoken and hyperbolic in theirs.

Despite the Republicans' initial reaction, I still held out hope that an attitude of conciliation on both sides might prevail. This was the message I delivered in my first address from the Senate floor as majority leader late that same week. But I could see that consensus was not going to be easy to achieve. The Republicans' anger was palpable. Their mood, far from cooperative, was confrontational. Meanwhile, the more liberal wing of our caucus, often led by Paul Wellstone, was urging a full frontal assault on Bush's entire agenda, from his judicial nominations to his plans to drill in the Arctic National Wildlife Refuge. Stop him in his tracks, this group urged. Block him at every turn, now that we really have the power to do it.

The problem with this approach gets back to the fundamental difference between the tactical position of the minority party and the responsibilities of the majority. When you're in the minority, you can serve as a check on the extreme elements of the majority's agenda. However, the majority leader is responsible for "making the trains run on time." Thus, no matter the outcome, the party in power is held accountable for *results*, or the lack thereof.

Some political tacticians went so far at the time as to suggest that we were actually hurt by Jim Jeffords's defection. If Jim had stayed a Republican, they argued, we could have fought a "holding action" until the following year's midterm elections and then blamed the GOP for its inaction. Now, however, as the majority party, we would have to shoulder a greater share of the blame if gridlock ensued.

This "blame game" became the immediate focus of the Republicans. Tom DeLay threw down the gauntlet, pointing directly at me as the new majority leader: "Blocking legislation is one thing," he told a reporter. "Running the Senate efficiently is quite another. We'll see if he can get results, not just throw up roadblocks."

One of Republican House Speaker Dennis Hastert's staff put it more succinctly: "He can no longer be Dr. No," said the staffer. "When you're in the majority, you have to produce."

We were ready to take on that challenge, but before we could begin, we had to deal with the "dream team" mentioned in Lott's memo. The power-sharing agreement that Trent and I had hammered out at the start of the year was now obsolete. A new organizing resolution had to be negotiated. A new agreement on the composition and structure of the all-important Senate committees had to be reached.

On the appointed day, Senators Gramm, Domenici, Hatch, McConnell, and Specter, grim-faced and stern, marched into my main conference room and sat down. They meant business. Trent had suggested that I also appoint five senators for these negotiations, but I felt that was unnecessary and too cumbersome.

These Republican senators were the same men who had been so irate about the concessions Trent had made in our power-sharing agreement five months earlier. Now they were out to avenge that deal, as well as to do everything they could to minimize the impact on them of Jim Jeffords's move. Their first order of business—and this was framed as a demand, not a proposal—was that we create co-chairs for each committee, so that power would be distributed equally between the two parties. Trent and the Republicans had refused to agree to co-chairs for us when the Senate was split fifty-fifty, so it was hard to understand the logic of them asking for it now, especially with us holding a fifty-one to forty-nine edge.

But then there wasn't much logic to this entire situation. They, as the minority party, were not in a position to be making demands. And they knew that I was not about to accept this particular demand. I understood their frustration, their anger, their need to vent. They could do that as long as they'd like, but nothing was going to change the fact that just as they had for the previous six years enjoyed the leverage that comes with the majority position, that position was now ours. There was plenty of room for compromise and concession, but when it came to the key issue of committees, we were not about to give up control any more than they had been willing to give it up five months earlier.

It was ironic in so many ways how the worm had turned here. For example, Trent had made a point back when we negotiated the power-sharing agreement that if the Senate's membership structure changed at all during this 107th Congress, we would revert back to the organizing resolution of the previous one, the 106th.

A key clause in the 106th Congress's resolution dictated that the majority party would have a one-member advantage on each committee, as compared to the equal memberships Trent and I agreed on with our power-sharing arrangement for the 107th. Trent had included this "revert" clause in our agreement, fully expecting that any membership change would be in the Republicans' favor and that they would then regain majority membership control of the committees.

With Jeffords's move that clause had backfired. Not only would the chairmanship of each committee now change from Republican to Democratic, but the memberships would be realigned as well, with Democrats enjoying a one-seat advantage across the board. This was tough for the Republican negotiators to accept.

That day was just the beginning of these negotiations. They wound up lasting for nearly a month, until the Fourth of July recess. In the meantime, as dictated by the existing power-sharing agreement, we reverted to the organizing resolution of the 106th Congress, which gave us both the chairmanships and majority memberships on every committee. With that, we got down to business.

I had emphasized "principled compromise" in that first press conference as majority leader, and I wanted to demonstrate that attitude as soon as I could.

It seems almost quaint and naive to think about it now, but one of my first concerns was how to assuage the anger and hurt feelings of our Republican colleagues. As a small but symbolic olive branch, I offered to have Republican senators continue to share the duties of presiding over the Senate. Prior to this, only the majority party handled the duties of the presiding officer, mostly because the duty of presiding (being the person who is addressed as "Mr. or Madam President" during debate) carried with it the power to decide which senator would be recognized during debate. I had hoped that this would serve as a daily visual reminder of the bipartisan spirit in which I thought the Senate should operate.

The Republicans graciously accepted. Then, after a month, they simply quit—a sign of things to come. My reaction was, So be it.

Meanwhile, within our own caucus, I wanted to establish the same spirit of conciliation that I hoped to attain with the Republicans. Payback is not a high priority with us. Within a caucus as fractious as ours, there are always plenty of disagreements, plenty of internal battles. Members come from both ends of the political spectrum. To some in my caucus, there are issues on which we aren't liberal enough. To others there are times we lean too far to the left. Guns, abortion, war: these and other issues find our caucus at times irreconcilably divided.

But more often than not, the Senate Democratic caucus is able to present a largely united front. And as we began that summer with a new majority, there was no confusion about our core agenda. At the top of our list were pending legislation for the Patients' Bill of Rights and a stronger commitment to public education. After months of battling the Republicans' versions, we now intended to bring both these bills to the floor—to try to improve an education bill that was largely completed and to introduce a patients' rights bill that had languished for far too long.

Also on our legislative list were a Medicare prescription drug benefit, an increase in the minimum wage, electoral reform, and an energy package based much more on conservation, efficiency, and alternative fuels than the President's oil-centric approach.

Besides pushing our own agenda, we were now in position to moderate President Bush's, where appropriate. With our new committee chairmen in place, the President's wish list was not going to be rubber-stamped by Republican committee chairmen and sent directly to the Senate floor, as it had been during Bush's first six months in office.

For example, with Carl Levin replacing Republican John Warner as chair of the Armed Services Committee, President Bush's proposed missile defense system, which is projected to cost hundreds of billions of dollars, would now be subject to serious public scrutiny and debate. Carl and

I both felt that, if deployed before being proven effective, this system would antagonize our allies, sap our budget, and make America less secure and the world less stable. Rather than simply signing off on the administration's request, we would debate whether it made sense to authorize the deployment of a missile defense system that had not yet been proven effective and whether we should provide money for deployment when we had much work still to do in development.

As for energy, with Jeff Bingaman from New Mexico replacing Alaska's Frank Murkowski as chairman of the Energy and Natural Resources Committee, there would be an increased focus on alternative and renewable sources of energy.

On the international front, with Jesse Helms replaced by Joe Biden as chairman of Foreign Relations, that committee would now become a more proactive participant in critical foreign policy debates, rather than a place where, under Senator Helms, treaties died and nominations languished.

The interesting thing about our entire agenda was that despite the election results of 2000, which put both the presidency and the House in Republican hands, public sentiment across America on the issues themselves was clearly leaning more toward our side than theirs. Even as President Bush was pushing his conservative education agenda toward us in Congress, voters in California and Michigan and Washington State were rejecting school voucher initiatives in their states. While we were debating the President's budget plan, tax cut initiatives in Alaska and Colorado and Oregon were defeated by large margins. That is partly why Trent Lott's "Declaration of War" was so stunning. Republicans were citing a "mandate" that they didn't have, and they were pursuing policies that the majority of Americans didn't support.

Just as encouraging to us was the fact that—dream teams and declarations of war aside—the grip on the Republican Party by the far right wing seemed to be loosening. Four of their more doctrinaire senators—John Ashcroft, Slade Gorton, Spencer Abraham and Rod Grams—had been replaced by Democrats during the 2000 election. The fifty-five Senate seats the Republicans had held when Trent Lott took over as their leader had now dwindled to forty-nine—yet another reason Trent was taking more heat all the time from his party's disgruntled hard core.

And Republican allies were beginning to move toward us from some unexpected directions, in unexpected ways. During the power-sharing discussions back in January, among the Republicans who argued for giving us equal representation on committees were three of their own chairmen—John McCain, Fred Thompson of Tennessee, and Alaska's Ted Stevens.

John McCain, in particular, is someone for whom I've developed deep respect. His character and integrity are apparent to anyone who merely knows his background and biography. And I can testify that he's the same person in private as he appears to be in the public eye—open, candid, and fearless. One of the rewards of this job is having the opportunity to get to know people like John McCain on a personal basis.

Back in the spring of 2001, when I was still talking to John about possibly changing parties—this was just before the Jim Jeffords split began to develop—John and his wife, Cindy, invited Linda and me to come spend a weekend at their home, near Sedona, Arizona. We set a date for early June, which turned out to be just after Jeffords made his switch.

I approached John on the Senate floor during a vote at that time and said, "Look, you're going to be under a lot of scrutiny. People are going to make a lot more of this than they should. Do you want to just cancel the trip?"

"Hell, no!" he said. "I want you guys to come as much now as before. Screw 'em."

When the Republican leadership found out about the visit, they were beside themselves—angry, worried, and, with the Jeffords move still front-page news, a little embarrassed. How would this look in the papers? They could see the headlines now: JOHN MCCAIN HOSTS TOM DASCHLE AT DESERT COMPOUND.

Well, they *did* wind up seeing headlines much like that. The story was widely reported, and I wish it hadn't been. When Linda and I arrived with police escorts at the outskirts of the McCain property that Saturday, we were met by a group of sign-carrying demonstrators who were angry about what Jim Jeffords had done and what John and Cindy were doing—hosting the new Democratic majority leader and his wife for the weekend.

It was strange to drive out into this gorgeous, expansive desert with a convoy of police vehicles in front and behind us. Stranger still was to approach a fork in the road, in the middle of nowhere, and come upon a group of about fifty men and women by the side of the road, all waving hand-painted signs attacking Jim Jeffords and me.

It was about a mile from there to John and Cindy's house—a mile in which the road dropped down from dry, brown-red desert into a lush, verdant arroyo where the McCain home stood by a blue, sparkling river flanked by hundreds of tall shade trees. It felt like a Garden of Eden right there in the Arizona desert.

John and Cindy greeted us with a wonderful picnic. We spent the afternoon strolling the property, and that evening, after John barbecued dinner, the four of us sat up late, talking into the night.

It was a wonderful night, sharing stories about our families, our children, and our lives. Unlike Linda, who is with me when I'm in Washington, Cindy prefers to stay in Arizona when John is in D.C. We talked about what that's like, for Cindy and their kids to be home and have John away, traveling so much—especially to be away as much as he was during the presidential campaign of 2000, when he was running against Bush for the Republican nomination. John talked about that, what it was like on the bus, traveling with the press, all of that.

We didn't talk politics at all until the next day, and then it was only to discuss what an incredible piece of history Jim Jeffords had just written. Nothing was said about John doing the same thing. I think we both knew that wasn't going to happen, not now.

My friendship with John McCain has lasted to this day. I admire John tremendously. He is an independent thinker who is willing to act on the courage of his convictions. He has the political courage to stand up to the leadership of his own party when he disagrees with their positions. He also has been a major factor in many of the legislative victories that we have won, in large measure because of his principles and that courage.

When I returned to Washington after that visit, we got back to work, with the first order of business being the Patients' Bill of Rights (of which John McCain was a prime co-sponsor). This legislation, which Trent Lott had done all he could to fend off a year earlier, was so compelling, so needed, and so *right* that it passed the Senate in less than two weeks.

Next we turned to the Elementary and Secondary Education Act reauthorization, which was a hugely important bill, the most significant rewrite of the federal education statutes in thirty-seven years. Our goal was twofold—to make our nation's public schools more accountable for the performances of their students (and, by extension, their teachers) and to increase the funding and support for teachers and administrators to help them do their jobs as well as we know they can.

It was appalling to me that while countries in Europe spend from 20 to 40 percent of their national budgets on education, America's contribution from our overall federal budget was 7 percent. *Seven* percent. This is not only shameful, it's dangerous. Everyone knows that the foundation of our future as a nation rests on the education of our children, who will grow to inherit and take the reins of this society, of this nation. On this point, I like to repeat a quote that was shared with me at the time that Henry, our first grandchild, was born. "Our children are a message to a future that we will not see. What kind of message do we want to send?"

The answer to that question lies directly in our ability to provide both universal education and universal health care for our children and grandchildren. And it lies in our need to recognize that it is far easier to build a child than to repair an adult.

That is why there has always been such a chasm between Republicans and Democrats when it comes to education. They favor federal school vouchers and assistance for private schools. We strongly favor public education because we believe it is so fundamental to the empowerment of our children—all children—regardless of race, region, religion, or economic background. We oppose vouchers because we think they drain important resources away from the limited funds that are now available for our public schools. Our divergent philosophies and the strong views we hold on education and our nation's responsibilities to provide it play themselves out in many ways over the course of a legislative session. That was certainly true with this particular bill.

President Bush, of course, had a particular interest in this piece of legislation, with the "no child left behind" promise he had made to America. He had promised during his campaign that education would be one of his highest priorities. Now he would use this bill, the name of which he had appropriated from Marian Wright Edelman and the Children's Defense Fund, as the high-profile vehicle to keep that promise.

The debate was principally over two things: the need for more accountability in schools and the need for more resources to deal with the problems additional accountability was certain to highlight. Democratic moderates joined Republicans in arguing hard for more school testing.

Their view was that unless there could be more testing, more accountability, there could never be more improvement in educational outcomes.

Democrats responded that reform without *resources* was no reform at all. Paul Wellstone argued that it was like taking a child's temperature and, finding that it was above normal, doing nothing to make the child feel better. "What good does it do," he asked, "to know you're sick if you don't treat it afterwards?"

What was fascinating during this process was to watch President Bush's ability to be such an affable individual one moment and turn so strident the next. Maybe we all have a little split personality in us, but watching George Bush from day to day really is like watching two people. The man Linda and I had dinner with that night in the White House was a completely different individual from the man who snidely belittled a reporter for having the gall to ask a question in French of the prime minister of France. Bush was very strident when it came to the tax cut battle that spring and summer of 2001. He was strident whenever the topic of energy was discussed. And he was beyond strident when it came to people who displeased him, such as Paul Wellstone, or Jim Jeffords . . . or, as time passed, me.

None of this, however, made Bush any less politically dexterous. He showed it that summer with the education bill. His tactic earlier that year with the tax cut had been to peel off, one by one, the number of moderate Democrats he needed to join his side on that vote. And he was successful.

With the No Child Left Behind bill, he used a different approach. Rather than focus on swing votes, he went right for the reigning icon of American liberalism, at least in the public eye—Ted Kennedy—and he began negotiating directly with Kennedy to reshape this bill.

For all his reputation as a diehard, intractable liberal, Ted is also a person who likes to get things *done*. Achievements are important to him, and he is a skillful legislator. Ted Kennedy has been around a long time. He understands that sometimes you may not get all that you want in a certain situation, that in some cases it's better to settle for all you *can* get rather than fighting to the bitter end and winding up with nothing. Call it the art of the "doable," and there's no one who does it better.

Negotiations on the No Child Left Behind bill went on for nearly six months. Finally, Ted and the White House reached an agreement. New requirements would be enacted that mandated rigorous new testing in every public school in America. Federal resources to help schools implement these standards and promote achievement were promised, but not actually provided in the bill. This was early that December. Time was running out on the first session of this 107th Congress. A decision had to be made: Do we pass the bill without a firm commitment of federal resources, or do we oppose it until that commitment could be locked into the new law?

I will long remember the meeting of Democratic senators who were involved in drafting this bill. The meeting was held in a room across the hall from my office. It was late in the afternoon. As is often the case, I invited each of the dozen or so senators in attendance to express his or her view of the current draft of the bill.

The moderates joined Ted in arguing that we had made great progress in negotiating many of the issues with the administration. The liberals, while acknowledging progress on these points, argued that we still had failed to lock in the resources necessary to help schools correct the deficiencies that this testing would certainly reveal. Paul Wellstone, in particular, was adamant about withholding support until resources could be guaranteed. To do less, he argued, would set public schools up for failure. Joe Lieberman, Evan Bayh, and others argued that we must be willing to accept this version of a bill as a form of down payment on meaningful reform. "Let's put this in the bank and work to get more," they argued.

Having listened to both sides, I had to make a decision. After a great deal of thought, and I must say some discomfort, I said that my heart was with those who argued for the resources, but my head was with those who felt that, particularly with this administration, we ought to bank this accomplishment and continue to work on the resources. With that, the meeting ended.

In retrospect, the experience with the education bill was another revealing demonstration of this president's approach to working with Congress. As the tax cut fight took shape and Jim Jeffords's move played itself out, as the spring of 2001 turned to summer, Bush had given up dealing directly with our Democratic leadership—with Dick Gephardt and me. He didn't have to worry about the House, where Tom DeLay and Dick Armey were in such clear control. So he focused all his efforts on the Senate, on picking off Democrats who, on a particular issue of importance

Chpt. 4 (cont)

99.

to them, would be willing to circumvent the normal legislative process to reach an informal compromise, thereby ultimately dictating the outcome of the formal Senate position.

In terms of the overall picture, however, these little battles were just skirmishes, small victories for George Bush on a much broader battlefield. As for the most important battle, the main event—taking care of the nation's economy—the Bush approach was foundering. As July drew to a close and the August recess approached, the stock market was plummeting. The nation's retail and high-tech sectors were laying off employees by the tens of thousands. Unemployment was pushing 5 percent, with more than one million jobs lost since the start of the year in the manufacturing sector alone. The value of the 401(k) plans so many Americans were counting on to finance their retirements was shrinking. So was public support for the President and for the Republican members of Congress who would be up for reelection the next fall. The federal surplus that Bush insisted his tax cuts would not affect was shrinking, and the economic turnaround that Bush insisted his tax cuts would stimulate was simply not happening.

This was the lay of the land on the domestic front at that time. As for foreign affairs, I was increasingly concerned about President Bush's apparent willingness to discard bipartisan foreign policies and international alliances that had served America well for decades.

This was something that had troubled me even before he took office. It was my understanding that during his father's presidency, George W. Bush's involvement in White House affairs, to whatever extent he was involved, had been restricted to domestic issues and politics. He had no involvement and demonstrated no *interest* in foreign affairs. During his campaign against Gore, Bush's responses to questions involving international affairs were long on attitude and quite short on substance. Since taking office, Bush had confirmed my fears on almost every international front:

- By disengaging from active involvement in the pursuit of peace in the Middle East.
- By rejecting the international Kyoto Protocol to limit greenhouse gas emissions into the atmosphere.
- By walking away from the comprehensive test ban treaty, the Biological Weapons Protocol, a global agreement to curb illicit sales

of small arms and light weapons, and a measure to create an international criminal court.

- By straining relations with our allies in Europe and Russia by aggressively pursuing development and deployment of an unproven missile defense system that would violate the Anti-Ballistic Missile Treaty of 1972.

My Democratic colleagues and I felt that reasonable people could disagree about the merits of each of these individual commitments but that no reasonable person could ignore the consequences of turning our back on international discussion on so many important fronts, in such a sweeping way, and offer no alternative solutions. We feared that instead of the United States asserting our leadership, we were abdicating it. Instead of shaping international agreements to serve our interests, we were removing ourselves from a position to shape them at all. Not only did we believe the administration's foreign policies were misguided, we also felt that they threatened to undo U.S. international relationships in many arenas where those relationships had taken years—in some cases decades, if not longer— to construct. In too many cases, we were turning allies into adversaries. At the very least, we were losing respect within the international community.

Late that July, as Bush was embarking on his first trip abroad as president—he was headed to London before continuing on to Italy for the annual summit of the world's leading industrialized countries—I shared my concerns about his foreign policy in a breakfast discussion with a gathering of *USA Today* reporters and editors at their headquarters building in Rosslyn, just across the Potomac from Washington.

Speaking of the Bush foreign policy, I argued that we were isolating ourselves and, in so doing, were reducing our influence over world events. I went on to say I was troubled by how tenuous our relationship with many of our allies around the world was becoming as the attitude and policies of this administration continued to alienate them. British prime minister Tony Blair, with whom Bush was about to meet, had recently offered, for example, to act as an intermediary for the U.S. in shoring up our relations with our European allies.

Since when, I asked, did we need a liaison with Europe? This fact alone, I asserted, spoke volumes about the effect of President Bush's foreign policy. His disengagement was creating a "global vacuum," which was being filled by others. A Russia-China treaty signed that very week, which pledged stronger military cooperation between those two nations and which criticized the NATO alliance, was, I suggested, a "wake-up call." It was a warning that instead of pulling back and circling our wagons in this world of increasingly interwoven, interconnected nations, we should be expanding our understanding of world affairs and building stronger international relationships. To many of us, Bush's rejection of proven policies and partnerships was disturbing and ominous. I suggested that if President Bush didn't choose to be involved in international affairs, that role was going to be filled by others.

By the next day, I was embroiled in controversy, not so much over what I had said as about *when* I had said it. Notwithstanding that the Republicans criticized President Clinton often when he was abroad, there is an unspoken tradition that the president is not to be criticized by members of Congress while he is engaged in diplomatic work overseas. I had violated that tradition, albeit inadvertently.

The truth is, I hadn't even thought about the fact that Bush was leaving that same day for Europe. That's not really an excuse, nor is it an apology. I could have picked a better time to make my remarks, but having made them, I stood firmly by what I had said. I don't think there's any question that subsequent events have borne me out.

At any rate, the White House immediately questioned both the propriety and substance of my comments. Ari Fleischer, the White House press secretary, said my remarks were "unseemly, unwise and inaccurate."

Condoleezza Rice, President Bush's national security adviser, telephoned me that afternoon to complain. We had met a few times before and had other telephone conversations in which she had laid out the administration's positions on priority issues. These conversations had always been cordial, but this one was not.

With a stern voice, Rice sounded very defensive. She talked at some length about all of the outreach efforts the Bush administration had initiated and the progress they were making. She was especially critical of the timing of my remarks and noted that the President was disappointed that they were made just as he was embarking on his foreign travel.

Trent Lott was naturally delighted by the controversy. When asked for his reaction, he noted to reporters that I had served as Senate majority leader for "only" six weeks. "That's the kind of thing that happens while you still have your training wheels," Trent said, hardly disguising a smile.

I didn't have to go back too far to find examples of the same thing being done to Bush's predecessor by the very people who were criticizing me now. Tom DeLay, during one of Bill Clinton's trips abroad in 1998, said, "The President of the United States cannot be believed. And I think it's reflected in his foreign policy." In late 1996, during the American air assault on Iraq, as President Clinton again was abroad, Trent Lott said flatly, "I cannot support this action in the Persian Gulf at this time."

That last comment is revealing, not just in terms of the inconsistency between the Republican reaction to my statements about President Bush's policies in July 2001 and their comments about President Clinton when he was abroad, but also when compared with their reaction to my statements about his policies in March 2003, as George Bush, not Bill Clinton, made the decision to attack Iraq.

So much was ahead of us as that summer of 2001 drew to a close—so much we could not foresee.

As the Senate adjourned for that August's recess, our caucus was more than satisfied with the year we'd had. We were feeling good. After struggling for eight years as the minority, we were back in control of the Senate, and now, finally, we were getting some important things done—the Patients' Bill of Rights, the education bill—with much more to come. We now had the opportunity to demonstrate the strength and effectiveness of our policies, rather than being forced to simply moderate the Republican agenda.

Meanwhile, George Bush's policies were demonstrating their fundamental flaws—especially his economic plans. As we reconvened that first week of September, Bush was back on his heels. His popularity in the polls was dropping. So were the prospects for his party's candidates in the following year's midterm congressional elections. Public confidence in Bush's handling of the economy was drastically low. A front-page story in the *Washington Post* that week reported that a nationwide survey showed only 33 percent of Americans had a positive view of the economy, compared to 70 percent who had a positive view back in January, when Bush assumed office. An editorial in that same day's *Post* addressed the President's befuddled approach to foreign affairs.

"When it comes to foreign policy," that editorial declared, "we have a tongue-tied administration. After almost eight months in office, neither President Bush nor Secretary of State Colin Powell has made any comprehensive statement on foreign policy. It is hard to think of another administration that has done so little to explain what it wants to do in foreign policy."

The date of that morning's newspaper was September 11, 2001.

End of chpt. 4

goes to pg. 118 = 14 pgs.

CHAPTER FIVE

September 11

I WAS IN MY MAJORITY LEADER'S OFFICE, just off the floor of the Senate, pulling together some notes for our weekly Democratic leadership team meeting, when John Glenn stopped by. John and his wife, Annie, have been good friends of Linda's and mine for quite some time. He's been retired from the Senate since 1998, but he still drops by occasionally to say hello.

John had just cut a public service announcement at the studios of CNN, not far from the Capitol, and was scheduled to do another one in the Capitol studios later that morning. We both remarked on what a gorgeous day it was, the September sun glinting off the reflecting pool just outside my office window, the Washington Monument in the distance gleaming golden white in the bright morning light. The sky was so clear and blue, it almost hurt to look up at it.

It was 8:45 A.M. Tuesday, September 11, 2001.

John hadn't been there more than a few minutes when Marty Paone, the secretary for the majority and one of my closest aides, entered the room. He said there had just been a bizarre incident in New York City. A pilot had flown a plane into a skyscraper. Marty wasn't overly alarmed, nor were we. But this was a strange piece of news, and the response from John—a man who had been awarded the Distinguished Flying Cross on five occasions—was immediate.

"Pilots," he said, "don't fly into skyscrapers."

Marty left, and John and I talked for another moment before walking out to my office's lobby. A half-dozen of my staff were huddled around a television that sits on one of the desks. The broadcast was confusing, not clear on just what had happened. All anyone knew was that an aircraft had definitely hit one of the World Trade Center towers. They were showing live footage of the black smoke billowing out from that building.

John said he thought for a moment that it might be a rerun of the movie *The Towering Inferno*. He also recalled an event in the mid-1940s when a B-25 actually did crash into the Empire State Building. But that accident occurred in foggy conditions. Today, it was as clear and sunny as any morning in New York could be. This was no accident.

As we stood there puzzling over this unnerving image—as most of America was beginning to gather at televisions in homes and offices across the nation—we were stunned by the sight of what looked like another aircraft banking in toward the second tower. Then impact. And the orange fireball.

Someone said it must be a taped replay of the first incident. But Marty pointed out the word *Live* on the top of the TV screen.

Seconds later, the television anchor confirmed it. The second tower had been hit.

Audible gasps filled the room.

This is an attack, I thought, and immediately wondered if we were about to see more such images. John, too, was thinking about this.

"I'm not sure you ought to be here," he said. "This would be a logical target."

The mounting anxiety was palpable as I looked at the faces and worried eyes of my staff. I glanced at the clock. It was now 9:10. My weekly leadership team meeting had been scheduled to start ten minutes earlier in room 219, just across the hall from my office.

When I entered the meeting room, everyone was there—Harry Reid, John Breaux, Barbara Mikulski, Jay Rockefeller, Dick Durbin, Byron Dorgan, Patty Murray, Barbara Boxer, and Bill Nelson—all watching the television we keep near the door of that room.

As we moved to the table and began taking our seats, I said, "Look, I don't know what's going on, but if it's possible for us to refocus right now, why don't we try to do that." Everyone agreed, but John Breaux asked that we leave the television on with the volume turned down, which we did.

The issue of the week was the ongoing debate about how to use the surplus revenues in the federal budget—and whether Social Security funds could be counted as part of the surplus. Just the Friday before, Senator

Pete Domenici, the top Republican on the Budget Committee, had publicly announced his support for using Social Security revenues for other purposes. We had been arguing for a "lockbox" for these funds, insisting that they should be used only for the purposes of Social Security retirement. We were convinced we had the high ground.

We were well into that discussion, trying to focus on issues, not airplanes, when everyone turned again to the TV, whose broadcast from New York had been interrupted with a report of a fire at the Pentagon.

At that same instant, Patty Murray looked toward the conference room's window and yelled, "Look. There's smoke!"

With that, we all rushed to the window. None of us could believe what we were seeing. There, beyond the Washington Monument, just across the Potomac, thick plumes of black smoke were billowing up from the spot where the Pentagon stands. I know it's a cliché, but I really could not believe my eyes.

It was surreal to be standing there, in the United States Capitol, looking out at the very image that the newscasters on the television screen behind us were struggling to describe. The network cameras hadn't yet reached the Pentagon to show the world what we in that room were watching.

It looked from where we stood as if the entire Pentagon had been destroyed. The smoke was so thick, and there was so much of it, that it was easy to assume the impact had been even greater than it actually turned out to be. Within minutes, we learned that the "blast" had indeed been yet another suicide aircraft.

I've heard people observe since that day what a prime target the Capitol Building makes for such an air attack—this brilliant white structure perched on its own terraced hill, its dome outlined against the sky, with the broad, sprawling expanse of the Mall leading up to it like a long open runway. Those details didn't occur to me that morning, but I did realize as soon as I saw the Pentagon on fire that the Capitol, as well as the White House, might now be a target of what was clearly a concerted attack.

Within minutes—it was not yet 10:00 A.M.—one of my staff handed me a message that my wife, Linda, was on the phone. I just about ran back to my office to take Linda's call—first to make sure she was safe and then to see if maybe she knew more than I did. I've talked to so many people who assume that senators and members of Congress—certainly the Senate's majority leader—have some kind of hot line to all that's occurring at a moment like this, that we're plugged into some top-secret, high-tech source of instant information. It's hard to fathom—or maybe we simply don't want to believe—that our leaders in the upper levels of government in Washington, the people we turn to for confidence and security in times of crises, might, at just such a time, be as utterly clueless as everyone else. But the fact is that while we often are privy to sources of communication and information that the average citizen does not have, we just as often get the only information we have from the same place everyone else gets it— in many instances, from television. Walk through the Capitol on any given day, and you'll see a TV in every House and Senate office tuned in to CNN or C-SPAN. Those sets are turned on from the moment the office is unlocked in the morning until the last person leaves late at night. In the chaos and confusion of September 11, I was as dependent on the network television reports—at least early on—as everyone else.

Linda was calling from her car. She has worked as a public policy analyst for the aviation industry for more than twenty years. In recent years, one of her major clients has been American Airlines. She said that she was on her way over to American's Washington, D.C., corporate headquarters. Both the airplane that had flown into the World Trade Center's north tower and the one that hit the Pentagon belonged to American. Later, Linda recalled how struck she was by the strength and professionalism of their executive staff as she sat among them that morning. Like everyone else, they were overwhelmed at the horror of the images they witnessed on television. But beyond that, they were also dealing with the horror of knowing that their own airplanes' crews and passengers were among the victims.

Personally they were devastated, yet as professionals they knew they had a job to do—now more than ever. They knew that the whole world— including, most of all, the families of the people aboard those airplanes— would soon be asking them to answer their questions. Who was on the flights? How could this happen? What did they know about who was responsible? The questions were likely to be unending. And for those first few hours, they had hardly any more information than the rest of us.

As I raced back to my office's lobby, Mark Childress, my chief counsel, was on the telephone with the White House. He told me that the White House staff was evacuating. Nancy Erickson, my deputy chief of staff, took a call from Dick Gephardt, who reported that he and the Speaker were evacuating the Capitol.

I turned to my staff, who had now gathered together, and said, "I think we need to get out of here," just as a Capitol Police officer broke into the room.

"Senator," he said, "we're under attack. We have word that an airplane is heading this way and could hit the building anytime. You need to evacuate."

That word had come through the Senate's sergeant at arms, Al Lenhardt, who had begun that job just seven days earlier. Our sergeant at arms is responsible for the Senate's security, just as the House's sergeant at arms is responsible for theirs. Both positions had come under increased scrutiny after two Capitol Police officers were shot to death by an armed intruder in July 1998. In the wake of that attack, Congress authorized extensive plans to increase security at the Capitol, which, considering the fact that some seven million people a year visit this building, is a massive challenge. We approved the construction of an underground visitors center, which will serve both a security and an educational function for visitors to the Capitol and is now in the process of being built, to be completed in 2005.

One of my first responsibilities after assuming the position of majority leader had been to choose the new officers of the Senate, including the Senate sergeant at arms. From the very beginning, I was extremely impressed with Al. Jeri Thomson, our secretary of the Senate, had recommended him. When I saw his qualifications—a retired army major general, with thirty-two years of military experience that included law enforcement and security duties, training in personal protection and counterintelligence, and a stint as the army's commanding general in charge of recruiting—I knew he was the man we needed in this position.

I also knew, when I nominated Al to be the Senate sergeant at arms, that he would make history as the first African American ever to serve as an elected officer of the Senate or the House of Representatives. What I didn't realize is what a crucial role he would play in the history that began that morning of September 11.

Al, though, had been initially reluctant to take the job. He said later on that it was his meeting with me—our conversation about the changing security needs here at the Capitol—that convinced him to accept the position. He also said, looking back at the timing, with all that transpired beginning that morning, that I must have been clairvoyant.

I don't know about that.

I do know that it looked unlike anything I had ever seen before as senators and staff rushed en masse out of the Capitol that morning. The scene was total chaos. The halls were filled with fear and confusion. One of the Capitol restaurant's cooks had been chopping vegetables and came out still carrying a knife. The fire alarm system, which was working in the nearby Senate office buildings, was never activated in the Capitol, so there were people who weren't aware that an evacuation was taking place— the first time in history that the entire United States Capitol had been evacuated.

Some individuals were reluctant to leave. Robert Byrd, true to his nature, did not like the idea of running away like this. It felt to him like retreat. As president pro tempore of the Senate, Byrd was number three in the line of presidential succession, behind Vice President Cheney and Speaker of the House Dennis Hastert. If anyone needed to get out of that building, it was Senator Byrd. Instead, he stood in the main hallway, waving others out like a captain evacuating his ship. It was all the Capitol Police could do to persuade him to leave.

There was nothing orderly about this evacuation. There was no procedure for something like this. Contingency plans (called COOPs, for continuity of operations plans) had been developed for all manner of possible attacks on or threats to the Capitol. Scenarios were on the books for everything from tornadoes to fires, from small bombs to nuclear devices. But no one had foreseen or planned for an attack from the air by a suicide jet.

As frenzied as the scene had been inside the Capitol, the confusion outside was even worse. No one knew what to do or where to go. People congregated on the grass and in the parking lot. Senators and staff were mixed in with tourists, all staring up at the sky, wondering what might be headed our way. People were punching their cell phones to no avail. The lines were jammed. Calls couldn't get through.

The wailing sound of police sirens from throughout the city filled the air. Government officers, some with drawn weapons, urged people to move farther back from the building. It was reported on some networks that a bomb had gone off outside the State Department.

At one point, a deep rumbling sound filled the air. There were screams, fear that yet another attack was occurring. We later learned that the sound came from two Air National Guard F-15s that had been scrambled from Falmouth, Massachusetts, and three F-16s that had taken off from Langley Air Force Base in Virginia. They had all initially been dispatched to the World Trade Center, then were rerouted to the skies over Washington. By the time we heard them overhead, American Airlines flight 77 had already hit the Pentagon. The fighter jets overhead were now looking for another plane possibly headed our way.

At another point during the evacuation, a Capitol Police officer shouted, "There's another plane coming!" For a moment, it looked as if there were. A large plane could be seen over the Capitol—a rare sight in any event, since this airspace is not part of any airline's usual flight plan. The aircraft looked huge—something like a 747. People pointed up at it and began hollering, "We're too close!"—too close to what looked like the next target, the Capitol. Some began running. The aircraft, we learned later, was most likely an Air Force C-130 cargo plane from Andrews Air Force Base that had been asked, in this emergency situation, to provide visual reconnaissance on a possible attack on D.C.—on the plane, it turned out, that had already hit the Pentagon.

My security detail, who had been by my side since leaving my office, herded me into the back of a black Lincoln Navigator and shot away from the plaza in front of the Capitol, leaving a streak of burned rubber on the pavement behind us. The streets were already gridlocked with traffic. Constitution Avenue looked like a parking lot. The entire city was shutting down. Major bridges and roadways were already closed. By the end of that day, Washington would resemble a ghost town under martial law, with Humvees and armed soldiers patrolling empty, abandoned streets.

Al Lenhardt later said how alarmed he was to see members of Congress and their staffs mixed in with visitors and passersby wandering in the open around the Capitol grounds. One of the tactics that terrorists have been known to employ is to create a diversion to move their intended target to the area where the actual attack will take place. Al imagined a bomb or gunfire erupting right there on the lawn outside the Capitol. He and the Capitol Police began urging House and Senate members to move to safe quarters. Some were openly angry with Al for not knowing more about what was going on. Others didn't recognize him—again, he'd been on the job only for a week. At one point later that day, Al joined Dennis Hastert to brief a gathering of House members, and Hastert was a bit puzzled by this man standing beside him, because Hastert had no idea who he was.

It was one thing to urge us to move to a place of safety, but quite another to know just where that place was. The COOPs for other emergencies directed us to convene at the Hart Senate Building, right next to the Capitol. But that was considered unsafe in this situation. Some members of Congress who lived in the area decided to simply go home.

Jay Rockefeller, for example, invited Bill Nelson to go with him to his house in the Rock Creek section of Washington, where the two of them spent the rest of that day and that night. Others convened at a nearby restaurant—the One Sixteen Club—which became a mini-command center of sorts. The remaining senators were finally directed to the Capitol Police headquarters a block and a half away, where it was decided members of Congress would be safest. That became Congress's central command center for the rest of the day.

When I got to the Capitol Police building—a fairly innocuous, somewhat decrepit brick structure—I was taken up to the seventh floor. It had been decided that the fourth floor was where the House members would gather. Through the course of that day, as many as 250 House members were there, crammed into several conference rooms and offices, working the telephones and watching the TV monitors for developing news.

When I got to the seventh floor, where the offices of Capitol Police chief Jim Varey and his staff were located, most of the leadership teams of both parties were already there: Dick Gephardt, Harry Reid, Trent Lott, Don Nickles, Dick Armey, Tom DeLay, J. C. Watts—about two dozen people in all. By the end of the day, as many as seventy-five senators and congressmen would fill those rooms. At some point someone asked, "Is this the safest place for us to be, on the top floor of this building?" With that, someone else pulled down the shades on the windows, which I thought was pretty amusing.

It was there, in the chief's office, that we stood transfixed, crowded in front of a television, watching the graphic images of destruction and death in New York and at the Pentagon. I was standing beside Don Nickles as we watched the first tower collapse. Shortly thereafter, we watched in horror as the second tower fell. I felt sick to my stomach.

After a little while, I was able to reach Linda on one of the office's hard

lines. She had already reached our family to let them know that we were all right. They had been trying to contact us since they saw the news, but had been unable to get through. In reaching my mother, Linda learned she had been evacuated from her house by the Aberdeen Police Department and been taken to a friend's home to spend the day and that night. The police told her that it was just a precaution, that they were concerned for her safety. I had no idea my mother in South Dakota would be evacuated in such a situation, but I'm glad that she was.

It was late morning now, not yet noon. After a brief discussion, our group there at police headquarters decided to issue a statement, to display bipartisan solidarity and reassurance to the American people and let the world know that these brutal acts were not going to weaken the United States or the strength of its democracy. We gathered in an adjacent conference room, where our staff had prepared a draft. Displaced as we were, we were still the United States Congress, and we still followed procedure as best we could. The statement was read aloud and approved immediately.

There was then some discussion about what to do next. Plans were forming to evacuate both the Senate and House leaders from Washington. Dennis Hastert, second in line of succession behind the Vice President, had already been taken away. Trent Lott felt strongly that we—the two leaders of each party in the House and the Senate—should go over to Andrews Air Force Base right away. He argued that it was a secure site with ample logistical support—something sorely lacking in the chief's office. I was concerned that by going to Andrews, we would be too isolated, too far apart from our colleagues and staffs.

Unable to agree, we each wound up making our own arrangements. Trent left for Andrews, and I contacted the office of one of our political consultants, located about three blocks away, where several of my staff had set up a temporary office.

It was there that I received a call from Al Lenhardt telling me that the congressional leaders were indeed being evacuated from the city. The House leadership was already gone. Al urged me to get over to the Capitol as quickly as possible.

When we—my security detail and I—arrived there, a military helicopter had already landed, blades still turning, surrounded by a circle of CERT officers (CERT stands for containment emergency response team).

The CERT forces are a specialized division of the Capitol Police. Unlike uniformed Capitol Police officers, they wear black battle-dress uniforms and carry MP5 automatic weapons. Seeing them arrayed around the helicopter was an imposing sight.

I climbed aboard along with Harry Reid and my administrative assistant, Laura Petrou. The leaders had each been told we could bring one staff member with us. Laura, one of the most senior members of my staff, was my choice. Don Nickles was already aboard.

As we lifted off, the scene below was jolting. The serenely familiar, manicured grounds of the Capitol had been transformed into an armed heliport. I thought of the last time I had been on that lawn—nine months earlier, for President Bush's inauguration. Now, instead of that joyful, ceremonial scene, I was looking at troops prepared for battle.

No sooner were we airborne than the pilot received a call on his radio from Andrews asking if we could swing by and pick up Trent Lott. Again, in a day filled with dreamlike images, here was another—using a military helicopter as a carpool, headed to a "secret undisclosed location."

It took only a few minutes to fly over to Andrews Air Force Base, and only a few minutes more to pick up Trent and one member of his security detail. Then we were airborne again, headed west. The pilot told us he wanted to see if he could get permission to fly directly over the Pentagon. By now the skies were filled with fighter jets, on alert to shoot down any threatening aircraft coming this way. We were denied approval for a fly-over, but we were cleared to come very close to the site.

The devastation was almost incomprehensible. We could see the rear section of an airliner jutting out from the rubble of what had been one of the Pentagon's exterior walls. Orange flames were licking out from the black gash where the aircraft had plunged into the building. Dozens of fire engines and rescue vehicles circled the scene, their lights flashing, uniformed figures darting this way and that. Interstate 395, which runs right past the Pentagon, was frozen solid with vehicles, none of them moving, the drivers transfixed by this nightmarish scene. It occurred to me as I watched the smoke waft over nearby Arlington Cemetery how ironic that was. And how heartbreaking.

We then banked toward our "secret, undisclosed location." It's been a well-reported fact for some years now that the federal government maintains dozens of "continuity of government" installations. Most of these "relocation centers" were built during the Eisenhower administration in

response to the cold war threat of a Soviet nuclear attack—specifically, an attack aimed at "decapitating" the nation's leadership in Washington. I was certainly aware of these installations, but I had never been to one before. There had never been any reason to go. Now, however, on this horrible morning, there was.

As the skyline of Washington and the smoke of the Pentagon receded behind us, Trent's face and manner reflected the gravity of the moment and the uncertainty about what lay ahead. I assumed my face was just as ashen. So I could understand Trent's anger and impatience as he peppered his escort and the pilot with logistical questions.

Immediately upon landing, we were met by armed guards who escorted us through two massive steel doors and down into the underground "secure location." The room we were first taken into was more bare bones than I had imagined. It had nothing in it but a couple of tables, a few folding chairs, and bright fluorescent lights. It could almost have passed for a police interrogation room.

We waited there a short while before we were led down a cave-like tunnel into a more spacious room, furnished with desks and cubicles and a console of television monitors arrayed much like a NASA command center. The other congressional leaders were already there: Hastert, Gephardt, DeLay, Armey, and the House Democratic whip, David Bonior.

We all felt anxious and frustrated, feeling responsible as Congressional leaders to both communicate and take action, but unable to do either. We talked among ourselves of our concern for our loved ones back in Washington and our need to be with them as soon as possible. It was hard to feel so responsible and at the same time so helpless, to have so little control over our situation.

We weren't there long before Trent began pressing the people around him—his own security detail and the facility's personnel—about his strong desire to get back to Washington. "I want more helicopters," he declared at one point. "There's no reason we should all be flying together like this. You get more helicopters, and if you have a problem with that, you tell them to call me."

We were still getting our bearings, calling staff and colleagues back in Washington, trying to figure out what to do next, when Vice President Cheney telephoned from his own secured location. We all picked up for a group conference.

Cheney basically told us what we already knew—that the President had been moving around since first getting word of the attacks that morning, and he was now at Offutt Air Force Base in Nebraska. I was familiar with Offutt, having been stationed there when I was in the service. Cheney also told us that all airline flights throughout the United States had been grounded temporarily, which we had already heard on television reports.

About five o'clock, Trent and I spoke by telephone to a gathering of about fifty of our fellow congressmen and senators, who had assembled in a first-floor conference room in the Capitol Police building. It had been a very difficult day for all of them, crammed into the tight confines of that setting, having to confer and debate some very important questions, with none of the privacy we are all accustomed to in the familiar surroundings of the Capitol and our offices.

There were mixed opinions and strong feelings about when we should reconvene. One camp was adamant that we should get back on the Senate floor that very evening. Others argued that it would be more prudent to wait until the next day. After quite a discussion, we decided that we would not reconvene until morning, but that our group would return to Washington that evening. We—leaders and members alike—would make a collective appearance on the steps of the Capitol, both to announce that we were reconvening the next day and to demonstrate our collective resolve, to show that the United States Congress had not been weakened in the least by these horrific and cowardly acts.

With that, we headed back to D.C. Trent got his wish—this time there were a number of helicopters. I took the last one.

As we neared Washington, our pilot was told that the President was also returning and was, in fact, about to land. We were ordered into a holding pattern a few thousand feet above the Pentagon. As we circled, I saw the black smoke continue to rise. The dozens of emergency vehicles had now grown to what looked like hundreds—including news satellite trucks, their dishes beaming images in every direction.

By the time we touched down, landing on the same Capitol lawn location from which we'd taken off that morning, with the same machine gun–armed CERT team on guard, the Capitol grounds were circled by yellow police ribbon and concrete barricades. The streets of D.C. were now deserted, with military units stationed throughout the city. Flags had been lowered to half-staff. It reminded me of the first time I had come to Washington, as a college student in April 1968. I was on spring break and wound up in the midst of the riots that besieged Washington in the wake of the assassination of Martin Luther King Jr. I was stunned at the time to see the nation's capital transformed that week into an armed camp, with soldiers and armored vehicles patrolling the streets. That's just how this felt.

As the hundred or so members of Congress still at the police headquarters building at the end of that day began walking back toward the Capitol, the Capitol Police were deeply concerned about the wisdom of so many of us gathering together out in the open. They were worried about the possibility of snipers or some other form of terrorist attack. The Capitol Hill area had not yet been secured to their satisfaction.

The suggestion had been made during our telephone consultation with the membership that afternoon that perhaps just the four leaders—Trent, Gephardt, Hastert, and me—should make this appearance. But that idea was immediately drowned out by the insistence of our colleagues that we assemble en masse. And so we did.

The sun was just setting beyond the still smoking Pentagon as we came together on the Capitol's east front steps—senators and representatives, Democrats and Republicans. I was struck by the vulnerability we all felt and showed at that moment, by our collective humanity and, yes, determination. In the face of the unspeakable horror of that morning's events, our entire nation had been drawn together that day in a way few of us have experienced in this lifetime.

Our differences, made so petty by the tragic enormity of what we had witnessed, fell away as our bare humanity drew us together, just as the American people were drawn together that day, neighbor to neighbor, colleague to colleague, parent to child, husband to wife, in homes and workplaces across this entire vast nation. I can't think of a time in my life when I have witnessed such deeply felt unity and connection among our countrymen as I saw and experienced that day—as we *all* saw and experienced.

That emotional nakedness was palpably evident on the steps of the Capitol as the men and women of Congress, so often divided by their beliefs, stood shoulder to shoulder in the dusk's fading light, some embracing, many with tears in their eyes, all joined together by sorrow and courage.

Dennis Hastert spoke first, and then I said a few words. When I closed with the straightforward sentence, "Congress will convene tomorrow," my colleagues burst into a loud cheer.

And then someone began singing.

This had not been rehearsed. This had not been planned. Even the most jaded cynic had to have been overwhelmed as these members of Congress all lifted their heads and their voices, singing "God Bless America" to a shaken nation in need of some faith and some hope.

To this day I don't know who started that song, but when it was finished we turned to one another like long-lost members of a large family and embraced once again.

And then we went home to face a new day.

And a world that was no longer the same.

end of chpt 5

CHAPTER SIX

goes to py.141=23 pgs

The Honeymoon

All is changed. Changed utterly.
— W. B. YEATS

WHEN HE FIRST FACED THE NATION that morning of September 11, after receiving word of the terrorist attacks while speaking at an elementary school in Sarasota, Florida, President Bush seemed shaken, unsteady, somewhat overwhelmed by the enormity of the events that had suddenly engulfed him—that had engulfed us all. Up to that point, Bush's presidency had been almost exclusively a domestic one. His blanket response to matters of foreign affairs had been essentially one of avoidance.

Rather than deal with the vexing diplomatic complexities of international entanglements, obligations, and agreements, he chose instead to simply withdraw. On six separate occasions in just six months, the administration walked away from agreements that had been embraced by many of our closest friends and allies and broadly supported by the international community: the Comprehensive Test Ban Treaty, efforts to create an international criminal court, the Biological Weapons Protocol, the Kyoto Protocol, and the Anti-Ballistic Missile Treaty.

Before September 11, Bush's approach to foreign policy had been to break treaties, pull out of alliances, ignore or offend our allies, and retreat behind a barricade of blustery pronouncements and faith in an unproven missile defense shield. That's what I had been talking about in my much vilified remarks to the *USA Today* audience.

Now, in his first response to this attack on America, Bush looked shaken and unsure. When he referred to the terrorists who had committed these acts as "those folks," I cringed a little. I couldn't imagine Franklin Roosevelt or John F. Kennedy referring to Hitler or Khrushchev as "those folks." Up to that point, Bush's lean-on-the-lectern informality had been a large part of his public appeal. It had gone over well with America's voters during the 2000 presidential campaign, especially when compared to the stiff formality for which Al Gore had unfortunately—and unfairly, I think—been ridiculed. Bush's folksy nonchalance played well in Washington, too, in terms of connecting to his anti–"big-government" Republican base. His straight-talking down-home populist pose, his scorn of all those fancy-thinking intellectuals and inside-the-Beltway bureaucrats, delighted his constituency—even as his actual domestic policies were wreaking ruin on almost all fronts. Now, though, that pose would be tested as it appeared to the world.

As for those domestic policies of Bush's—as well as the domestic policies we Democrats were proposing—they had been subsumed by the enormity of these events. Social Security, aid to education, so many issues that had been at the forefront of our national debate just twenty-four hours earlier were immediately overtaken. All that mattered to every American who looked to the President that day for guidance and strength in this time of crisis—and that included me—was that he display the wisdom and courage and grace that we've come to expect from our commanders in chief throughout history. Lincoln at Gettysburg. FDR in the wake of Pearl Harbor. JFK during the Cuban missile crisis. It is crises like these that become crucibles in which great men are forged. These crises are challenging, fearsome, and frightening indeed. But they are opportunities as well, watersheds where true leaders rise to the occasion and make their mark on history.

I wanted to see George Bush rise as well. Our differences, I can honestly say, were obliterated when that first airplane hit the first tower that morning. Those differences would eventually return, but that day I turned to our President just as every American did, to provide the leadership we all needed. And I was ready to help with that leadership in whatever way I could.

George Bush stumbled that morning. By the end of that day, when he addressed the nation again, this time from the White House, where he declared, "We will make no distinction between those who planned these acts and those who harbor them"—a statement that meant far more for America's foreign policy than we realized at the time—he was beginning to transform into a surer man. But he still seemed dazed, and his words didn't sound as if they were his own.

Within the next seventy-two hours, that transformation would become complete. Bush's resolve, his demeanor of certainty, his confident tone, the "moral clarity" that would take shape by the end of that week, were just what America needed at that point. Later, in the morass of complex realities that the "war on terrorism" eventually entailed, that same certainty would evolve into a dangerous arrogance. But at that point, that second week of September, I was as glad to see it as were most Americans.

The morning after the attacks, Wednesday, September 12, the congressional leadership, along with the most senior members of the appropriations committees, met with President Bush in the White House Cabinet Room, just off the Oval Office. It was 11:30 in the morning.

As each of us sat in the large, high-backed chairs around the mammoth, leather-covered elliptical table, the President looked drained both mentally and physically. He was very somber. But as he began to speak, he took on an authoritative tone as he provided a briefing on the events of the day before and the aftermath. He laid out what was known—which was very little. We talked about the ongoing rescue efforts at the World Trade Center and the Pentagon and the heroic efforts of the police and firefighters and the passengers who overcame the terrorists on United flight 93. We were told that there was still hope of finding survivors at the World Trade Center.

Each of us was overwhelmed by the demonstrations of sympathy from the millions of people in cities and countries around the globe. Never has the world witnessed such an outpouring of sympathy. People all over the planet held candlelight vigils and laid bouquets of flowers on the steps of our embassies. World leaders sent heartfelt messages of support while millions of ordinary people from virtually every country did the same with faxes and e-mail messages of their own.

People in my own state of South Dakota stopped what they were doing to help people they didn't know in a city that many had never visited. One manufacturer of heavy-duty cutting supplies had 175 employees volunteer to work around the clock, producing eight tons of equipment that were picked up by an Air Force cargo plane and brought to New York. One ranch couple, themselves struggling, sold one hundred calves and donated the proceeds—more than $40,000—to help victims of the attacks. All over South Dakota, and America, we were beginning to hear stories like these.

We talked about the available intelligence we had and about the need to demonstrate that all government operations would continue. Discussion then turned to the need for new, emergency legislation: a use-of-force resolution to go after whoever orchestrated the attacks; additional powers for national law enforcement to address domestic security needs; more resources for a range of emergency spending, including the cost of debris removal and reconstruction.

As the discussion continued, many references were made to this new "war" in which we found ourselves. That's when it fully struck me: The horrific events of the last twenty-four hours meant that our country was now at war.

But the question was: With whom?

How can one be at war without knowing the enemy?

And if it was a war on terrorism, how would we define success?

I expressed my concern about the unintended semantic consequences of employing the term "war" in this context. Over my time in public life, we have used the term "war" to describe our efforts to eliminate poverty (the war on poverty) and to reduce drug trafficking (the war on drugs). Yet in spite of our efforts to engage in these "wars," in many ways our country has actually lost ground since each of these "wars" was declared. This kind of wholesale and often indiscriminate use of the term "war" can minimize its meaning. As a society, we've forgotten that war typically calls for sacrifices to be made, and not just by those doing the fighting. So-called declarations of war that cannot be defined in traditional terms present very real possibilities that these efforts are ultimately perceived as failures, since victories, as we understand them in clear-cut terms, cannot be achieved. We risked this possibility as we now considered the "war on terror."

Yet our situation was clear: For the first time since the attack on Pearl Harbor, a surprise attack on United States soil had taken American lives. The parallel was obvious. So was the American reaction and response. There was a tension . . . a sense of urgency . . . and a strong feeling of uncertainty about what the future now held.

Would they hit us again and, if so, where and how? Who were "they"? Why now? What was their motivation?

Whoever they were, there was complete unanimity that we would do all in our power to find them and to bring them to justice.

But the powers of the President to carry out this effort were limited. President Bush justifiably argued that he needed additional authority to use military force as well as to expand the authority of all law enforcement officials to meet this new threat. While there was no disagreement about our changed circumstances—especially in those first days of unity and common purpose—there was skepticism about providing new authority without limit either in scope or in time.

Later that evening, we received a fax from the White House congressional liaison. It was a draft of what the administration wanted in a resolution authorizing the President to "use force" in pursuit of the perpetrators of terror. All resolutions begin with what are called the "whereas" clauses. These clauses essentially lay out the facts that lead up to the "resolved" clause—the description of what action it is resolved that we will take. In this case, the "whereas" clauses were pretty clear—we were attacked, the attack was unprovoked, and Americans were killed. However, even in the shock and emotion that attended those days immediately after these attacks, the administration's draft of the "resolved" clause gave us pause. Here is how it read:

S.J.Res. 23 Resolved Clause
Resolved by the Senate and the House of Representatives of the
United States of America in Congress assembled,

That the President is authorized to use all necessary and appropriate force against those nations, organizations, or persons he determines planned, authorized, harbored, committed, or aided in the planning or commission of the attacks against the United States that occurred on September 11, 2001, and to deter and preempt any related future acts of terrorism or aggression against the United States.

While the first part of that paragraph contained exactly the power the President should be granted, the second, we feared—the clause containing "to deter and preempt any related future acts of terrorism or aggression against the United States"—was a blank check to go anywhere, anytime, against anyone the Bush administration or any subsequent administration deemed capable of carrying out an attack. I assumed it was an overstep born of the heat of the moment.

Senator Byrd wasn't so sure. He noted that he was present and accounted for when the use of force was authorized in the Gulf of Tonkin resolution prior to our increased involvement in Vietnam. He warned that he would not be party to any declaration of war or any resolution authorizing the use of force that did not have clear limits on the designations of authority.

I shared Senator Byrd's concern. The Constitution is very clear about the responsibilities of the legislative and executive branches in times of war. Only Congress can declare war. Only the president can be the commander in chief. The question comes, of course, when military action occurs without the declaration of war. At what point can the president assume his role as commander in chief?

After Vietnam, Congress attempted to answer this question with the War Powers Resolution. That resolution authorizes the president to introduce U.S. forces into hostilities or imminent hostilities abroad, but it says that the president must keep Congress and the public informed of that action and that Congress must vote to specifically authorize the use of those forces within sixty to ninety days or those forces must be withdrawn.

In this case, there was near unanimous agreement that a Use of Force authorization was required and would be provided. The only questions were: Given the language the administration initially proposed, would Congress grant the President only the authority he needed to deal with those responsible for September 11, or would it give in to the administration's initial proposal to seek something much broader and more open-ended—and how quickly could the resolution be drafted and passed?

After a frenetic series of discussions with the White House and congressional Republicans (many of whom shared our concerns that the resolution was too far-reaching), we were able to agree on language that gave the President the authority he needed without making that authority unlimited. We wanted him to focus on the people responsible for September 11. By that Friday, September 14, we were ready to pass the resolution.

As the House and Senate debated this use of force, tens of thousands of military reservists were being activated to respond to the domestic security needs the United States now faced both on land and in the air. They would also help with the massive recovery efforts at the Pentagon and in New York City, where the mountainous ruins of the World Trade Center and surrounding structures sat like a smoldering funeral pyre. Tens of billions of dollars in federal emergency funding would be needed in New York at once, with more to come as, literally and metaphorically, the smoke cleared.

Discussion and votes on these issues began when we returned from the White House on Wednesday afternoon.

Meanwhile, the Capitol's security remained a concern. The nation's military alert status was now at "DefCon 4," lowered one level from "DefCon 3," which had been declared Tuesday, September 11. "DefCon 1," the highest alert, is declared in the event of an all-out war.

The Capitol was, for the time being, closed to the public. It was still surrounded by yellow police tape and concrete barricades. Nerves were still jittery. F-16s were still patrolling the skies overhead. By now we knew that the plane that had gone down in Pennsylvania, based on its trajectory before crashing, had been intended for a target in Washington—either the White House or the Capitol. No one was sure if other attacks might be imminent.

Late Thursday afternoon, as a vote was in process on the Senate floor, I was in a meeting with Robert Byrd, Trent Lott, and Ted Stevens when we were interrupted by a member of my security detail. "Sir," he said, "we need to get you out of here."

We could hear some commotion out in the hall. Someone yelled, "We've got a ten one hundred!"

I had no idea what a "ten one hundred" was. I later learned that it's Capitol Police code for a suspicious package, possibly a bomb. Within minutes, the scene in the hallways resembled the scene two days earlier as people began panicking. Staff spilled out of offices. The Senate floor emptied. The halls were filled once again with men and women rushing toward the exits. Somebody yelled, "It's a bomb!" Others urged people not to panic, to slow down, while still others yelled, "Run!"

Once again we found ourselves standing outside the Capitol, where we waited for forty-five minutes while the building was searched. It turned out that a Capitol employee's locker, in a stairwell not far from Senator Byrd's office, had aroused the suspicion of one of Byrd's staff. The police were called, bomb dogs were brought in, and the dogs got a "hit" on the locker. When they began barking, the alarm to evacuate was triggered. It turned out that the "10-100" was an old pair of boots made with a petroleum-based product that tripped the dogs' scent.

That alarm was a false one, but our fears, and the fears of the entire nation as that week wound toward an end, were quite real.

The next day at noon, under a dark gray sky, in a steady downpour that fit the subdued grief of the occasion, members of Congress, the cabinet, representatives of all branches of the federal government, and former Presidents Ford, Carter, Bush, and Clinton filed into downtown Washington's National Cathedral.

I've been in the National Cathedral several times, and each time I'm overwhelmed by its splendor, its gothic majesty. It's a breathtaking edifice, with its massive stained-glass windows and soaring arches. Its grandeur is at once both inspiring and humbling, as such a place of worship should be. On this day of sorrow and loss, it was meant to be a place of healing and strength as well.

This was the first time I felt truly inspired by our President. His remarks were quite brief, but they were pointed and strong. He referred to the "kinship of grief" that had united us all. I thought that was a wonderfully succinct phrase. When he declared, "This conflict was begun on the timing and terms of others," and, "It will end in a way, and at an hour, of our choosing," I thought he summarized well the situation to which we, as a nation and as a government, were now compelled to respond.

E pluribus unum—Out of the many, one.

These words are inscribed in our Senate chamber wall. I have looked at it hundreds, if not thousands, of times. But never have I felt its meaning as I felt it at that moment. We were many. We were Democrats. We were Republicans. We were white and we were black, urban and rural. We were many. But now—perhaps for the first time in my lifetime—we were truly one.

The only portion of Bush's remarks that afternoon that made me uncomfortable was his reference to our duty "to answer these attacks and rid the world of evil." Answering these attacks was unquestionably our responsibility. But ridding the world of evil was something else entirely. What "evil" were we talking about here? The particular "evil" that had unleashed the attacks of September 11 was going to be difficult enough to identify and deal with. But Bush's phrase wasn't limited to just that. It referred to the entire *world* and to what sounded like *all* "evil"—a disturbingly unfocused and ill-defined mission, if ever there was one. Even this early, in the first days after the attacks, Bush was already setting the stage, with his use of the language of religious conflict, for going much farther in response to these acts of terrorism than just finding their actual perpetrators. The Pandora's box of broader targets and deeper agendas was already beginning to creak open. The word "evil" would reappear many times in the coming months, culminating in Bush's linchpin "axis of evil" State of the Union address that January, in which he would draw Iraq, Iran, and North Korea into the fray. But on this rainswept September afternoon, that address was still more than three months away.

The concerns that I felt as I heard Bush target all the world's evil that day were subsumed by the inspiration and pride I felt as I watched him return to his seat at the end of his speech and I saw his father reach over to squeeze his son's hand. I was seated in a pew just across the aisle, and I was deeply touched by that discreet gesture. It was such a genuine moment, so poignant, not from one president to another, but simply from father to son. It reflected the human connection I talked about earlier, that kinship of grief that united us all in those early weeks after September 11.

Six days after Bush's speech at the National Cathedral, Trent Lott and I led a delegation of about fifty senators as we boarded a train at downtown D.C.'s Union Station—a train bound for New York City and ground zero.

Other than Chuck Schumer and Hillary Clinton, who had already visited the site in their capacity as New York's senators, this was the first trip for all of us, the first opportunity to witness firsthand the enormity of the devastation that had occurred there.

The train trip took three hours. When we arrived at New York's Penn Station, a gentle rain was sweeping down as dark clouds rolled in from the west. A bus took us to the Hudson River, where a boat was waiting to take us to the site. As we sat there idling, Mayor Rudy Giuliani climbed aboard. He was clearly exhausted. There wasn't a word said, but as he looked up at us, everyone gave him a standing ovation. He raised his hand to motion us to stop, but instead wiped away his tears. We were all crying.

It was a short ride, only a matter of minutes to the site.

And then we were there.

We docked about a block from the site, at the tip of Manhattan's North Cove Marina. Even from that location you could look up and see the absence of what had been there before. Where there once rose an uninterrupted forest of skyscraper peaks and spires outlined against the sky, there was now a gap, an expanse of open gray, smoky air where the World Trade Center had stood.

It is hard to convey with mere words the immensity of what we stepped into as we entered the site. It was like leaving the world we know and walking into a terrible dream, a monstrous canyon of wreckage and ruin. It was what I imagined Hiroshima might have looked like. It was like entering hell.

The odor of smoke, dust, and ash filled the air not just there but for miles around. We had smelled it on the boat, a pungent and acrid smell that had a strange hint of sweetness to it, perhaps brought on by the rain. Plumes of that dust and ash billowed from the smoldering wreckage, the mountains of steel and debris that rose as high as five stories around us. Inside those mountains, and down seventy feet more to the subterranean foundation of what had been the twin towers, were the crushed remains both of those buildings and of the bodies of the nearly three thousand people who perished inside them.

More than 1.5 million tons of steel and debris had been driven by gravity into this ground. The massive, bulldozer-like, grappler-clawed orange-and-yellow excavating machines picking at the jagged slopes of those mountains looked like small toys. The more than three thousand firemen, police officers, engineers, construction workers, and volunteers spread out over the site, spraying with hoses and working by hand and with buckets, looked like long lines of ants. These workers had already given the site a nickname—"the Pile"—and for more than a few of them, the Pile contained the remains of relatives and friends.

Mayor Giuliani showed us the way, along with a contingent of reporters and photographers who pressed in close with their cameras each time one of us would stop and speak with or embrace one of the workers. In trying to capture and record the intimacy of these moments, the photographers were intruding upon them, but then the workers there were already becoming used to this. Even in a setting as vast and as sprawling as this, it was hard, I imagined, for anyone here to find privacy. The whole world was watching every move they made.

At one point we were taken to a wall on which photographs of the missing—hundreds of them, along with letters and leaflets and even some personal effects—were displayed. It was heartbreaking to look at these faces and to see them look back, all so happy and alive, before they became victims.

We had lunch with some of the workers, men and women so shaken by what surrounded them that grief counselors and psychologists were on standby to help those who needed it. The enormity of the sadness enveloping that hole in the heart of Manhattan was as vast and as heavy as the wreckage itself.

The trip back to Washington that afternoon lasted the same three hours it had taken to get to New York, but it felt much longer. And the day wasn't done. As soon as we reached Union Station, we all went straight to the Capitol to prepare for that evening's address by President Bush to a special joint session of Congress.

It had now been nine days since September 11. We had spent those days in a landscape of grief, but as a nation it was time now to move beyond grief. It was time to move forward with resolve, to respond to this attack and the damage it had done with forceful concerted action, both at home and abroad.

It was apparent, from the moment that we—Trent Lott and I, joined by the other members of the House and Senate leadership—met with President Bush in the Speaker's office across the hall before escorting him into the House chamber that evening, that he had now made that transition from uncertain grief to the sureness of action. He *looked* more like a commander in chief than ever before. It was as if he had actually grown a suit size or two.

By now, Bush had sharpened and refined the vision that had been so roughly shaped in his previous speeches in response to these attacks. The vaguely defined "evil" out there in the world that had been his target at first was now honed to a "global terror network." The President laid down the gauntlet that night, challenging the entire world to make a decision. "Either you are with us," he declared, "or you are with the terrorists."

This was Bush at his best—and at the same time, at his most worrisome—distilling a complex situation into a clear, simple decision. His closest advisers admit that Bush is uncomfortable with complexities and layers of meaning. In our meetings, I've seen that he likes things boiled down to their essence. Black or white. Good or evil. With us or against us. It's easier to be certain when things are made simple. And clarity—particularly moral clarity—is extremely appealing in times of crisis and confusion.

Leaders throughout America's history have been able to provide such clarity at precisely the times it's needed most. Patrick Henry was speaking not just to his colleagues in the First Continental Congress when he declared in 1774, " I know not what course others may take, but as for me, give me liberty or give me death." He was speaking to an emerging, uncertain American people, many of whom would indeed have to die for that liberty. Nearly a century later, over the fallen at Gettysburg, with the fears of a divided nation filling the air, Abraham Lincoln resolved, "that these dead shall not have died in vain . . . that government of the people, by the people, for the people, shall not perish from the earth." Seven decades after that, Franklin Roosevelt fortified an America unnerved by economic depression by pronouncing in his first inaugural speech that "the only thing we have to fear is fear itself." Eleven years later, General George S. Patton strengthened the resolve of U.S. troops on the eve of the invasion of Normandy by telling them, "Death must not be feared. Death, in time, comes to all of us."

Words like these galvanize and inspire. They pull people together, pointing the way toward a common goal, a common target. In the case of Bush's joint session speech, the target was terrorism, and we were all moved by the moment, by the power of the President's words. It remained to be seen how those words would play out in action, but like tens of millions of Americans who watched Bush speak that evening, I was stirred by his speech. I wanted him to do well—we all wanted him to do well—and he did. He hit a home run, and I wanted to tell him I thought so.

As he stepped down from the dais and we—the escort delegation—rose to accompany him back out of the chamber, the room resounded with a standing ovation. As President Bush moved toward me, he reached out and we embraced each other. We looked at each other without saying a word, like brothers who understand the meaning of the moment. There was no thought behind this. It was an impulsive, heartfelt expression of the feeling we shared at that instant.

"The Hug"—as it was called in the next morning's newspapers and in political commentaries written for days thereafter—symbolized the unity not just of our nation, but of our government, which had been so rent by partisanship. Here were the leaders of the two sides in this long-running domestic political "war" embracing each other in a warm, wordless way, with a look in each other's eyes that said, "We're in this together."

That's what I felt at that moment. At that moment there wasn't a Democrat or a Republican in that room. There were only Americans.

First thing the next morning, the President and I talked on the phone. I can't recall who called whom—we were often speaking more than once a day at that point—but he asked, almost sheepishly, "Did we get into trouble last night for hugging each other?"

"I don't think so," I told him. "It just seemed like the natural thing to do. I think that was what the American people expected."

That was the beginning of our "honeymoon" period. Before September 11, Bush's purpose had been to break up our caucus's rank-and-file in order to advance his agenda. But now, at least temporarily, we shared the same agenda. Now there was no need for Bush to try to peel off Democratic senators to support his proposals. Now we could work directly as a true team.

Earlier that year, during the budget debate, I was having a conversation with Mort Kondracke, the executive editor of the *Roll Call* newspaper on Capitol Hill. We were talking about the tension that had grown between the President and me, and I recalled to Kondracke how Dwight Eisenhower used to routinely call the leaders of both parties to the White House to meet together with him and discuss issues. That was Eisenhower's way of trying to generate an environment of cooperation with Congress. I wondered aloud to Kondracke why Bush didn't try that.

Well, Kondracke went and wrote a column suggesting Bush do exactly that. There had been no response from the White House before September 11. But now was a good time to begin, and the White House called to schedule the first in what became a series of regular leadership breakfasts.

We met on September 25 in the small dining room just off the Oval Office—President Bush, Dick Gephardt, Trent Lott, Dennis Hastert, and me. As time passed, Dick Cheney would occasionally join us as well. Much of the material we discussed was highly classified. All staff and aides were left outside the room. No words were recorded. No notes were taken. The breakfasts would begin at 7:00 A.M. sharp. At 8:00 on the dot, no matter where we were in our discussion, Andy Card, the President's chief of staff, would step in and that was our signal that time was up.

The tone was congenial and relaxed, although the buttoned-down standards of formality demanded by Bush of his own staff in the White House applied here as well. I remember Dick Gephardt arriving at one of these breakfasts carrying his suit jacket on his arm—Dick prefers not to wear his jacket when he doesn't have to. As he entered the room, President Bush stopped him and said, "You know the rules here. Put your coat on." For a moment, Dick wasn't sure Bush was serious. Then he saw that he was, and with a small, awkward "Oh," Dick put on the jacket and we went ahead with the meeting.

In a strange way, it was our level of comfort and honesty that made the breakfasts quite productive. We discussed everything from emergency disaster relief for New York City to economic relief for the shattered commercial airline industry, from military action against the terrorist network to increasing airport security, from addressing the needs of the nearly one million American workers who would wind up losing their jobs between September 11 and the end of that year to somehow stimulating the stock market, which had been sinking before these attacks and was now dropping like a rock off a cliff. In the first few weeks after the attacks, we were able to put aside our differences and find agreement on most issues. In a very short time period, we authorized a string of critical pieces of emergency legislation.

What people watching Congress saw in those months was the legislative machinery of their government operating in overdrive. Virtually every day brought with it the passage of a new law—much of it passed unanimously. Though we all ended up in the same place on many of those bills, we often didn't start there. On many issues, our differences were much more fundamental.

One of those issues was aviation security. The aviation security fight went on for some time and resulted in a fierce battle between House and Senate, but only one issue of importance truly divided us, and that was the federalizing of almost thirty-thousand employees conducting airport security in the newly created Transportation Security Administration. As anyone who had gone through security at large airports in the days before September 11 knew, the attention to detail was desultory at best. Security screeners had incentives to get people through as quickly as possible—and many of the screeners were woefully underqualified. Some even had criminal records. It was protection by the lowest bidder, and it often felt that way. But security didn't feel particularly important, either—not until September 11. After that day, it became a top priority.

Democrats—and a fair number of Republicans—felt that the best way to professionalize the security screeners was to federalize them. The Republicans in the House, and in the White House, much less openly, were adamant that the legislation oppose the federalizing of airport screeners. This put the GOP in the untenable position of defending the record of private security firms such as Argenbright Security. Argenbright, at the time, was the largest private contractor of airport screeners. The company had paid a $1.5 million fine in federal court in 2000 for hiring criminals and for fraudulent billing. The General Accounting Office had also issued reports citing the poor performances overall of such contract workers; the private screeners' pay was miserable, morale was terrible, and the turnover rate was astounding.

Despite all these obvious problems, and very negative media coverage, the House stuck to its guns in blocking a bill that federalized the aviation security workforce. Their arguments tended toward the ridiculous—it often sounded as if they felt that federal workers (and the possibility that they might join a union) were a graver threat to America than the terrorists. The Senate passed a bill that federalized security screeners on October 12. Our vote was unanimous, and Senators McCain and Kay Bailey Hutchison—Republican leaders on the Commerce Committee—were vocal in their support for the Senate position. The House, however, refused to act until November, despite significant criticism. When the

House finally did act, it passed a bill that, just as the President called for, left the primary responsibility for screening in the hands of private contractors such as Argenbright. It was not until November 16 that the House ultimately relented and passed what was essentially the Senate bill.

The White House seemed especially inept in its handling of this bill. The President had been clear in his strong opposition to federalizing workers, but his staff signaled that this was not necessarily his final position. In that vein, his staffers and the Department of Transportation officials were constantly telling us that they were going to come up with some new compromises. But they never did. In fact, it became something of a standing joke among the staff working on this issue that Michael Jackson, the Department of Transportation expert, was supposedly coming up to Capitol Hill with a new proposal . . . anytime now.

The White House actually had a compromise we might have accepted involving some kind of partial federalization targeted at the largest airports. They told Senators Hollings, McCain, Hutchison, and Rockefeller that they wanted to meet to discuss the proposal, and even went so far as to schedule a meeting. But at the last moment it was called off. We later learned that the administration staffers had stopped by the House before the Senate meeting to "inform" the House Republican leadership of the deal they were going to offer to us. Congressman DeLay vetoed the offer and the meeting with the senators was canceled.

This kind of Keystone Kops legislating by the White House was an example of the dangerous power they were willing to cede—even on issues of security—to the extreme elements of the Republican Party. In this case, it happened to work in our favor, both in terms of sound policy and in terms of politics. By refusing to allow good faith negotiation, Tom DeLay assured total victory for the Senate and a greater level of security for the country with the passage of a fully federalized screening force.

Another major legislative initiative was the USA Patriot Act. The Patriot Act was legislation designed to provide law enforcement officials with greater powers and authority to conduct investigations and apprehend suspected terrorists living within the United States.

On September 17, Attorney General Ashcroft publicly demanded that the Congress pass the administration's counterterrorism proposals by

September 21. The impossible demand was made even more unreal by the fact that Ashcroft did not even make a draft of the legislation available to Congress until two days later.

This approach exemplified the administration's desire to push through sweeping changes that would allow law enforcement agencies to conduct business with minimal scrutiny. Attorney General Ashcroft's original proposal asked for the ability to detain indefinitely any noncitizen suspected of having a connection to terrorist activity. He didn't want to have to press or prove charges—he just wanted the ability to hold them. We were ultimately able to change that so that charges would have to be pressed within seven days of arrest. As we sought to work out these concerns, contrary to the bipartisan climate created by most government officials in the wake of September 11, Ashcroft went to the microphones and attacked Democrats for delaying passage of this bill. It is important to remember the environment at this time. Our country was extremely tense, and in this climate of high anxiety, the attorney general was implicitly suggesting that further attacks might not be prevented if Democrats didn't stop delaying. John Aschroft seemed to have two goals—securing greater power for the Department of Justice and scoring political points for the Republican Party.

There were tortuous negotiations between the White House and Senate staffs on this legislation. Ultimately, for reasons of efficiency and because of disagreements on amendment strategy between Senators Hatch and Leahy, I introduced a Senate alternative to the Ashcroft bill on October 4. Senators Leahy, Hatch, and Lott were the prime co-sponsors, and on October 11, it was passed by the Senate.

Meanwhile the House stuck mostly to the Ashcroft version. We spent a long time working with Speaker Hastert's people to try to figure out how to work out the differences between the Senate and House versions of this bill. Two decisive issues were major sticking points: the "sunset clause" and the money-laundering provisions. While most members were willing to support new counterterrorism proposals, we in the Senate feared that even though we had made positive changes to some of the original Ashcroft proposals, we were still talking about giving law enforcement significant new powers. Many of us wanted to give future Congresses—who would perhaps be operating in a different security environment—the ability to go back and look at the changes we made, to see if they were effective, to evaluate whether these powers were being abused, and to modify them if necessary. Therefore, the idea was proposed that instead of permanently enshrining these new authorities, we authorize them for a limited number of years, after which most would lapse, requiring Congress to then make a new determination of the merits. This caveat came to be called the "sunset clause."

Not surprisingly, Attorney General Ashcroft was bitterly opposed to any such limitation. In the final meeting in Hastert's office, where we crafted the deal that ultimately passed both Houses, the sunset clause was the last major obstacle. There was debate about whether the sunset should take effect in five years or four. Democrats supported four.

The deputy White House counsel, Tim Flanigan, made a long and impassioned attack on *any* sunset provision. After some consideration, we decided he was bluffing, and I made the decision to ask him whether the President would veto the bill if the sunset clause was included. Clearly there was a risk in asking this in the open meeting, as all Hastert needed was the excuse of a possible veto to kill the sunset.

This was high-stakes poker, but I was confident that Flanigan was bluffing. After a long pause, he gave a wry smile and acknowledged that, no, it was not the administration's position to veto over the sunset. With that, all the air went out of the anti-sunset balloon, and we got it knocked back to four years.

Money laundering was an especially maddening challenge. Terrorists, in an effort to hide the real nature of their activities, often set up fronts and disguise their resources to avert detection. The Republican negotiators—except for Senator Phil Gramm—publicly acknowledged that anti-money-laundering provisions were vital to the success of counterterrorism efforts. But even as they extolled the virtues of cracking down on money laundering, they tried to keep the provisions out of this bill.

Money-laundering provisions had passed the Banking Committee the previous year, but Republicans argued that we should pass those separately and not "hold up" this new counterterrorism legislation—a move that would effectively allow Republicans to ignore the provisions were they to come up again as a stand-alone measure. Phil Gramm, who was dead set against such provisions, would simply kill any freestanding legislation, as he had been more than willing to do in the past. The administration stood with the Republican congressional leadership, arguing that in order to avoid any delay in the passage of this legislation, we should forgo efforts to include money-laundering provisions.

We decided that, on this issue, we needed to be very direct with the President. So I brought it up at our next breakfast meeting. I made it clear to him that no bill would pass unless money-laundering provisions were included. It was only after delivering this blunt message that the Republicans finally relented. When the money-laundering provisions were finally passed, the administration was quick to take credit for assuring their inclusion. Their ability to pivot from active opposition to boastful support amazed me, and, again, it was a sign of things to come.

Another major piece of legislation in the wake of the September 11 attacks involved our efforts to "stabilize" the airlines. It was drafted in a white hot environment amid warnings that any number of commercial airlines were on the verge of collapse. Airlines had received formal notice that their liability insurance would be canceled. There was genuine concern by most economic experts that a critical U.S. industry was about to go completely under.

The legislation was simple, at least at the beginning: $5 billion in direct aid for losses stemming from September 11, and $10 billion in loan guarantees administered by a newly created Air Transportation Stabilization Board. It also allowed for airlines to tap into the federal war risk insurance program and reimbursed the airlines for six months for any increase in insurance.

But in this case, too, two major issues were fought out in the short negotiation process—providing for aviation workers who had lost their jobs and creating a Victim Compensation Fund.

Democrats in both Houses thought it outrageous that we would bail out the aviation industry with billions of dollars and yet provide nothing for the 150,000 aviation workers who had lost their jobs in the month following September 11. We felt that the least we could do was help those workers and their families get unemployment insurance, maintain their health insurance, and get some training so they could find new jobs that would allow them to support themselves and their families. The White House and congressional Republicans were not only opposed to this, they became increasingly strident about the pressing need to pass the bailout for the airlines and abandon the workers.

As much as we tried, it became clear that we simply were not in a position to get the House to agree to anything. Dick Gephardt told me that he had a personal commitment from Speaker Hastert to bring up the workers issue soon, and he believed that Hastert would keep his word. Because I was in a position to ensure that we would have a vote in the Senate on the workers' provisions when the House bill came to the Senate floor, we allowed the bailout to go forward.

Senator Carnahan and I put together an amendment to the bill that would guarantee health care and unemployment insurance for these workers. We went to the Senate floor, pleading for Republicans to help the economic victims of September 11. Unlike on aviation security, on this issue Republicans drew a hard line and held firm. They filibustered our amendment, and on October 11, our side was four votes shy of the sixty needed to overcome their filibuster. I was devastated for those workers and deeply disappointed in the senators who refused to do anything to help them.

The other major issue in the airline stabilization bill was the effort to provide a compensation fund for victims of September 11. The basic principle was simple. The airline bailout bill specifically limited the liability of the airlines whose planes had been hijacked by terrorists to the relatively small amounts of insurance on the aircraft themselves. This would almost certainly have left thousands of victims' families without any means of compensation, other than through a lawsuit.

However, having a mass of lawsuits going on for years seemed like a bad idea, particularly given the traumatic nature of the loss. Our solution was to allow the airlines a measure of liability relief but also to be realistic about the fact that anyone who went to court would be fighting over an ever dwindling pot. Therefore, we suggested creating a federal fund administered by a special master at the Justice Department who would determine the appropriate level of compensation and ensure fair and rapid payout to victims and their families. Unlike several similar efforts in the past that had been subject to what can be a long and contentious congressional appropriations process, we drafted the fund to allow payouts to come directly from the Treasury to avoid the possibility of Congress short-changing victims. Tom DeLay and some of his Republican colleagues were furious at the whole concept.

The Republican solution to this issue was, of course, to do nothing other than do away with any liability at all that the airlines might have. We talked about how one puts a monetary value on a human life. I said that it would be a very difficult thing to do. Mitch Daniels turned to one of his staff and asked, "We do that all the time at OMB [Office of Management and Budget], right? We have to put a dollar value on people's lives all the time."

After fighting all night and into the morning, first DeLay and then Daniels finally relented. Daniels did so only after we rejected his offer to pay $75,000 to each victim's family and talk about further compensation sometime in the future. The final bill, which was passed on September 21, included the federal fund almost exactly as we had drafted it, and despite controversies, that fund today has compensated scores of victims and survivors of that awful day's attacks, allowing shattered families to go on with their lives without having to go to court.

With all the successful negotiations on each of these issues over several weeks, our differences finally came to a head in mid-October with the White House's proposed economic stimulus package, shaped by Bush's chief economic adviser, Larry Lindsey.

We all—Democrats and Republicans alike—agreed with Federal Reserve Board chairman Alan Greenspan's assessment that, having been careful not to rush in to "fix" the economy too soon in the wake of the attacks, the government should now, after a month of plummeting consumer spending in almost every sector of sales throughout the country, step in with some combination of new spending and tax cuts.

In the weeks following the September 11 attacks, we had several conversations with the people widely considered the economic experts— including Alan Greenspan and former Treasury secretary Robert Rubin—and we asked them what would be the most effective steps we could take to shore up our economy.

What they told us was basically this: Put money into the hands of low and middle-income workers; they're the ones who will spend it quickly. Make sure that workers who have lost their jobs receive unemployment benefits, again because they need the money and will pump it back into the economy—which is the definition of a stimulus. They said tax cuts for businesses could be effective, as long as we limited the tax cuts to those that actually help create jobs. In those uncertain days after September 11, they told us that confidence was critical, and therefore any plan to stimulate the economy should help people regain the sense of security they need to shop, travel, and invest. Finally, they said our plan should be affordable and temporary. If something isn't temporary, it isn't stimulus, they said. Most important, they warned us, the baby boomers will start retiring in less than a decade, and we shouldn't be taking on major long-term spending or revenue obligations that will make it even more difficult to meet our responsibilities to Social Security and Medicare. The developing consensus was that something in the ballpark of $75–$100 billion would do it.

Up until this moment, everything we had done in the wake of the attacks had been handled at the leadership level, usually in the Speaker's office. We negotiated the bills, often late into the night, and ultimately would reach an agreement on the final wording. But as the economic stimulus package became the focus of our next legislative effort, the Speaker informed me that we would now be using "regular order," which was code for the normal legislative process. The legislation would be drafted in the Senate Finance and the House Ways and Means Committees and then sent to the Senate and House floors for debate and amendment. Recalling how politicized that process had been in the highly charged partisan atmosphere of pre–September 11 Washington, we knew that the work on economic stimulus was about to get politicized, too—not only politicized, but extended indefinitely as both sides postured for their traditional political bases.

Immediately, the debate over how best to stimulate our economy brought us right back to one of those baseline differences that defined us. The Republicans wanted the bulk of that relief to be directed toward tax cuts for businesses and individuals, to "kick-start" the economy from the top, as it were. We believed that those benefits should go directly to the people who needed them most—to the nation's middle- and lower-income workers and to the unemployed.

More egregiously, they tried to use the stimulus debate as a Trojan horse to eliminate the corporate alternative minimum tax, called the

chpt. 6 (cont)

141.

AMT, which would have given billions of dollars to some of the most profitable companies in America and a lot of money to some not-so-profitable ones as well—including an estimated $254 million to a company called Enron.

What's more, we had put money into our stimulus bill to strengthen homeland security, feeling that immediate homeland security spending would not only make America safer, but boost consumer confidence as well. Republicans immediately labeled it "pork."

The honeymoon, as they say, was over.

As if to make it official, *Time* magazine ran a lead story titled "The End of Unity." The date of that issue, October 15, 2001, is one that I will never forget—not because of that story, but because of the story that was about to unfold in my very office. On that same day an envelope was opened by a young intern in my Hart Building office, releasing a cloud of white powder.

The fine, talcum-like substance contained highly refined, highly lethal spores of a bacteria called *Bacillus anthracis.*

Anthrax.

End chpt. 6

CHAPTER SEVEN

goes to pg. 188 = 46 pgs

In Cipro We Trust

BY MID-OCTOBER 2001, the wounds of September 11 were still raw. It had been only a month since the most horrifying attack on U.S. soil, and Americans were still struggling to cope with their new reality. Then, as if to test a nation's strength, an already jittery public was hit with a new cause for alarm: anthrax. A word once used only by ranchers and scientists, anthrax had fast become a topic of speculation and fear in offices, schools, and living rooms throughout the country.

At the beginning of that month, a sixty-three-year-old man had been driven by his wife to a medical center emergency room near West Palm Beach, Florida. Robert Stevens—a photo editor for the company that owns the *National Enquirer* magazine—had been aching and feverish for several days, nothing serious. But then, according to his wife, he suddenly took a turn for the worse. His body temperature spiked, he began vomiting, and his speech became incoherent. Not long after arriving at the medical center, he suffered a massive seizure. Three days after that, on October 5, despite the efforts of doctors who had initially thought they were dealing with some form of meningitis, Robert Stevens died of what turned out to be inhalation anthrax—the first such death in the United States in a quarter century.

For weeks following September 11, there was a somewhat fatalistic expectation in the minds of many that we would be attacked again. The only question was where and how. One day I walked in on a discussion taking place in Pete Rouse's office among several of my staff. In what had become a morbid parlor game, they were debating whether the next attack would be anthrax or smallpox—anthrax because it could be mailed and smallpox because it would be far more devastating. They were convinced that I and other members of Congress secretly had been given the smallpox vaccine—I hadn't.

These weren't just idle discussions, either. Since September 11, we had talked about the various methods terrorists might choose for another attack—not just anthrax or smallpox, but the potential of a raid on a nuclear power or a chemical plant or the simple explosion of a bomb in a public place. It was those talks that helped shape the homeland security funding proposal we were working on.

At the same time, we were very conscious of the fact that we—Congress—were a likely target. After I heard the news of Robert Stevens's death in Florida, my first thought was that this might be "round two." If the first attack employed jetliners, was the second anthrax? We had known for some time that anthrax existed in the former Soviet Union and was susceptible to being stolen or sold. And I had little doubt that terrorists had the desire to use it.

My confidence in this thinking, however, was tempered by questions that had no answers. Why the office of a tabloid newspaper? If they wanted maximum impact, like that produced with the World Trade Center, why not something bigger, more prominent? And while the tragedy of September 11 produced the loss of American life of an unprecedented magnitude, this incident appeared to be limited to one victim. The inconsistencies argued against a connection with the attacks on the World Trade Center and the Pentagon. But whether an act of international terrorists or a lone domestic madman, my greatest concern was how we could defend against an anthrax attack like this. We had no procedures in place. We were completely defenseless.

Despite Health and Human Services Secretary Tommy Thompson's suggestion that Robert Stevens could have contracted anthrax from water in the North Carolina woods he'd visited recently, the news of Stevens's death gave many of us the sense that al-Qaeda's next phase had begun—that they were out to prove they could attack us whenever and wherever they chose.

While we were trying to anticipate and prevent potential attacks against our nation, the Senate's sergeant at arms, Al Lenhardt, whose predecessors had never faced anything like the challenges we were currently facing, worked long hours to anticipate and thwart any attacks on the Capitol itself. After the death in Florida, anthrax moved up the list of likely attacks, and we had started to put in place new measures to protect the mail coming into the complex.

Within a week of Stevens's death, another employee at that same Florida magazine office was hospitalized for the same infection, an anthrax-laced letter was discovered in the offices of the *New York Post,* the seven-month-old son of a freelance photographer at the Manhattan offices of ABC News came down with a relatively mild form of the illness contracted through the skin, and an NBC News employee was also diagnosed with cutaneous anthrax after opening a letter addressed to Tom Brokaw.

The Brokaw news broke on Friday, October 12. Linda and I heard about it on our way up to New York City, where we were headed for the weekend with four of our closest friends—my North Dakota Senate colleague Byron Dorgan and his wife, Kim, and Chip and Betsy Barclay. The six of us often spend time together, especially to celebrate birthdays, holidays, and wedding anniversaries. This weekend was particularly special, since Betsy was celebrating her fiftieth birthday. But the news about Tom Brokaw cast a pall over everything.

Tom is from South Dakota, too. He grew up in a small town not far from my hometown. Slightly ahead of me in years, Tom went to the University of South Dakota before launching his remarkable career in broadcast journalism. (USD is the rival of my alma mater, South Dakota State.) His wife, Meredith, is also from South Dakota.

I didn't know Tom before coming to Washington. But over the years, we have come to know each other and share a number of mutual friends. I've watched with admiration the charitable work that he and Meredith do out in South Dakota, and I recently had the opportunity to "roast" him for a good cause back in D.C. Whenever I sit to be interviewed with Tom, we catch up on South Dakota gossip before the cameras start rolling. We often joke about the long odds that a national news anchor could be interviewing a Senate leader and both of them would hail from South Dakota. The one thing I haven't gotten—or expected—from my friendship with Tom is any special treatment on NBC News. It's a testament to what an objective newsman he is.

Friday afternoon, while CNN ran constant reports of the anthrax found in Tom's office, a group of Alaska natives dropped by my Hart office to thank me for my opposition to drilling in the Arctic National Wildlife

Refuge. As a token of their appreciation, they wanted to present me with fur from the Alaskan musk ox, a species they said would be endangered by drilling.

When they asked the intern who greeted them in my absence to grab a handful of fur from their plastic bag, she, having learned from so many reports that anthrax can be found in the hides of infected animals, offered up an envelope and asked them to place the fur in it. A little nervous, she thanked the visitors and, once they were gone, reported the incident to another member of my staff, who asked the Capitol Police to test the fur to ensure it was safe. By all reports, the visitors were extraordinarily gracious and respectful. It didn't occur to them that such a gift might arouse suspicion. They probably weren't as focused on the bioterrorist threat as we were. Still, several of my staff joked that a simple "thank you" would have sufficed.

Given the Brokaw news and the fact that the Senate was planning to institute a new mail security protocol, my staff had stopped opening mail until they could be briefed on the new Senate procedures. Our Friday afternoon mail delivery sat unopened on our sixth-floor mail table. The top letter in the bundle was from the "4th Grade, Greendale School, Franklin Park, New Jersey."

Late Friday, my office manager met with the staff and interns who open mail to train them on the new procedures. My systems administrator, Tim Mitrovich, assured the interns, half-jokingly, "If you're going to be exposed to anthrax, this is the best place for it to happen," explaining that, unlike Robert Stevens and Ernesto Blanco, the two men infected in Florida, we knew we were targets and were on the lookout for white powder.

I tried to call Tom to see if everyone there was okay and to find out more about what had happened, but I couldn't reach him. All I could think was, My God, this is incredible. Why would anyone send Tom Brokaw anthrax? What could have motivated them?

I was still thinking about that on Monday morning, on my way to—of all places—the hospital. For several weeks I'd been struggling with terrible headaches. I didn't know what was causing them, but I had begun to fear that they might be indicative of something more serious. The Capitol's attending physician, Dr. John Eisold, had decided we should run some tests, so I was scheduled for an MRI at Bethesda Naval Hospital on that Monday morning, October 15. I remember sitting alone immediately after the test, not knowing how serious this might be. The tests showed nothing wrong, a clean bill of health. I was relieved.

I wasn't able to enjoy that feeling for long. No sooner did I get back to my Capitol office—it was close to 10:30 A.M.—than Pete Rouse came in and, in his rough, understated way, said, "The staff over at the Hart office just opened a letter that appears to have a toxic substance in it. We don't know what it is, but it may be anthrax."

I couldn't believe it. One of the first things I had intended to do that morning was to finally track down Tom, to find out how he and everyone else in New York was doing with this anthrax thing, and now this "thing" had hit home right here, with my own staff. I told Pete I had to get over to the Hart Building right away. "You can't do that," he said. "They've quarantined everyone in the office. The Capitol Police are on their way over there now to investigate."

All that we knew at that point was that several of our interns had been opening mail that morning on the sixth floor of our Hart office, where our mail arrives several times each day. The area, which has since been reconfigured, was essentially a wide-open space with a table where mail was opened, surrounded by five or six open workstations. Later it was determined that thirteen people were on the sixth floor around the time the letter was opened.

In the regular course of sorting and opening mail, the same intern who had greeted the Alaska natives the Friday before, Grant Leslie, opened a letter, noticing it was from a New Jersey elementary school class. Contrary to later media reports, the letter was not heavily taped and didn't appear unusual in any way. She cut about an inch into the envelope and, much like talcum powder squeezed out of its container, a fine white powder, accompanied by a cloud of white dust, spilled out. Powder landed on her skirt and shoes, on the clothes of Bret Wincup, the intern standing next to her, and on the floor.

Grant realized immediately what this might be and sat frozen, trying to keep the envelope closed. One staffer ran down the office's internal staircase to notify my assistant office manager, Shannon Lane, while another staff member called the Capitol Police. Shannon posted herself at the top of the stairs to keep anyone else from entering the area.

The first police officer arrived within minutes and instructed Grant, still motionless, to place the envelope on the floor on top of the white powder that had settled there. A few minutes later, three more officers arrived—none in protective gear. After surveying the situation, the police instructed all those on the sixth floor to gather in an adjacent room where my staff that deals with health care issues sits. Grant was isolated in another nearby room.

My office manager, Kelly Fado, called the Senate superintendent's office, reporting that they had a suspicious substance in the office and asking them to shut down the ventilation system to the area (we later learned that that process takes forty-five minutes). Another staffer called Pete Rouse to let him know what was happening.

By this time, two of the police officers had donned HazMat suits as they prepared to conduct a rapid "field" test to detect the presence of a range of dangerous substances. Over the preceding weeks, the Capitol Police HazMat team had been called in to check, on average, one suspicious package or substance per workday. None had ever tested positive. On Monday, October 15, ours was their third call of the day.

The initial field test was positive for anthrax. Incredulous, the police repeated the test. It came back positive a second time. The police took the twelve staff gathered in the adjacent room into the sixth-floor hallway and told them they suspected the letter contained anthrax but that the test results were preliminary. In the hallway, doctors from John Eisold's office in the Capitol collected nasal swabs from each of them. Next, they were instructed to wash their faces and hands and were then taken to a large conference room on the ninth floor of the Hart Building—where they joined Russ Feingold's staff from next door (our offices share a back hallway)—and the police swabbed their clothing.

The nasal swabs were sent to the lab at Bethesda Naval Hospital to determine the likelihood that any of these staff had inhaled anthrax spores. My sixth-floor staff was held on the ninth floor to separate them from the rest of my staff, who were gathered in my office on the fifth floor and presumed to be unexposed.

Grant, still isolated, heard the police reading the text of the letter aloud. "You cannot stop us. We have this anthrax. You die now. Are you afraid? Death to America. Death to Israel. Allah is great."

The doctor attending to Grant collected her nasal swab, and the police swabbed her clothes. The doctor advised her that she needed to prepare herself for the news that her nasal swab would be positive, even if others' weren't. He asked her if she wanted to go to the hospital. Shocked by the suggestion, she asked if he thought she needed to be hospitalized, and he responded, "It's up to you."

She felt fine—at least physically—and worried that her arrival could cause a big scene at the hospital, so she chose to go home. First, because her clothes tested positive for the presence of anthrax spores, Grant washed her face and hands, wet her hair, and changed clothes.

Then the FBI took her to an office down the hall to question her about the letter. By that time, the hallway was filled with people—doctors, Capitol Police officers, Al Lenhardt, and FBI agents—and confusion. Most of the FBI's questions weren't answerable, but Grant, and later others on my staff and I, did our best to answer them.

To evade the hordes of media stationed outside my office, Grant and the police took a back route through the Hart Building to the Hart garage, from which the police drove her home. She and the others from the sixth floor each had been given a twenty-four-hour supply of a drug called ciprofloxacin—Cipro—the only FDA-approved medication recommended by the Centers for Disease Control and Prevention (CDC) for inhalation of anthrax spores.

I felt helpless, extremely concerned for Grant and everyone else over there. As many as forty people worked in that office at any one time. I didn't know how many were there at the moment, but I needed to talk to them right away, which we were able to do over a speakerphone. At their end of the line, with investigators in hooded white biohazard suits already probing the desks and walls around them, my "fifth-floor staff"— the twenty-five people who were on the fifth floor when the letter was opened—gathered together for a conference call unlike any we'd ever had before.

Kelly, who set up the call, had just reported to the group that the letter had tested positive for anthrax in two field tests. When they got on the phone with me, they were a little stunned and very worried about their colleagues on the sixth floor, but considering everything, they were amazingly calm.

In retrospect I can say that ignorance truly is bliss, because none of us— not them and certainly not me—realized at that point how incredibly *chpt. 7 (cont.)*

150/

lethal this poison could be and how much danger they were actually in. "Don't worry," I told them. "I'm sure everything's going to be okay."

But I wasn't so sure.

No sooner did I hang up the phone than President Bush called. We had a lot to discuss—the Senate had passed anti-terror legislation at the end of the previous week that included anti-money-laundering provisions that the House failed to include. I had recently voiced my reservations about making the administration's proposed tax cuts the centerpiece of an economic stimulus plan. Things were moving at a furious pace. When I picked up the phone, I apologized for being distracted but explained that a letter containing anthrax had just been opened in my office. The President immediately began asking me what I knew—and I shared what little information I had.

The President happened to have a joint appearance scheduled just after our phone conversation. He was welcoming the Italian prime minister, Silvio Berlusconi, to Washington and thanking him for Italy's partnership in the war on terror.

I had just begun the process of calling the families of my staff to tell them what had happened when, on the television near my desk, I saw the President standing in the colonnade of the White House, taking questions from reporters.

The second question was, "Have there been any other reports of anthrax-tainted mail being received by U.S. businesses or government offices today?"

The President responded, "There has been today. I just talked to Leader Daschle. His office received a letter, and it had anthrax in it. The letter was field tested. The staffers that have been exposed are being treated. The powder that had been field tested is now, obviously, going to the CDC lab.

"Beyond that, I don't know more about it. I spoke to the leader; he is, obviously, concerned, as am I. The key thing for the American people is to be cautious about letters that come from somebody you may not know, unmarked letters, letters that have got—that look suspicious . . . "

I didn't know the President was going to repeat on national television what I had told him minutes before. But now most of the staff families I

Top: A thirty-one-year-old congressman Tom Daschle receives the "Landslide Award" from House Speaker Tip O'Neill. The award was given to the representative who won the election by the smallest margin. Tom Daschle won by 14 votes, a margin that grew to 110 after a year-long recount.
(Courtesy of Tom Daschle)

MIDDLE: Texas governor George W. Bush; his father, former president George H. W. Bush; and his brother, Florida governor Jeb Bush, watch the 2000 election night returns come in from Florida.
(Stephen Crowley/New York Times)

LEFT: Vice President Al Gore tells Governor Bush that "there is no reason to get snippy" while informing him that he will not be conceding the election. Looking on are Senator Joe Lieberman, Tipper Gore (with camera), campaign chairman Bill Daley, and other family members and staff.
(Callie Shell/White House)

With the Senate race of Maria Cantwell in Washington State yet to be decided, Senator Daschle holds a news conference announcing the possibility of a historic fifty-fifty Senate. (*Justin Lane*/ New York Times)

In early January, Tom Daschle and Trent Lott negotiate the final details of the fifty-fifty power-sharing agreement for the 107th Congress. (*PF Bentley/PFPIX.com*)

On May 24, 2001, Senator James Jeffords returns to Burlington, Vermont, to announce that he will become an independent. (*Vyto Starinskas*/ Rutland Herald)

Tom Daschle sits on his balcony doing paperwork in the relatively calm days before September 11. This photo was taken on September 7, 2001. *(PF Bentley/PFPIX.com)*

A series of never-before-seen photos documents the panic that surrounded the evacuation of the U.S. Capitol on September 11.

TOP LEFT: Here, a woman has literally run out of her shoes in her haste to leave the Capitol. TOP RIGHT AND BOTTOM: Capitol Police CERT members form a perimeter on the west front of the Capitol as House and Senate leaders are evacuated from Washington in a convoy of helicopters.
(Office of the Architect of the Capitol / C. Stephen Payne)

Members of the House and Senate gather on the steps of the east front of the Capitol on the evening of September 11 and spontaneously sing "God Bless America."
(Office of the Architect of the Capitol / C. Stephen Payne)

Congressional leaders visit the crash site at the Pentagon on September 13, 2001. *(PF Bentley/PFPIX.com)*

On September 20, 2001, members of Congress tour ground zero in New York. They are led by Fire Commissioner Thomas Von Essen and New York City mayor Rudy Giuliani. *(Mike Albans/Reuters)*

Senator Daschle and Senator Wellstone discuss bioterrorism issues with Michael Osterholm from the University of Minnesota. Six days later, Daschle's office received a letter containing anthrax. Senator Wellstone was killed in a plane crash in late October 2002. *(PF Bentley/PFPIX.com)*

A copy of the letter and envelope sent to Senator Tom Daschle's office on October 15, 2001. The release of one to two grams of highly concentrated anthrax spores from the envelope marked the biggest bioterrorist attack in U.S. history.
(Federal Bureau of Investigation)

Workers prepare for aggressive air sampling of Senator Daschle's suite: Efforts are made to dislodge potentially hidden spores, and negative air machines are used to vacuum and filter air from the room. *(Environmental Protection Agency)*

After Senator Daschle's suite was fumigated with chlorine dioxide gas, a team of Marines folded the U.S. flag that stood in his office. Later the U.S. Marines, the Coast Guard, and the EPA returned the flag to the senator in a ceremony that commemorated America's strength and resilience following the anthrax attack. *(Environmental Protection Agency)*

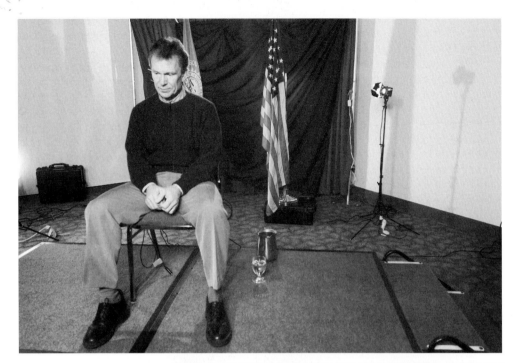

Tom Daschle participates in a series of television interviews the morning after the 2002 elections. At that point, Tim Johnson and Mary Landrieu's elections remained undecided, but it was clear that the Democrats had lost control of the Senate.
(*Val Hoeppner*/Argus Leader)

Tom and his wife, Linda, enjoy a quiet moment in the U.S. Capitol.
(*PF Bentley/PFPIX.com*)

was trying to call were going to learn this horrible news from the television rather than from me. The phones in our office immediately began ringing off their hooks. The Capitol press corps was outside my door within minutes, armed with dozens of questions for which we had very few answers. I continued calling the families, to let them know that we had this potent antibiotic and that everything was going to be all right. Some of the relatives were distressed because, like us, they were trying to digest and sort out this cascade of information on something they knew little or nothing about before that morning.

We were in constant communication with the Hart staff over the telephone. It was now noon. Reporters and staff members in other sections of the complex could see, through our office's interior glass windows, technicians in hooded HazMat suits and Capitol Police officers and members of John Eisold's physician staff wearing lab coats and latex gloves moving around the office—until one of the technicians, noticing the onlookers, drew the blinds.

Soon several Department of Defense technicians arrived on the scene. Al Lenhardt was already there, assessing the immediate situation in terms of what should be done to isolate and secure the premises and make sure this thing didn't spread. One of the jobs Al had held in the Army was commanding general of the military police and chemical schools at Fort McClellan, Alabama, so he was familiar with various protocols for responding to chemical and biological attacks. Still, those situations were scenarios. This was real. And the setting—the offices of the United States Senate—was, to say the least, unique.

One of the first things Al did, using plans from the architect of the Capitol's office, was order that the ventilation system for the entire southeast quadrant be shut down. He didn't learn until later that the building's ventilation system had been modified and rerouted in the years since those original plans had been drawn and that some of the ductwork connecting that quadrant to the rest of the complex was still open. As Al later remarked, "We were just darned lucky."

By early that afternoon, Al was on the phone to, as he put it, "my friends over in that five-sided building," trying to piece together what to do next. The people he spoke to at the Pentagon routed him to the U.S. Army Medical Research Institute of Infectious Diseases (USAMRIID) at Fort Detrick, Maryland, who instructed him, among other things, to have the letter sealed and sent there immediately for analysis and testing. Al instructed the Capitol Police to call the FBI, who assumed jurisdiction over the case.

An FBI hazardous materials team arrived and, under armed escort, drove the letter, sealed inside a biocontainment package, to the Fort Detrick lab. Concerned that there could be more dangerous letters in the mail system, Al ordered the immediate collection of all unopened mail in every Senate office, and mail delivery was suspended until its safety could be ensured—something that would take several months. Al was initially criticized by some for "overreacting," but his decision soon proved to be the right one.

Meanwhile, the networks were all over the story. Around 1:15 P.M., accompanied by Lieutenant Dan Nichols of the Capitol Police and Dr. Eisold, I held a news conference on the Capitol lawn, sharing what I knew about the situation. Over in the Hart Building, my sixth-floor staff had been allowed to return to my Hart office to join the fifth-floor staff, who had been quarantined since about 10:00 A.M. It was a chaotic, confusing, surreal situation.

The Hart staffers watched as their own story scrolled across the television screen. Some of the news was true, some wasn't, and some, if true, was news to them. They saw the President tell the world that they'd been exposed to anthrax, information that some of them hadn't yet been able to give their own families. They wondered if it was really safe to stay in an office where anthrax had been spilled.

It was past lunchtime now, and it was unclear when they'd be allowed to leave, so they were given permission to order pizza. Although an elaborate plan had been devised to accept the pizza without anyone else entering my office, in all the confusion the delivery man somehow got beyond the police checkpoint in the hallway. His steps across the threshold of our front door later earned him a sixty-day supply of Cipro.

Because one of the sixth-floor staffers had gone to the fifth floor immediately after the letter was opened, the Capitol Police decided to test the fifth-floor staff's clothes for anthrax contamination. Although those tests were negative, several members of my staff felt that nasal swabs should be obtained from my fifth-floor staff, just as they had been from those on the sixth floor.

The doctors felt that wasn't necessary, since at that time no one had any reason to believe that the anthrax spores could have traveled down an internal stairway and around several corners to reach the fifth floor, where much of my staff had been quarantined for hours. Insistent, the fifth-floor staff developed a list of those who wanted nasal swabs, and, as soon as they were allowed to leave the Hart Building—around 3:00 P.M.—they went to John Eisold's Capitol office to get them. In retrospect, that decision by my staff was a pivotal one.

To avoid the media gathered in the hall outside the fifth-floor entrance, these staffers took a circuitous route of back hallways and tunnels out of the Hart Building and over to the Capitol. After getting swabbed, some came to my Capitol office to work, and some went home. Later, we would spend hours retracing their steps to determine if they'd tracked anthrax into the Capitol complex.

By the time that day ended, I didn't know what to think or feel. Reporters kept asking me what it felt like to know that someone was trying to kill me. I was obviously a target, but I wasn't sure how to interpret it.

I don't know if the perpetrator(s) had any real expectation that the mail would reach me, but it was clear they were trying to kill someone. Those who have argued that the person or persons who did this were merely sending a wake-up call to the government about the threat of bioterrorism—and did not intend to hurt anyone—are, in my judgment, naive. This wasn't a statement. It was the largest bioweapons attack in United States history.

The anthrax contained in that letter was far more sophisticated and dangerous than the anthrax in the letters sent a few weeks earlier to New York and Florida, and Robert Stevens had already died after exposure to the less-engineered anthrax—before the letter to me was even postmarked. There is no question that the intent was to kill. And the fact that this attack might have been directed at my staff made it even worse.

By Tuesday morning, all of America was on anthrax alert. Warnings were on their way from the U.S. Postal Service to 135 million homes, cautioning them about possible "biological hazards" moving through the U.S. mail. Virtually all of the postal service's 1,900 inspectors and 1,400 security officers were reassigned to investigate and guard against this particular threat.

The American public, along with my staff and me, had learned more about anthrax in the previous twenty-four hours than they had ever known before—and there remained much more to learn. I knew a little bit about anthrax already, but just a little. I knew that it occurs naturally in the form of bacteria found in the infected remains of farm animals like goats and sheep. That's why almost all cases of anthrax infection on record—until now—had been in factories where goat and sheep hair was handled and, to a lesser extent, among farmers and people who worked with farm animals. That's why one of the common names for anthrax is "woolsorter's disease."

But I didn't really know what anthrax spores actually *do* once they enter the body.

When inhaled anthrax spores reach the lung, the body's immune cells surround them in an attempt to consume and destroy them. The spores then germinate and replicate inside the immune cells and begin attacking the body. The immune cells carry them into the lymph nodes and eventually the blood. Once anthrax hits the bloodstream, there is little that can be done, as the bacteria spread throughout the lungs, brain, and other organs.

The anthrax toxins they release are so potent that they have names like "lethal factor" and "edema factor." And there is a lot more anthrax in the world today than just what can be found on prairies and farmland. Anthrax bacteria have been cultivated in laboratories for decades by researchers at universities and zoos and public health clinics all over the world. The Los Alamos National Laboratory in New Mexico alone has more than 1,200 different strains of anthrax in storage.

Those germs, if they fell into the wrong hands, would be deadly enough, but even deadlier is anthrax that has been developed for years in the military bioweapons laboratories of different nations. Milled and refined to a fine powder, these aerosol forms of "weapons-grade" anthrax are intended to be used in an attack, the spores so minuscule that they dissipate and hang in the air once they are sprayed, dumped from an airplane, or otherwise injected into the atmosphere.

During the cold war, the Soviet Union had a lab in a place called Sverdlovsk dedicated to developing weapons-grade anthrax. In the spring of 1979, a worker in that lab forgot to replace a ventilation filter, and the lethal "aerosolized" anthrax spores—approximately two grams—were accidentally released into the city's air. According to the Soviets—and we don't know how accurate these numbers are—hundreds of animals and more than sixty people died in that accident, and dozens more were hospitalized. When I considered what two grams of these weaponized spores did in Russia when released over an entire city, the thought of what the two grams of anthrax spores released from the letter in my office could do to my staff was mind-boggling.

With an appreciation for how lethal this substance can be, the FBI was on the scene Tuesday morning at the Trenton, New Jersey, postal facility where both the letter addressed to Tom Brokaw and the letter addressed to me had been postmarked. FBI agents were also investigating possible cases of anthrax infection at a Microsoft office in Nevada and at a Ford Motor Company plant in New Jersey. The Planned Parenthood Federation of America, which had been a target of hoax mailings for some time, reported that day alone that ninety family-planning offices and clinics across the country had received envelopes containing powdery substances—all of which turned out to be harmless.

Federal agencies were flooded with thousands of calls about "suspicious" white powdery substances that turned out to be brick dust or talcum powder or NutraSweet. Doctors were besieged by patients demanding prescriptions for Cipro. And the nervousness wasn't limited to America—a bank in France, a nuclear authority office in the Czech Republic, and U.S. embassy offices in Australia all closed temporarily owing to reports of "suspicious substances."

Some residents at the apartment building of one of our interns, fearing that she had "infected" them, suggested that everyone in the building be tested. At the Senate's day care center, parents demanded that their children be tested because a member of my staff had picked up her child on her way home on Monday. Americans had been told repeatedly that anthrax wasn't contagious and that secondary exposures were unheard of, but fear often trumps rationality, and several of my staff, struggling with their own fears, spent untold hours calming the fears of others.

Meanwhile, my office suite was taped shut and sealed with plastic, and the southeast quadrant of the Hart Building was cordoned off. In a hearing room of another section, on the building's second floor, hundreds of

Senate staffers lined up for hours for nasal swabs and to be given a preventive three-day supply of Cipro by Dr. Eisold's team of physicians.

That same Tuesday morning, we arranged a briefing for all senators to share what we knew so far. It was held in the Senators' Dining Room in the Capitol. Major General John Parker from USAMRIID, Dr. Eisold, Al Lenhardt, Secretary of the Senate Jeri Thomson, and the FBI were there.

General Parker explained that the letter had been tested at USAMRIID and that it was indeed anthrax. He praised my staff for the way they handled the situation. The FBI assured us that everything possible would be done to investigate the crime. I had to focus on my obligations as Senate leader—to keep the Senate running, to protect the people who work there, and to keep everyone calm.

But I was also numb, unsure of so much, including the answer to a question I didn't even want to ask—whether my staff would live through this experience. My colleagues were extremely supportive, asking how I was holding up and expressing concern for my staff. And they were worried. They had lots of questions about how they could protect their own staffs and how our security could be improved.

They knew that one man had already died of inhalation anthrax and that another had miraculously survived. At that point there weren't many answers, and people hadn't yet learned one of the crucial lessons of this ordeal: When you aren't sure, admit it, and err on the side of safety.

Lots of misstatements added to the confusion. There were conflicting pronouncements about how dangerous the anthrax in this letter actually was. Someone said it was "weapons-grade," an assertion that was both contradicted and confirmed several times over the weeks that followed. Senator Bill Frist, a heart-lung transplant specialist, tried to reassure everyone, saying he was confident that no one else in America would ever die of inhalation anthrax. I wondered how he could be so sure—I certainly wasn't. One statement that did hold up over time was General Parker's succinct description of the anthrax. "The sample is highly concentrated," he said. "Pure spores."

Monday afternoon, John Eisold had called the chief of infectious diseases at Bethesda Naval Hospital, Dr. Greg Martin, and asked him to come to the Capitol early Tuesday morning to help with the effort to collect nasal swabs and address the general health threat on the Hill. I knew Greg through the attending physician's office and had great admiration for him. John's decision to assign Greg to this crisis turned out to be one of the godsends of the whole experience.

Before he left Bethesda for the Capitol Tuesday morning, Greg stopped by the lab to check the blood agar culture plates of the nasal swabs collected from my staff. Cultures are generally held for forty-eight to seventy-two hours, but the plates usually get checked for growth at the twenty-four- and forty-eight-hour marks. It had been less than twelve hours since the cultures were plated, but Greg checked them anyway. He was amazed to find the cream-colored colonies of rod-shaped *Bacillus anthracis*—anthrax bacteria—well on their way to completely covering about a dozen of the plates. Suddenly, it was a whole new ball game.

The anthrax spores my staff and others had been exposed to had spread farther—through the air—than anyone had thought. For the first time, Greg realized there was a strong possibility that despite all medical interventions, some of my staff could develop inhalation anthrax. He quietly reserved four beds at Bethesda for them—something we didn't learn until much later.

Tuesday night I was at a fund-raiser for Mark Pryor, who was challenging Tim Hutchinson for his Senate seat in Arkansas, when at about 7:00 P.M., Pete Rouse called me from Jeri Thomson's office with the news that he'd just gotten the initial test results of the nasal swabs taken from our Hart office staff and that I should get back to the Capitol immediately because, as he put it, "We've got a problem. Some of the nasal swabs came back positive, and we don't know if the Cipro's going to work."

I went straight to the secretary of the Senate's office in the Capitol, thinking, Now what do we do? Pete, Jeri Thomson, Al Lenhardt, and Dr. Eisold had gathered to deal with the fallout. Later we were joined by Dr. Martin and Mark Childress and Laura Petrou of my staff.

When I arrived, Pete handed me a piece of paper with twenty-five names on it. Seventeen of them were members of my staff, one was a member of Senator Feingold's staff, one was a worker at the P Street mail facility—later determined to be a false positive—and the rest were Capitol Police officers and other first responders.

Later I would assure the nation, as the doctors had assured me, that testing positive for exposure to anthrax does not necessarily mean that you have the disease. But at that moment, as I stared at those names—staff members I'd known for years and young interns who'd just arrived within the past few weeks and had already endured the horror of September 11—such statements provided little comfort. There was no escaping the reality that some of them might die.

Another startling discovery was that four of the people who'd tested positive for exposure were on the fifth floor of my office when the letter was opened up on the sixth. The final count of "positives" included seven from the fifth floor. The implication was clear—the anthrax had not been "contained," as so many had assumed. The experts were dumbfounded. We were in uncharted waters.

Floating through my consciousness were comments like "This is special stuff" and "It's highly concentrated and finely milled." It was hard to think of anything other than the danger these men and women were in. The enormity of it was overwhelming, but there were so many things to do.

Even though we weren't certain the antibiotics would work, we had to make sure that the people who tested positive were actually taking them. We knew that the sixth-floor staff was already on Cipro, but we weren't sure about those from the fifth floor. Pete and Laura called them. They woke some of them up, since by this time it had gotten late. We didn't want to alarm people—and we didn't explain the situation to them until the next morning—but we weren't going to take any chances.

I asked the doctors about the anthrax vaccine and whether these people should be vaccinated. They said that Department of Defense protocol in such a situation was to provide the vaccine post-exposure along with the antibiotics. I said, "Then that's what we'll do." They explained that the Defense Department's vaccine wasn't available for civilians, that the CDC had the civilian stocks, and that we'd need to get special approval for it. I called Tommy Thompson, who didn't know all the details but assured me, "Whatever you need, Senator, you'll have."

Then we received yet another disturbing report. Throughout Tuesday night, different pieces of information were coming in from various sources—from Bethesda Naval Hospital, the Naval Medical Research Center, the Defense Advanced Research Projects Agency (DARPA), and USAMRIID. Among these reports was word that a woman in my *Capitol* office, Michele Ballantyne, had tested positive for exposure.

The implications were enormous. Greg Martin was immediately skeptical, but we explained to him that several of the people from the Hart office had come to the Capitol office after they were allowed to leave on

Monday. People were hugging each other, and anthrax might have been on their clothes. The theory of possible secondary exposure was a terrifying one—for that could involve a whole new universe of people.

Greg kept asking questions, and a program manager from DARPA eventually discovered that someone had confused the environmental samples with the nasal swab cultures. The police had swabbed the clothes of my Capitol staff on Monday afternoon, because some of the Hart staff had been in the Capitol office, and it was Michele's *clothes* that had tested positive.

Laura called Michele around midnight, and Michele confirmed that she hadn't even had a nasal swab. We told her that her clothes had tested positive but that there was suspicion that this was a false positive and a confirmatory test was going to be run. She was instructed to start on antibiotics, just in case, and was told to bring her clothes in the next morning for more testing. The outfit Michele wore that day was probably tested more thoroughly than any person or object throughout this entire ordeal. Fortunately it turned out to be a false positive, but it was several days before we got that news.

Given the possibility of exposure in the Capitol, Dr. Eisold decided that my Capitol staff and I needed to be swabbed and to take Cipro, at least until we knew more. Bruce Clemons, another Navy physician from Dr. Eisold's office, and Greg Martin swabbed each of us and handed out three-day supplies of large white Cipro caplets. By this time, "Cipro" was a household word in America and "nasal swab" was part of the Capitol Hill community's vernacular. All over the Capitol complex, people asked one another if they'd been "swabbed" yet.

Many Americans probably don't understand what a nasal swab feels like. The words suggest a relatively delicate procedure, but it's far from that. Tuesday night I learned this firsthand. The "swab" is essentially a six-inch Q-tip. Since they are actually taking a "nasopharyngeal" culture, the doctors push it far back into the nasal passages, causing many people to gag, sneeze, or cough. The doctors call it "tickling your tonsils," but some on my staff called it a "nasal lobotomy." It's not comfortable.

In any event, it was clear that this situation was developing faster than we could react to it. I wasn't sure what we'd ultimately be facing, but I was sure that members of Congress were not experts in this highly specialized area. Our decisions needed to be informed by accurate information. We had to ensure that we brought in the right experts and then we had to trust them to advise us.

My only directive to the experts was to put health and public safety first and to follow the science. To gather the scientific evidence we needed, it was clear that we would have to do more environmental testing to determine if anthrax could be found anywhere else in the complex. We didn't want to cause a panic, but we needed to make sure these buildings were safe, and we needed to know if there were more letters out there.

I consulted that evening with Trent Lott about when we should close the Senate office buildings for testing. We decided we would close them around 5:00 P.M. Wednesday, so that people would have time to collect things they might need and vacate their offices in an orderly way. We hoped and expected that this evacuation would be for just a short time.

Dr. Eisold charged Dr. Martin with the care of the high-risk group: my staff, Russ Feingold's staff, and the first responders involved in the incident. We had to give the test results to the staff, and we talked about how to break the news to them. At this point, it was after 1:00 A.M. We decided that Pete and Laura would call each of them in the morning, and Greg Martin agreed to come to our Capitol office at 7:00 A.M. to coach Pete and Laura through the calls.

That night, on Tom Brokaw's news broadcast, Homeland Security Director Tom Ridge called the bioterrorism threat we now faced "the number one priority this week and for the weeks ahead."

I, for one, had no question about that.

The following day—Wednesday—Al Lenhardt and his staff discovered the Hart Building's rearranged ventilation system. Although they had been assured by experts from DARPA and USAMRIID that it was extremely unlikely that even highly refined weapons-grade anthrax would be able to spread through the system without quickly becoming diluted, the decision was made to shut down the entire building. The nasal swabbing continued, but now the lines began forming inside the Capitol at the attending physician's office and outside the Russell Senate Building's Caucus Room—the same room in which the McCarthy, Watergate Committee, and *Titanic* Commission hearings had been held. By the time the testing that week was finished, more than six thousand Capitol Hill employees had been swabbed.

That morning, I attended the regular Wednesday breakfast with the President and congressional leaders. Meanwhile, Pete and Laura, with Greg Martin there to address medical issues, began to call the people who had tested positive and ask them to attend an 8:30 A.M. meeting in my office in the Capitol.

Most weren't given their test results over the phone—we wanted Greg to do that. Then Pete and Laura called the rest of the Hart staff, telling them to report at 9:00 A.M. The plan was to protect the confidentiality of those who had tested positive by telling them first and then having a full staff meeting to give everyone the information they all needed.

Around 8:00 A.M., Dr. Martin, who'd been on the phone with the lab at Bethesda, finally got some good news. The anthrax was sensitive to Cipro— and to a number of other antibiotics, including penicillin. As dangerous as this strain of anthrax was, it was not resistant to antibiotics.

By 8:30 A.M., I was back from the White House, and the "positives" trickled in for the first meeting. Some brought their spouses. Most, at the urging of the FBI, carried the clothes they had worn on Monday. They looked like refugees, coming in with these black plastic bags filled with their "anthrax-day" clothes. I couldn't understand why this was a good idea—and it caused quite a stir among others in the Capitol—but I assumed that somebody who knew what he was doing had decided that it was. Having lived through the uncertainties of September 11, I should have understood that we were once again in a situation where nobody knew quite what to do.

Ironically, by Wednesday morning, the FBI had decided they didn't want these clothes after all, and that led to an absurd series of events in which the clothes endured a journey through multiple government agencies, multiple dry cleaners, and a drive up and down the East Coast. It ended about six months later, when the staff finally got their clothes back—at least most of them.

The first meeting was held in my conference room. I introduced Dr. Martin to the group of "positives" and assured them they were in good hands. Greg was just fantastic. Not only was he extremely knowledgeable about anthrax, which was reassuring in itself, but he was also a very calming presence, an easygoing personality. He explained that each of them had tested positive for anthrax exposure.

If someone's nasal swab tested positive, that did not—and Greg emphasized this—did *not* mean that he or she was infected with the disease or would become infected with it. Simple penicillin, said Greg, can kill most strains of anthrax, as can a host of other familiar antibiotics, such as tetra-cycline. The "gold standard" medication for inhalation of anthrax spores, however, is Cipro.

If anthrax spores were found deep in their nasal passages, Greg told us, we had to assume that some had penetrated their lungs, so they would have to adhere to a strict course of antibiotics that should prevent them from actually developing an anthrax infection. They were cautioned to report any flu-like symptoms, such as a fever or a cough. To complicate matters, the early symptoms of inhalation anthrax are essentially these same flu-like symptoms—fever, body aches, and cough—and we were just entering the cold and flu season. Greg assured everyone that if they did develop the disease, it would be recognized quickly and treated aggressively.

However stunned these first seventeen people must have been to hear that they had been exposed to the deadly spores that all of America feared, they were still amazingly calm. Most of them were concerned that they might have taken anthrax home to their families or friends or tracked it to other areas of the Capitol complex.

While this meeting was going on, the rest of my staff were gathering in the LBJ Room of the Capitol, where more bags of clothing were deposited. Between the two meetings, Dr. Martin took another call from the lab at Bethesda. Six more culture plates had turned up positive, including three more of my staff members who had been on the fifth floor when the letter was opened and another Feingold staffer.

At that morning's full staff meeting in the LBJ Rroom, Dr. Martin, Linda, and I joined the entire "Daschle 38" who had been in my Hart office on Monday—including two pregnant women and another staffer who'd recently survived cancer. Al Lenhardt had arranged for General Parker to be there, and he and Al reported everything they knew. Greg Martin explained that those who had tested positive for exposure had already been notified, and he repeated his crash course on anthrax.

He then told us the limitations of the nasal swab results, explaining that an individual nasal swab can prove that exposure has occurred, but it can't prove that it has *not*. As an epidemiological tool, nasal swabs are used to define an area within which people may have been exposed to anthrax spores. He also told us that anthrax as finely milled as the sample in the letter mailed to me spreads like a gas. He asked us to imagine a container of gasoline opened in a large, enclosed room. Within a few seconds, he said, anyone in the room will smell the gas and inhale its fumes. When aerosolized, odorless anthrax moves just as far and just as quickly as those fumes.

Given the fact that people on the fifth floor had tested positive for exposure, we had to assume that everyone in the entire suite had been exposed. The same principle applied to those in Senator Feingold's office next door. Greg explained that he and Dr. Eisold would work with the epidemiologists at the CDC, using all the nasal swab results, to identify a perimeter, later dubbed the "hot zone," within which everyone would be presumed exposed and put on sixty days of preventive antibiotics.

Those in the Daschle and Feingold suites—and the first responders who had arrived at the scene—were all considered to be at high risk, and Greg spent the next several months ensuring that they survived the ordeal. Over that first two-day period, we had shifted our attention from just one or two people who might be endangered to twenty-five, and now, to sixty-three—with the possibility that that number could climb even higher.

Obviously, this was difficult news to hear, but again, my staff inspired me with their courage and their stoicism, their concern for one another and the rest of the Senate community, and their ability to do their jobs under the most difficult circumstances. Some of them were working to protect the country from bioterrorism at the very time that they were wondering if they themselves would survive it.

That Wednesday morning, we all made a crucial, collective decision—and I know Russ Feingold and his staff made the same one: to tackle this challenge as a group. We were all in this together. I am so proud—and I know Russ is, too—of the way our staffs pulled together and supported one another. They, along with the first responders who were exposed, also committed themselves to the effort to further public health and bioterrorism research efforts, with the vast majority of them—joined by other Senate staff who served as "controls"—volunteering for studies conducted by the CDC, the Navy, and others.

We also agreed that no one would divulge anyone else's "positive" or "negative" status. In fact, everyone agreed not to divulge their own status to anyone beyond their close friends and families, since we realized that people could be "outed" by the process of elimination. While we were beginning to understand that the distinction between positive and negative nasal swabs wasn't relevant for those in my office—they had all been exposed—we understood it was a nuance that wouldn't make its way clearly into media accounts. So we provided information to the media that was important for public health, but we made a pact to protect one another's privacy.

Others weren't always so respectful. A few overzealous reporters went to incredible lengths to root out the "positives." When my staff went home on Wednesday night, most of them were welcomed with multiple telephone messages from reporters pleading to talk to them. Unable to get my staff to identify the "positives," some reporters started to track down their parents.

One persistent reporter even tracked down a staffer's grandmother in a nursing home, where she innocently divulged the information about her grandchild.

After the Wednesday morning meeting, Greg Martin met with Russ Feingold's staff and later with the affected first responders. Then Dr. Martin set up camp in another room near my office, and until about 9:00 P.M. that night, he met individually with each of the "Daschle 38," answering his or her questions, giving most of them flu shots—which we hoped would lessen the likelihood that they would contract influenza but fear they had contracted anthrax—and handing out sixty-day supplies of Cipro.

Laura Petrou, who'd been out of the office on Monday, served as Greg's makeshift physician's assistant and coordinated the staff's care with him for the next several months. Several members of my fifth-floor staff were given their first dose of Cipro that morning—in retrospect, two days after they should have gotten it.

At the same time, a team of epidemiologists from the CDC was interviewing each staff member to map out what the scene in my Hart office had been on Monday morning and to retrace their steps until each of them had gone home that day. Greg was pulled away at various times throughout the day for press briefings or to answer senators' questions. It was an extraordinary scene.

It's hard to explain just how frightening and pressure-filled this time period was—how fast intractable problems and incomprehensible data were coming at us. The anthrax was scary enough. Even scarier was the fact that every day "experts" were contradicting one another and mostly proven wrong. Interagency politics was clearly at play, which was one of the great disappointments of this whole experience.

It was almost impossible to know who to trust, yet trust was necessary for us to move forward. Decisions had to be made, and they had to be made fast. People's lives depended on them. Washington is a big city, and we had access to any number of private doctors and to the National Institutes of Health (NIH) and the CDC. We chose Greg Martin. Individually and collectively, we made a decision to trust him. He was calm, steady, and straightforward—and he was perhaps the only person who never misstated anything. We really believed in him. This turned out to be a sound, possibly lifesaving decision.

While we were dealing with all this, Al Lenhardt was facing the frustration—and in some cases, the open defiance—of senators who were upset that their Hart offices had been shut down. A few senators insisted on going back into the building to retrieve items from their suites and conference rooms.

They dared the Capitol Police to stop them. Some were familiar with the anthrax found on ranches across the country and thought, It's not that big a deal. They didn't yet comprehend how different this anthrax was from the "garden-variety" anthrax.

Most displaced senators, however, began making do without complaint. By that afternoon, makeshift offices were set up all over the Capitol, as staffers with cell phones and laptop computers began working in whatever spaces and on whatever surfaces they could find. Chuck Schumer took his work home to his Capitol Hill town house.

John Edwards arranged himself on a bench in the hall outside the Senate chamber. Barbara Mikulski told a reporter, "If you see me at a Starbucks with a yellow legal pad, it could be the Veterans, Housing and Urban Development budget." And she wasn't joking.

Over the next forty-eight-hour period, fifty senators and thirteen committees from the Hart Building were relocated. This extraordinary feat— which involved, among other things, setting up temporary offices at a new building, connecting 600 new telephone lines and 650 new LAN lines, setting up 73 new routers, and connecting over 700 PCs and 100 printers to them—was accomplished because of the tireless efforts of the staffs of the sergeant at arms and the Senate Rules Committee. During this period—

and for weeks on end—these people and many others worked without a break to keep the Senate functioning so we could fulfill our constitutional duties and send the world a clear message that we would not be defeated by any form of terrorism.

By that Wednesday evening, we would all be finding alternate office space, at least for the next few days, as the Russell and Dirksen Senate Buildings, as well as the Rayburn, Longworth, and Cannon Buildings on the House side, were shut down for environmental testing.

The shutdown that drew the most attention, however, was Dennis Hastert's decision to adjourn the House of Representatives through the weekend while that side of the Capitol was scanned for anthrax. Earlier that day, at breakfast at the White House, Trent and I had told Speaker Hastert and Congressman Gephardt, the House leaders, our decision to shut the office buildings for testing. Somewhere in the conversations among the four of us, and our subsequent conversations with our caucuses, the fact that we were shutting down the office buildings—but not adjourning the Senate itself—was lost. As a result, Speaker Hastert decided to shut down the House entirely. The next day, the headline of the *New York Post* had a picture of Hastert and Gephardt underneath the blaring headline WIMPS—THE LEADERS WHO RAN AWAY FROM ANTHRAX. It was unfair. We didn't think they were wimps—or that we were acting with bravado. We were just trying to make sound decisions based on what little we knew.

On Thursday, October 18, we learned that Dan Rather's personal assistant at CBS News had been diagnosed with cutaneous anthrax after opening an anthrax-laced letter, presumably of the same quality mailed to the other media outlets. By then, the incident command team meetings were in full swing, with an interagency group—consisting of representatives from Secretary Thompson's office, the CDC, the surgeon general's office, DARPA, EPA, NIOSH, and the District of Columbia's Department of Public Health—meeting several times a day, seven days a week, with the House and Senate sergeant at arms, the secretary of the Senate, and representatives of the four House and Senate leaders.

Al Lenhardt, sensing an urgent need to bring together the various authorities and their expertise to address all aspects of the crisis, had formed the group the night before. For almost two weeks—until the meetings were eventually moved to a conference room at the U.S. Botanic

Garden—the incident command team met in the office of the secretary of the Senate to coordinate the health and environmental responses as well as the effort to disseminate information to the public. It was essential to bring all these people to the table, though it wasn't always easy to tell who was in charge of this multidisciplinary crisis. Nothing like this had ever happened before.

The CDC, with help from my staff and others, continued the enormous task of identifying the people who had been in the "hot zone" that Monday. CDC epidemiologists worked tirelessly with my staff to identify and contact the hundreds of people—including the man who had delivered the pizza to my suite—who needed to begin taking their sixty-day courses of antibiotics. Regular briefings for senators and staff were held, and news briefings were conducted daily, sometimes several times a day.

Another epidemiological effort was to determine whether the "hot zone" should be extended beyond the fifth and sixth floors of the southeast quadrant of the Hart Building. The EPA experts started at my office and, working backward, traced the steps the letter had taken to arrive there.

Trace amounts of anthrax had been found on one of the strapping machines (used to bundle mail for the Senate offices) in the post office in the Dirksen Building, and in the Ford Annex on the House side, but none of the employees from either facility had positive nasal swabs. In fact, from the thousands of swabs taken, the only positive results were those of the original twenty-eight—twenty Daschle staffers, six first responders, and two members of Russ Feingold's staff.

When the trace amount of anthrax was found on the Dirksen strapping machine, the incident command team, including representatives from the D.C. Public Health Department, discussed the possible implications for the P Street and Brentwood mail facilities, which handle all mail coming into the Capitol complex. If the postal employees in the Dirksen Building were on antibiotics—even if only temporarily—shouldn't postal employees all along the letter's trail be on them? We wanted to make sure that the postal workers—and anyone else at potential risk—were taken care of.

The CDC, along with the D.C. Public Health Department, assumed responsibility for the postal workers. They had considered whether to swab or prescribe antibiotics for Brentwood workers but felt that since they knew of no postal workers in Florida or New York who had gotten sick, there was no reason to be overly concerned about the people at Brentwood or any other mail facility. Even if cutaneous anthrax—the skin form of the disease—was a possible threat to postal workers, that was treatable. The CDC simply didn't believe inhalation anthrax was a risk for these workers.

Nasal swabs were of questionable value at this point. It is believed that swabs are only somewhat reliable during the first twenty-four hours following an exposure, and it had been almost a week since the Daschle letter passed through the Brentwood facility. Every member of my staff who had positive nasal swabs on Monday, October 15, had negative swabs when they were retested one week later.

Whether or not the postal workers needed antibiotics was a more difficult call, but the CDC's experts felt reasonably sure they did not. Otherwise, they argued, we would already have seen postal workers getting sick, since the letter had been postmarked more than a week earlier. To build confidence in its decision among increasingly worried postal workers, the CDC held a press conference at Brentwood on Thursday, October 18, suggesting they wouldn't be there if it weren't safe. Unknown to them, an e-mail had been sent from the Canadian Defence Research Establishment at Suffield to the CDC, alerting them to the Canadians' study detailing the high aerosolizability of finely milled anthrax.

The study found that such highly refined anthrax spores are small enough to penetrate even the ten-micron holes in standard mail envelopes. The message had gone unnoticed by the CDC's overwhelmed and overworked staff. Furthermore, the CDC didn't know that a routine method for cleaning some of Brentwood's mail-processing machines was to spray them with high-pressure air hoses.

At the end of that week, with all the fear and alarm gripping Capitol Hill and with more than twenty thousand Americans on Cipro, the only actual death from what FBI investigators were now calling "Amerithrax" was that of the photo editor in Florida. But that Saturday morning, the incident command team got the first report of postal workers hospitalized with symptoms consistent with inhalation anthrax. The room fell completely silent as the implications sank in. An update later that day suggested that anthrax likely wasn't the cause of the postal workers' illnesses, but the clinical tests had not been completed.

On Sunday, October 21, Thomas Morris, who worked at the Brentwood facility, died of inhalation anthrax. Now this disease, in all its grotesqueness, had hit home.

We got the news of Thomas Morris's death on Monday, October 22. Greg Martin had just concluded another meeting with the staff, congratulating them on surviving the first week, saying they had cleared at least one major hurdle. He didn't tell us that he had expected the anthrax might overcome the antibiotics in some of the most heavily exposed people. The staff had asked more questions—the kinds of questions you'd think of after you'd had a few days to overcome the initial shock. Greg had answered every one, and people were feeling very upbeat. The meeting broke up, and a few people noticed one staffer staring at the TV and crying. The news on CNN was that a worker from the Brentwood postal facility had died of inhalation anthrax the night before. The smiles vanished from the staff's faces.

This news was devastating, for them and for me. It clearly demonstrated that we weren't necessarily out of danger, and at the same time, it brought the guilt that so many survivors struggle with: Why did this man die instead of me?

As difficult as our ordeal was, we knew we were lucky, because we knew when and how my staff had been exposed, and we could address it. The postal workers had no way of knowing what had happened until it was too late. Joseph Curseen, another worker at the Brentwood facility, died later that day, and several other postal workers remained hospitalized and gravely ill.

Those cases of inhalation anthrax led to a massive testing and preventive treatment program for the Brentwood workers, who were understandably terrified and angry. The CDC staff who had held the press conference at Brentwood several days earlier were put on antibiotics, and the CDC's leadership was put on the defensive. Environmental testing at Brentwood found anthrax throughout the vast space that held about 2,400 workers.

There is debate to this day about whether the deaths of Thomas Morris and Joseph Curseen—or the debilitating illnesses of Leroy Richmond, Norma Wallace, George "Fairfax" (a pseudonym), David Hose, Jyotsna Patel, and others—could have been prevented. I don't know the answer.

Neither do I question the commitment of the CDC or the D.C. Department of Public Health to give the postal workers at Brentwood—and the other affected workers at P Street and in the State Department's off-site mail facility—their best advice. I know that the CDC's human resources were already stretched beyond capacity. They were still responding to the crises at the World Trade Center, Florida, New York, and the Capitol. As soon as they had a confirmed case of anthrax linked to Brentwood, they shifted all their resources to the postal facilities. Still, there's no denying that, for too many mail handlers, their best advice at the time simply wasn't good enough. As the district's health director, Ivan C. A. Walks, put it, "What were sound CDC recommendations based on prior knowledge and science had left the Brentwood workers unprotected."

In other words, the system failed them.

The next Tuesday, October 23, both the House and the Senate went back into session. By the end of that week, all congressional office buildings except for the Hart Building were reopened. The fifty senators and their staffs—including my own—with Hart offices were looking at weeks, perhaps months, before the building would be decontaminated and declared safe.

There was a light aspect to this, and a real sense of camaraderie, as members ad-libbed to create working space. Storerooms and conference rooms became headquarters for some. Dianne Feinstein and Barbara Boxer converted their Capitol "hideaways" into staff offices. Chuck Hagel made room in his Russell Building suite for several members, including Ben Nelson, whom Hagel had defeated in their 1996 race for the Senate. Debbie Stabenow greeted constituents and visitors in a refitted storage room next to a loading dock. She and Barbara Boxer teamed up at one of our Tuesday Democratic caucus lunches and performed a rewritten version of the song "Heart," from the Broadway musical *Damn Yankees*. One verse went like this:

> *We're not being mean,*
> *Just can't wait for that chlorine.*
> *Just get back to work, the President says,*
> *But face it, it's difficult to start,*
> *So we gotta have Hart.*

"Chlorine" referred to the chlorine dioxide gas that the EPA was considering using to fumigate the Hart Building. Chlorine dioxide had been effective in killing the tiny bacteria that cause Legionnaires' disease. As October turned to November, however, the EPA's plans were far from confirmed.

No building of this size—nine stories high, with more than one million square feet of floor space and more than ten million cubic feet of volume—had ever been decontaminated before. Al Lenhardt and EPA advisers were awash with suggestions from industry experts and everyday people who thought they had a sure cure for sterilizing the structure. Some said a bleach foam should do it. Others proposed a hydrochloric acid disinfectant. Al Lenhardt got a call from one well-meaning person who insisted that "essential oils" would kill all the anthrax—oil of coconut, to be precise.

Lenhardt's office issued daily updates to let members and staff know how the work was progressing. Early on, those updates included the EPA's projections about when the work would be finished and the building reopened—a big mistake, as it turned out. One of the first of those projections was November 13. "Our lucky day, I'm sure," I told reporters at the time. Another key lesson: Predictions can be perilous. As it turned out, it would be two more months—well into January—before we were finally allowed back into that building.

When November 13 came and went and the building was still closed, more than a few angry members confronted Al and the EPA leadership. While the vast majority of senators were more concerned about safety than convenience, there were those who berated the EPA and Dr. Eisold for keeping them away from their offices.

Some insisted they be allowed back into their offices to retrieve their Christmas lists and cell phone chargers. At one point, Dr. Eisold reversed himself, and they were given brief access to their offices to retrieve a few "essential" items. I couldn't help noticing that some senators who'd scoffed at the danger and insisted on going back into the building now sent their staff to retrieve their belongings for them.

EPA and the Department of Health and Human Services researchers spent the lag time conducting experiments in their new, perfect laboratory—my Hart office. On November 10 and 15, they tested whether normal activity in such a space could cause the anthrax spores spilled there on October 15 to reaerosolize.

Dressed in protective gear, they placed seventeen blood agar culture plates (the same type of plate used to culture my staff's noses a month earlier) in my suite and, during the first experiment, moved carefully around the office in an attempt to leave the anthrax undisturbed. Even with very little disturbance, anthrax was found on five of the plates. In a second test, after placing seventeen new plates in my suite, the researchers moved around freely, attempting to simulate normal office activity. In that test, anthrax was found on sixteen of the seventeen plates, and the concentrations were significantly higher.

The researchers were stunned to confirm not only the high aerosolizability of this anthrax, but its ability to reaerosolize so readily a month after the original spill. They were also surprised to find that the spores floated up to the "breathing zone" about four to six feet off the ground. In previous studies, rearosolization had been limited to only a few inches from the ground.

These spores were still as potentially deadly as they had been the day the letter was opened. Scientists at USAMRIID charged with analyzing the original sample from the letter had reported the uniquely dangerous "floaty" nature of this anthrax, too. In fact, they had trouble keeping it under the microscope long enough to examine it.

Around that same time, Greg Martin, who, unlike the CDC, had reviewed the Canadian Defence study and understood its implications, was becoming increasingly worried that sixty days of antibiotics wouldn't be enough to protect those most heavily exposed to anthrax—whether they were exposed in my Hart office or at Brentwood.

Tommy Thompson had never provided the anthrax vaccine we'd requested that first Tuesday night and, frankly, I'd forgotten about it. I guess I'd gotten a little overconfident. My staff seemed to be healthy, and I wasn't as worried as I had been. But, after reviewing the Canadian study, Greg explained to Laura Petrou and then to me that it was clear that some members of my staff might have been hit with over 3,000 LD_{50}s—that is, three thousand times the dose of anthrax spores scientists estimate is needed to kill 50 percent of those exposed. Furthermore, there was nothing magical about the CDC's recommendation of a sixty-day course of antibiotics.

There were no human studies to rely on—and the monkey studies dated back to the 1950s and 1960s, so those exposed on Capitol Hill were breaking new scientific and medical ground. And this wasn't just a theoretical exercise. If we made cavalier assumptions, there would be real human consequences. If we stopped the antibiotics and sufficient spores remained in their lungs, my staff would develop inhalation anthrax.

In animal studies, at the seventy-five-day mark, only about 1 percent of anthrax spores were still present in the animals' lungs. One percent of 1 LD_{50} is probably harmless, but 1 percent of 3,000 or more LD_{50}s is still over thirty times a potentially lethal dose. Greg believed the vaccine was necessary to help develop antibodies to anthrax, so that when the antibiotics were completed, natural antibodies would clear any remaining spores from the system.

While there were no explicit studies of the vaccine's effectiveness as a post-exposure treatment, studies of U.S. troops had proven the vaccine's effectiveness in raising protective antibody levels in humans—the exact result Greg was looking for. He assured us the vaccine was safe—far safer than the smallpox vaccine—and that side effects were minor and generally confined to the injection site. Three doses of the vaccine would be given—the first as soon as we could get it, the second two weeks later, and the third two weeks after that. The antibiotics would need to be continued throughout that period.

I was now completely convinced of the need for the vaccine, but we had no access to a supply.

Greg told me that if our group had been U.S. Marines exposed on a deployment, he would have started them on vaccine the next day and continued their antibiotics for thirty to sixty days. Absent the vaccine, Greg felt a longer course of antibiotics was essential, though he couldn't be certain how long would be long enough.

The CDC refused to provide the vaccine or to change its recommendation regarding the antibiotics. It was a classic clash between the statistical world of public health and epidemiology and the flesh-and-blood world of clinical medicine. The CDC seemed prepared to stick to its recommendation unless and until someone got sick. Meanwhile, Greg had direct responsibility for sixty-three patients, and neither he nor I wanted to take that chance.

It turned out that he'd been quietly working to secure the vaccine since that initial Tuesday night—ideally, the vaccine should have been given the day of the exposure—but the vaccine was caught up in a controversy over past problems at the manufacturer's facility, and the CDC, which had control of all the civilian stocks, wouldn't release it. As the sixty-day mark approached, the CDC was still refusing to make it available.

Dr. Eisold agreed with Greg and, overriding the CDC's recommendation, extended the antibiotic treatment for another thirty days. That was a courageous decision, and the right one. Meanwhile, we intensified our efforts to secure the vaccine. Laura made two calls—first to Colonel Art Friedlander, the Army infectious diseases physician who spearheaded the key clinical anthrax research at USAMRIID and is perhaps the world's foremost authority on anthrax. Dr. Friedlander agreed that my staff was a unique population that did indeed need the vaccine. Now, even further convinced, we still had to find a way to get it.

Laura then called Lieutenant Colonel John Grabenstein, deputy director of the Defense Department's Anthrax Vaccine Immunization Program. Grabenstein told us that if we asked Secretary Rumsfeld for access to a limited amount of the Pentagon's vaccine stocks, he thought the answer would be yes.

I wrote Secretary Rumsfeld, explaining that unless the CDC reversed its decision immediately, we were requesting that he provide post-exposure vaccine to the high-risk groups from the Capitol and the postal service and anyone else believed to be heavily exposed. We couldn't be sure who was most heavily exposed at Brentwood, though we hoped that the CDC and postal officials, based on the environmental testing at the facility, could identify those individuals at the highest risk.

My letter to Rumsfeld had more of an impact on the CDC than anything else we had tried. Not wanting the Pentagon to usurp its role, the CDC was suddenly interested in helping us. Each day for several days, we were promised by the CDC and officials in Secretary Thompson's office that we would have the vaccine the next day.

While the CDC's people on the ground seemed to agree that the vaccine should be given to those who were highly exposed, the CDC's decision makers weren't as forthcoming. We also had reliable reports that someone from the NIH, who had no official role in this process, was fighting the vaccine's release and causing the last-minute delays. This person, with no clear authority, was forcing revisions in the consent form—revisions with which the CDC experts and Greg Martin strongly disagreed.

Again, it was impossible to tell who was really in charge. All of this was happening at the same time the media were starting to focus on Secretary Thompson's attempt to impose central control on information coming from the CDC, the NIH, and other health agencies. Following the lead of John Eisold and Greg Martin, the CDC finally altered its recommendation on antibiotics, suggesting that those on Capitol Hill and the postal workers extend their antibiotic treatment to one hundred days.

At this point, Greg began to psychologically prepare his patients for the vaccine. For the first time, he explained in explicit detail just how serious their exposures might be. They heard from him—and later in a detailed *USA Today* story—that some of them "had more anthrax in their noses than were found in entire buildings" and that they had been exposed to hundreds, if not thousands, of lethal doses of the bacteria.

Greg wanted to be sure their bodies could clear any spores that might remain after the antibiotics were gone. The vaccine would be completely voluntary, but he was recommending it for the Daschle and Feingold staffs and for the first responders at the scene.

Those who didn't want the vaccine could take antibiotics a little longer, or they could be on a "close watch" program with Greg for a week or two after they discontinued the antibiotics. Greg did not recommend the vaccine for those on Capitol Hill beyond that small group. The CDC, for its part, offered no judgment or recommendation regarding the vaccine, though they announced that they would make it available to anyone who might have been exposed to anthrax spores in the mail.

The vaccine was already delayed more than sixty days—it was now getting close to Christmas—and we would have to wait even longer before it finally arrived. In the meantime, we heard people call it an "experimental vaccine"—which it wasn't—and we watched Dr. Tony Fauci, the head of the National Institute of Allergy and Infectious Diseases at the NIH, go on national television to undermine the anthrax vaccine, saying that "there is no definitive data that say it is going to work."

We also read Senator Frist's comments in a *National Journal* publication: "I do not recommend inoculation for people with the vaccine in the Hart Building. . . . There are too many side-effects." The *National Journal* wrote, "Frist added that very little exposure to the anthrax took place in Majority Leader Daschle's office."

These inaccurate comments were as disappointing as they were confusing. It was disappointing to see the CDC—and others who were responsible for actual patients—failing to fulfill that responsibility, while others with no direct knowledge or responsibility stepped in with misinformation.

No wonder people were angry and confused about how to respond to this crisis. But I was confident that the advice we were getting from Dr. Martin and Dr. Friedlander was correct, and we pushed until the vaccine was made available—on a voluntary basis—to all who might need it.

The CDC's seemingly endless delays were almost unbearable. Clearly, they had been badly burned by the experience with the postal workers and now seemed paralyzed by the fear of making another mistake. It seemed they feared getting blamed more than anything else. Of course, they did wind up getting blamed—for their indecision. We just wanted professional medical help, for the people on Capitol Hill, at Brentwood, and everywhere else. If the CDC wasn't willing to lead, we wanted them to get out of the way. This wasn't about winning a power struggle; the CDC's actions—or inaction—had serious medical consequences, with people's very lives at stake.

These people should have been vaccinated on the day of their exposure or close to it. That's what the Pentagon would do for any of our troops exposed in combat, and that's what any American deserves. Had people gotten the vaccine when they should have, there's a real possibility they could have discontinued the antibiotics after thirty to sixty days, which would have put an end to the very unpleasant and potentially dangerous side effects that many suffered on those drugs. In the case of one staff member, the "side effect" was that the Cipro masked the fact that he had appendicitis. Shortly after he stopped taking it, he had to have surgery to have his appendix removed. As it happened, some were on antibiotics for 120 days. Furthermore, my staff and the postal workers were put through the psychological stress associated with the CDC's delays and indecision.

Meanwhile, in mid-November, another letter laced with anthrax was discovered by FBI agents searching through the tons (literally) of Capitol Hill mail that had been quarantined since the day our office was shut down.

This one was addressed to Pat Leahy, with the same block handwriting used on the envelopes sent to me, to Tom Brokaw, and to the *New York Post*.

The letter, which was found in the mail that Al Lenhardt had ordered quarantined beginning October 15, contained the same highly refined anthrax spores as those in the toxic powder sent to my office.

By this time, the FBI had more than one thousand agents working on the case, and they were beginning to shape a profile of who might have mailed these letters. Naturally the first thought most people had was that the letters were somehow connected to the September 11 attacks, that they were the work of a terrorist group such as al-Qaeda. Several of the September 11 hijackers had passed through New Jersey, where the letters to Washington and New York had been postmarked, and a dozen of them had lived at one time or another in south Florida, where the first anthrax death occurred.

Some in the administration concluded, however, that the small scale of these mailings—a network like al-Qaeda had the organizational ability to mail thousands of such letters, not just the handful that had been discovered—along with the nature of the written messages inside them, pointed away from such a group. Others continued to pursue possible connections to suspected stockpiles of anthrax in Iraq.

For its part, the FBI was leaning toward the theory that these mailings were the work of an individual, a "lone wolf," as agency behaviorists put it. There was a great deal of debate about whether this "angry male loner," as he was described in newspaper headlines, was American or foreign. The jumbled syntax and spelling in some of the other letters ("penacilin," for example) would suggest, at first glance, someone unfamiliar with the English language.

But then again, argued some of the many behavioral, linguistic, and handwriting experts studying the notes, such manglings might have simply been an attempt to mislead investigators by, as one FBI behaviorist put it, "dumbing them down a bit." The idea that this individual might be a "Unabomber" type of person, someone who was angry for one reason or another at the federal government, was supported by the targeting of Pat Leahy, whose primary work in the Senate is with domestic social and law enforcement issues. When the letters were mailed, Leahy was chairman of the Senate Judiciary Committee.

One reason the FBI was focusing so heavily on behavioral and linguistic profiling was that the forensic evidence was so limited. The highly refined, professional quality of the substance in these mailings suggested that this individual had extensive knowledge of this pathogen—or had access to laboratories that did.

As the focus shifted to individuals with expertise in microbiology gained, perhaps, from a scientific or military background, and as the FBI began scouring the personnel and records of government, university, and medical laboratories that dealt with anthrax, it became public that the U.S. Army's Dugway Proving Ground outside Salt Lake City had been processing a particularly virulent strain of anthrax for some years—a strain that genetically matched the contents of the letters sent to Pat Leahy and me. It turned that out this "Ames" strain, obtained in 1981 from the remains of a dead cow in Texas, had been cultivated for years by U.S. military researchers and other scientists around the world.

No sooner did the FBI descend on Dugway than DNA tests on the spores contained in the letters sent to Capitol Hill revealed that they matched not only the Dugway anthrax, but also a *sub*strain of anthrax that had been cultivated at the U.S. Army's Medical Research Institute of Infectious Diseases at Fort Detrick, Maryland—the same laboratory where the FBI had taken the anthrax mailing from my office to be examined. It was another sign of how little control any of us had over the situation.

Was the perpetrator influencing the investigation? What kinds of people were running our research program? It was also a painful reminder of the consequences of our government's past mistakes, like authorizing sales by U.S. companies in the 1980s of technology and equipment that assisted Iraq's efforts to develop weapons of mass destruction.

None of these leads, however, necessarily meant that the person who had mailed the letters had ever actually worked at any of these facilities. What the FBI discovered as it pursued this information was that these laboratories lacked adequate security procedures. Over the years, for example, scores of visiting scientists and individuals had access to these labs and could easily have passed viable cultures or information to a third party. Until recently, the transfer of actual specimens from lab to lab—a common practice in the research community—was made, it turns out, with very little record keeping.

All of which added up to very little evidence and a lot of guesswork on the part of FBI investigators. With the recent controversies over its mishandling of the espionage suspect Wen Ho Lee, and of Russian spy Robert Hanssen, and of the shoot-outs at Waco and Ruby Ridge, the agency hadn't inspired a lot of confidence from the American public, but now it decided to turn to them for help.

By mid-December, the FBI had broadcast the anthrax killer's psychological profile on *America's Most Wanted* and was preparing a mass mailing to every home owner in the region of the New Jersey post office from which the letters had originated, hoping that someone out there—a neighbor, a friend, maybe a family member of the person behind these attacks—would step forward and help point the way for authorities.

But as the year wound to a close, virtually all the FBI had in terms of finding this perpetrator was hope.

Once we had been assured the arrival of the vaccine was imminent, we set up briefings for Senate staff with John Grabenstein, deputy director of the Defense Department's Anthrax Vaccine Immunization Program, who explained the risks of the vaccine. John also made himself available to the postal service and briefed senior management representatives and several national postal union presidents. Because the FDA had not yet approved these particular lots of the vaccine, and because it was being given after exposure, the CDC made the vaccine available as an "IND," or investigational new drug. In yet another disappointment, the CDC wrote a consent form that would have scared most people away from the vaccine and took a long time to do it. The program initiation date was delayed several days in a row while this form was written. Again, it was no wonder the postal workers were skeptical.

The three interns who had been opening mail in my office on October 15 had already finished their internships and gone home for the holidays. Greg Martin and Laura Petrou had been trying to figure out how the interns, now spread across the country, would be vaccinated. One of them was preparing for an overseas trip.

Again the CDC resisted, and again the only thing that seemed to spring the CDC into action was our desperate plea to the Pentagon for help. After a series of late night calls between Laura and CDC officials, the intern leaving for Europe was finally vaccinated just hours before her transcontinental flight. The other interns were vaccinated at their college health units. All three were on antibiotics for almost 120 days because it took so long to get them vaccinated.

On December 18, we were again told the vaccine program would be initiated the next day. On Wednesday, December 19, we waited all day, with Greg Martin and Navy nurses on hand, for the CDC and the infamous consent forms to arrive so the vaccine could be given to my staff, Senator Feingold's staff, and the first responders who had been exposed. All day I was told that the consent forms were an hour or two away, but they never came. The vaccine couldn't be given without them.

On December 20, the CDC medical team arrived with the forms. More than two months after their exposure, my staff, along with postal workers up and down the northeast corridor, were finally given access to the anthrax vaccine.

By then, many of the patients had left town for Christmas vacation, and my confidence in the CDC had reached an all-time low. I also worried about how our government would respond to a larger public health crisis. It was widely felt that we were getting "special treatment." I kept thinking, *If this is special treatment, I'd hate to see the alternative.*

Meanwhile, the fumigation of the Hart Building had begun. While the other congressional office buildings had been decontaminated with liquid chlorine dioxide and chemical foam before they were reopened, it was decided that the most effective way to deal with the Hart Building—without damaging or destroying the records and files that had been left behind the day the building was evacuated—was to seal the entire structure, using duct tape, plastic sheeting, plywood, and urethane foam; pipe chlorine dioxide gas into the building; wait twelve or so hours for the chlorine dioxide to do its work; and then "scrub" the gas with a sodium bisulfite solution that would neutralize it.

Nothing like this had ever been tried before, and there were some serious safety concerns, not least of which was the reported but remote possibility that the whole thing might explode. People living in the neighborhoods surrounding the Capitol were understandably worried, both about the building blowing up and about some of this toxic gas leaking out. Trial runs were conducted off-site in trailers, and a peer review committee of scientists and doctors was called in to assess the plan. The reviewers agreed that my suite should be fumigated with chlorine dioxide gas, which would not create any explosion risk under the conditions the EPA outlined, but they weren't yet ready to sign off on fumigating the entire building. Based on the peer review committee's recommendations, the EPA decided to move ahead with plans to fumigate our suite and to do more environmental testing outside our suite to determine if other areas of the building required fumigation.

Based on what they knew about the special nature of the anthrax in my suite, the EPA and other experts suspected that anthrax spores had been tracked throughout the building—by my own staff or by mail carts that might have been contaminated. The environmental testing showed that the contamination was not as widespread as originally thought and that the affected areas outside my suite and the Dirksen mailroom were good candidates for more localized treatment. Under the EPA's revised approach, liquid chlorine dioxide, HEPA-filtered vacuums, and cleansing foam would be used throughout most areas of the building where anthrax spores had been detected, including elevators, stairwells, hallways, various senators' mailrooms, and the sixth floor of Russ Feingold's office. My office, as well as the heating, ventilation, and air-conditioning (HVAC) system in the southeast quadrant of the building, would be sealed and fumigated with the chlorine dioxide gas.

In the days before the fumigation began, the EPA and the incident command team assembled experts from throughout the federal government and partnered with private contractors to meet the many challenges of the cleanup effort. Key among them were the U.S. Coast Guard National Strike Force, the U.S. Marine Corps, Chemical Biological Incident Response Force, and the U.S. Army Center for Health Promotion and Preventive Medicine. Throughout the building's contaminated areas, files and other "critical items" were bagged and tagged for safekeeping or separate remediation. In my suite, the EPA collected a seemingly endless supply of bags of loose papers and valuable items that might not have fared well if subjected to the chlorine dioxide gas or the heat and humidity needed to ensure its effectiveness. They also removed the desk and several Native American artifacts from my private office, including a painted buffalo skin that has always had an honored place on my wall. Much of my office, though, remained as it was left on October 15, though file drawers and closet doors were opened so that the chlorine dioxide could reach every nook and cranny in the office. After the fumigation, special care was also taken with the U.S. flags in my suite, which were folded carefully and removed by the Marines in a moving ceremony that was captured on videotape.

On Friday, November 30, teams of specialists in HazMat suits began positioning throughout my suite test strips containing "surrogate" spores of harmless bacteria with characteristics similar to, but more resilient than, anthrax spores. In preparation for the fumigation, three thousand spore strips were positioned on the walls, floors, and surfaces in my suite—almost one for every square foot of space. The strips were used to determine the efficacy of the fumigation effort and to help ensure the safety of the space for reoccupancy. Optimal conditions had been determined to be at least 75 percent humidity and a temperature of at least seventy-five degrees.

By early Saturday morning, it was clear that the Hart Building was so dry—about 10 percent humidity—that the portable humidifiers the fumigation team was using weren't going to do the job. They were going to have to improvise. In the middle of the night, they found a live steam line on the ninth floor of the building, scavenged for pipes at a building supply store, and jury-rigged a system to pipe steam into my suite on the fifth and sixth floors. It worked.

While the temperature in the suite was held above seventy-five degrees relatively easily—it was closer to ninety degrees—the fumigation crews initially had trouble holding the humidity at 75 to 80 percent, which was their target. On December 2, when the necessary conditions were met, the fumigation began in earnest. The scene was like something out of a science-fiction movie. Several squads of EPA scientists and engineers, Coast Guard personnel, and private contractors, including a five-man team of technicians wearing HazMat suits stationed just outside my office and another team posted just outside the building, began pumping chlorine dioxide into my suite as a mobile laboratory/bus circled the building at a crawl, testing the outside air for traces of escaping gas.

Almost twelve hours later, the crews began pumping a solution of sodium bisulfite into the suite to break down the chlorine dioxide. Although spot decontamination with liquid chlorine dioxide was still necessary in a few areas of my suite—including the area of the floor covered by the piping used to pump in the chlorine dioxide gas—the fumigation was a success. That success was proven by the "kill rate" on those three

thousand test strips and the post-fumigation environmental sampling. By the end of the process, there were no detectable live anthrax spores.

Now, nearly two months after my office had been evacuated, the contents—everything from file folders to computer disks to staplers, pencils, and plants—were ready to be sealed, crated and removed for further fumigation with ethylene oxide—an industrial chemical used to sterilize medical equipment. A company in Richmond, Virginia, was contracted for this work. Two weeks before Christmas, several trucks filled with sixty-four-cubic-foot, six-hundred-pound containers of our office's contents pulled out from Capitol Hill and headed south on I-95.

Meanwhile, another key remediation task still remained: ridding the HVAC system of anthrax spores. Again, the EPA led the effort, with chlorine dioxide gas as the weapon of choice. From December 14 through December 17, the fumigation crews focused on the HVAC system, but a water blockage in the two-inch flexible tubing used to feed the chlorine dioxide into the HVAC system foiled that plan. A "U" had formed in the tubing. Both the crews who had been working inside the building around the clock that entire month and the senators and staff who were itching to get back into their offices began to get impatient and irritated.

There was a brief break in the decontamination effort at Christmas, and the crews resumed the HVAC remediation effort on December 27.

Finally, fittingly, the job was completed on December 31—New Year's Eve. It would still be three weeks before follow-up testing was finished and the building was deemed safe to be reoccupied, and my own office wouldn't be ready for us until April, but it seemed that the Hart Building was now anthrax-free.

Just as the medical situation we faced was unprecedented, so was the task of remediating this huge building. The Capitol Police had issued credentials to four thousand people involved in the cleanup, and each one of them contributed to the massive effort. I will be forever grateful to the crews from the EPA and countless other agencies and private contractors who worked long hours, often in extremely high temperatures. They withstood the anxiety associated with exposure to a deadly bacteria, the absence of standard operating procedures or a straightforward command structure to guide them, and the stress of being away from their families for months on end. Luckily for them and for us, the EPA's lead on-scene coordinator, Rich Rupert, navigated the murky waters—whether they

were scientific or political. He did exactly what I asked so many weeks earlier—he ensured that the entire team followed the science and put people's health and safety first.

Three days later, while most of the "Daschle 38," the Feingold staff, and affected Capitol Police were in the basement of the Capitol getting their second in a series of three anthrax vaccine shots, our sense of relief was tempered by the arrival in our Capitol office of a letter bearing a London postmark. By this time, all mail arriving at the Capitol was being screened and irradiated at privately contracted facilities in Ohio and New Jersey, then examined by newly trained Senate mail handlers before final delivery. Still, when this envelope was opened by my receptionist and white powder fell out, the whole office sprang into action. It was October 15 all over again, but we were determined to avoid the mistakes made earlier. We quickly evacuated the immediate area. Dr. Eisold's physicians were ready to swab and decontaminate the staff. The Senate side of the Capitol was locked down and cordoned off—no one was allowed to enter or leave. HazMat-suited specialists from the Capitol Police arrived with on-site testing apparatus. The letter and its contents were rushed over to Fort Detrick.

Both the letter, which was written in block lettering similar to the October 15 mailing, and the powder, which turned out to be talcum powder, were found to be harmless, a hoax. But the fear we all felt, the anxiety gripping the entire country in this new post–September 11 world of possible terror at every turn—those things were all very, very real.

By this time, despite the seemingly endless delays and disappointments, the crews over at the Hart Building and its previous inhabitants were all actually beginning to believe that the building would reopen soon. The night of January 16 brought one last twist that, in hindsight, is almost humorous but at the time was both demoralizing and potentially catastrophic to those who had dedicated the previous three months to the massive anthrax cleanup effort—the first ever of its kind. The Hart Building had been cleared for reoccupancy, and the architect of the Capitol's cleaning crews were hard at work catching up on three months of accumulated grime, exacerbated by the mess the remediation crews had created.

Carpenters were removing the plastic sheeting, duct tape, and urethane foam that had been used to prevent the chlorine dioxide gas from escap-

ing during the fumigation of my suite. As they chipped away at the hardened foam in the ceiling, they encountered a garbage bag that had been
used to fill a void and provide backing for the foam. A carpenter's knife
ripped the bag, and a plastic HazMat suit literally fell from the ceiling.
Alarmed, the carpenters contacted their supervisor and cleanup team personnel. One of the cleanup team members responded and, not recognizing the suit or its potential significance, assumed it was harmless. The
carpenters returned to their shop in the Dirksen Building, taking with
them any potential contamination and using compressed air to blow the
dust off their clothes. Soon, to everyone's great despair, it was determined
that the protective gear could have belonged to one of the Capitol Police
officers who had responded when the infamous letter was opened in
my suite.

The implications were immediately clear. That suit could have been
one of the most heavily contaminated items of the whole experience. The
carpenters who found it could have tracked finely milled, highly reaero-
solizable anthrax spores all the way from the Hart sixth-floor hallway to
the Dirksen carpentry shop. Rich Rupert wondered anxiously whether the
entire remediation effort would have to begin all over again, and the carpenters were given nasal swabs and Cipro while the HazMat suit was
tested, the HVAC systems were shut down, and the affected areas were cordoned off.

Some relief came when field tests for the deadly anthrax spores were
negative, but it would be twelve more hours before the laboratory analysis
could confirm those results.

For once, luck was with us. The laboratory results indicated no anthrax
was present. It turned out the suit that had "fallen from the sky" belonged
to the police officer who had decontaminated the officer who had field-
tested the original letter. His suit also would have been decontaminated
before it was put in the garbage bag, which was inadvertently left at the
scene and mistaken for one of the many bags used to fill the voids in the
ceiling when the area was sealed. All was well, but the cleanup crews, Al
Lenhardt, and I spent several stressful hours before that became clear, and
the reopening of the Hart Building was delayed yet again.

On January 22, after the CDC and EPA again declared the Hart
Building safe for reoccupancy, fifty senators and several committees—and
all who work there—were finally allowed back into their offices. Outside

my suite, most people's desks were just as they'd left them, and many returned to find the October 15, 2001, edition of *Roll Call* still on their desks. That day's front-page headline: HILL BRACES FOR ANTHRAX THREAT.

That same day, my Hart staff filled a temporary suite in the Hart Building, where they stayed until April 3, when we jubilantly returned "home" to my office in Hart. I'm very proud of the fact that every one of my permanent staff who had been there on October 15 was back there again.

They had survived a terrible ordeal, and they were as committed as ever to the cause that brought them to Washington in the first place: serving South Dakotans and the nation. Grant, the intern who opened the letter, also returned to our office once she graduated from college—this time as permanent staff. Every time I see her in a meeting or a briefing, I'm reminded of how lucky I am to be surrounded by such dedicated people. A few weeks later, in a ceremony I'll never forget, the Coast Guard personnel and Marines who had protected the U.S. flags in my office returned them to me.

The "anthrax days" had been extraordinarily difficult and chaotic. Events had transpired far more quickly than we could deal with them. There had been no precedents for the situations we faced. Nothing like this had ever happened before. Mistakes—in some cases serious ones— had been made. The costs, in both human and financial terms, had been high. The hope is that we will take important lessons away from this experience. Be prepared. Put safety first. Follow the science.

To this day, we still don't know who mailed those anthrax letters. Five people, including a ninety-four-year-old Connecticut woman and a sixty-one-year-old New York City hospital employee, are dead. For more than two months, the entire nation was terrorized by whoever did this.

The best that investigators could do was identify a "person of interest" in August of 2002, a former Army scientist, but no one has been charged, and we've learned, from the "D.C. sniper" case and others, in what misguided directions some assumptions can lead us. There are still those who believe that al-Qaeda or Saddam Hussein was behind this. Although the FBI has not yet, as of this writing, formally charged anyone in these cases, they tell me they have good leads, they're making progress, and they are confident they will solve the case.

* * *

A small footnote to this episode speaks to the heightened sense of threat we all feel in this post–September 11 world. I certainly felt invaded by the anthrax "attack," to be targeted so directly in such a manner and to have so many others affected because of it.

Personally, I made peace with this kind of threat several years ago, when, after one in a series of assessments of security here in the Senate, I realized that if I worried as much as the security staff about the risk of my position and public exposure, I would hardly be able to function at all. So I made a conscious decision to embrace a kind of fatalism, a willing acceptance of the fact that my time is going to come when it comes and I can't live my life worrying about when that time might be. I don't believe in taking foolish chances, of course, but neither do I believe in taking no risks whatsoever.

I'm a pilot and I love flying, for example. The only reason I haven't done much of it lately is lack of time, not danger or fear. Linda and I have wanted for some time now to skydive with the kids. We had actually arranged to do it in late 2001, for my daughter Lindsay's birthday, but then September 11 and the anthrax attacks occurred, and those plans were suspended. So much has happened since then that we still haven't been able to reschedule it, but we intend to.

My attitude about such things doesn't make my security detail particularly happy. But then that's their job, of course, to be scrupulously careful about every move I make, every step I take. Wherever I go, they go, too.

Which is where they were early one morning during that winter of 2001. As I've said, Linda and I often brought them coffee and doughnuts or pastry to start out the day. This particular morning we came out and they had sheepish looks on their faces. I asked them what was going on, and they told me they'd found a suspicious package outside the back door during a sweep of the grounds late the previous evening. Linda and I had both been asleep. The package—a tightly wrapped box—had the word *JERK* written on it in large letters, they explained. They immediately called in some dogs to sniff it, then cut it open to examine the contents.

They didn't need to finish the story. I realized what had happened. A couple of years ago, during one of my annual "unscheduled driving" tours back in South Dakota, I stopped by the largest business in the town of Alpena—an operation called Jack's Links. Fewer than three hundred people live in Alpena, and over four hundred people work at Jack's Links, which specializes in jerky of all kinds: beef jerky, turkey jerky, buffalo jerky. After I finished a tour of their plant, they asked me if I'd be interested in joining their "club." For a pretty fair price, they'll mail you a different box of their meat products—sausage, beefsteaks, jerky—each month for a year. I signed up that day and since then have been a member of what they call their "Jerk of the Month" Club.

Which is where that box came from. And which is why my security unit was so apologetic that morning. The box, they said, was a total loss. But the beef, they assured me, was saved.

End of Chpt. 7

CHAPTER EIGHT

gres to 19223-35 pg

"The Obstructionist"

O NE MORNING IN LATE SUMMER of 2001, I was out for my daily run, think-ing about the legislative session that had just come to a close—about the Jim Jeffords switch, about George Bush's reaction to that event, and about so much more. One thought led to another, until finally I began mulling over the future, in particular the autumn of 2004, when I would be up for reelection to my fourth term in the Senate.

I realized that this would be a watershed point in my life, a time when I would be faced with an extremely difficult decision about my political future. As I saw it, I had three choices. One was to run once again for my Senate seat, a job I found extremely rewarding. Another was to retire from the Senate and move on to new professional challenges. And the third was to run for president of the United States.

In order to consider these options as clearly as possible, I decided that day to begin keeping a diary. The date on the journal's first page is August 11, 2001—exactly one month before the terrorist attacks on New York and Washington.

It's stunning to look back through those pages and see how innocent the entries leading up to that date appear compared to the drama of the weeks that ensued. Reading through the month of September and on into that October, I'm struck by how hopeful and inspired I was by the soli-darity and teamwork displayed by Congress and the White House in the wake of such tragedy, how refreshing it felt to see partisanship and politics put aside as our government and our people stood together to respond to the needs of our nation. Just as striking, and deflating, is to read on as the pages turn to November, then December, and to see how rapidly the conflicts between our two parties returned with a force and a level of acrimony greater than ever before.

I wonder, in reading those pages, whether I had been simply naive to believe that a sea change had taken place that September, that we were actually stepping into a new world of unified purpose in Washington and in our culture at large. It was hard for me to imagine what some journalists and pundits had begun to assert—that this administration would actually exploit this situation to advance the broader agenda that had been slipping from its grasp before September 11.

Right-wing think tanks and publications unabashedly urged the Bush administration to seize the moment to advance long-favored tax cut plans and a roster of right-wing federal judicial nominees. Neo-conservatives pushed the administration for huge increases in the Pentagon's budget and began talking about an invasion of Iraq. And of course, the likes of Pat Robertson and Jerry Falwell weighed in with their opinions that these attacks were somehow connected to gays and abortion rights activists.

No sooner did I begin to question the President's economic stimulus plan and other aspects of his domestic agenda than I, too, became a target of these groups in a way and with a force that I had not previously experienced in my career. By that November, virtually all of the goodwill and teamwork displayed by the White House and the Republican leadership had disappeared, evidently replaced by a strategy of blaming Democrats and me in particular for "obstructing" the President's policy agenda.

Newspaper ads, paid for by a right-wing organization called the Family Research Council, appeared early that month in South Dakota, comparing me to Saddam Hussein because of my opposition to the administration's plans for oil drilling in the Arctic National Wildlife Refuge. When I first saw that ad, I just smiled and shook my head. I thought it was a joke— a tasteless joke, but a joke nonetheless. In fact, it was heartening that most South Dakotans saw it in the same way. Later, as I saw the depth of the anger and vitriol that advertisement aroused in people who were inclined to disagree with me politically, I realized that what would be political hyperbole to many could be a call to action for others.

A radio campaign funded by another Republican group called the Tax Relief Coalition assailed me for holding up the President's economic plan because Dick Gephardt and I went to visit Mexico's president, Vicente

Cht 8 (cont)

191.

Fox. The ad conveniently ignored the fact that my visit had taken place over a weekend (when Congress was not in session) and was intended to give new life to immigration reform talks between the United States and Mexico, something President Bush himself said was a priority.

In fact, as Congressman Gephardt and I prepared to leave, J. C. Watts, one of the Republican leaders in the House of Representatives, put out a press release full of what he seemed to think were clever uses of Spanish phrases. It began with "Today I open the paper and find out the top two Democrats are packing their bags and going to Mexico. Aye caramba [sic]." It went downhill from there.

Congressman Watts's release so angered Congressman Ciro Rodriguez from Texas that he accused Watts of using ethnic slurs and went on to say, "This type of 'Taco Bell' diplomacy has no place in the modern American political landscape." Congressman Watts may have ended up with egg on his face, but he made my trip enough of a story for other right-wing groups to latch on to it—which they did.

Osama bin Laden was also coupled with me in some ads, as was the American Taliban soldier John Walker Lindh.

In all, South Dakotans were subjected to nearly twenty different paid advertising campaigns attacking me—an unprecedented assault on a senator who wasn't even up for reelection.

A long memorandum issued to right-wing Republican groups the first week of December by a pollster named Frank Luntz—Luntz was one of the chief architects of Newt Gingrich's 1994 "revolution"—offered not only a blueprint for that winter's attacks on me personally, but also the Republicans' new signature "message" for the party. The single word that they continue to intone to this day like a mantra, fanning the flames of fear and anxiety that were lit on September 11, is "security."

That single word has been the linchpin of virtually every speech President Bush has made since that date, and it is the centerpiece of Luntz's memo to the armies of the Republican right wing (the bold lettering is the memo's, not mine):

> **"The National Unity Agenda"** that you develop over the coming weeks and months should involve three segments: **"national security"** (defense, foreign policy, intelligence, energy), **"personal security"** (crime, immigration reform, etc.) and **"economic**

security" (tax relief, small business regulatory relief, predatory lawsuit protection, etc.).

To help drive this message, Luntz suggested in his memo setting me up as the antithesis of all that was good and right about the Republicans' agenda:

> **Americans want economic intervention, but they don't want interference or obstructionists. That's why it is time for someone, everyone, to start using the phrase "Daschle Democrats" and the word "obstructionist" in the same sentence. It's time for Congressional Republicans to personalize the individual that is standing directly in the way of economic security, energy security, and even national security.** Remember what the Democrats did to Gingrich? We need to do exactly the same thing to Daschle.

The Bush administration immediately set out to implement the Luntz strategy. On December 9—eight days after the memo was issued—Vice President Cheney, appearing on *Meet the Press,* stated, "Tom Daschle, unfortunately, has decided . . . to be more of an obstructionist." The next day, Karl Rove, while visiting Sioux Falls, in my home state of South Dakota, declared that I was "obstructing" President Bush's domestic agenda. Two days after that, Karen Hughes, one of the senior communications strategists in the White House, complained to reporters that there was a leadership "void" in the Senate. Trent Lott echoed Hughes's imagery, saying that the Senate chamber had become a "black hole." Lott's colleague Rick Santorum wrapped things up nicely that week by comparing me to a "rabid dog."

By the second week in December, Capitol Hill journalists and Republican sources were reporting that this wave of anti-Daschle attacks was being directly ordered and orchestrated by the White House. According to the *Washington Times,* "The White House is escalating its attacks against Senate Majority Leader Tom Daschle. . . . [W]ith polls showing the Republican Party is losing some support in its handling of the economy, President Bush last week ordered senior advisers to take the gloves off and sharpen their rhetoric." (*Washington Times,* December 7, 2001)

The *Washington Post* reported that "Republican sources . . . said Bush had ordered the tougher public line [against Senate Majority Leader Daschle] shortly after Thanksgiving. Officials in both parties noted how unusual it is for the Bush administration to issue attacks as blistering as those on Daschle."

We had only second- and thirdhand reports about the involvement of Rove and others in the White House. Several prominent Republicans, some elected, others who have been friendly over the years, volunteered to me that these attacks were coming from Rove's office.

One of these sources told me that my appearance at a nationally televised benefit concert in late October in New York for the police and firemen who fought so valiantly on September 11 had been a catalyst for the Luntz strategy. Linda and I were asked to attend, in part because of our own tragedy earlier that week—the anthrax attack on my office.

The concert, which was held on October 20, was intended to be a recognition of and benefit for those who lost their lives on September 11, as well as those who put their lives on the line that fateful day. The lineup they had assembled was amazing. It included, among many others, Paul McCartney, David Bowie, John Mellencamp, and the Who.

Billy Crystal introduced me as "someone who has had a tough week"— a reference to the anthrax attack. I spoke of our gratitude and our great empathy for those heroes of that tragic day. I called the thousands of police officers and firefighters who were there "New York's other twin towers." And then I spoke about how we were all in this together—not as South Dakotans or New Yorkers, Republicans or Democrats, but as Americans, and that we were going to get through this as Americans. The response I got was breathtaking. There was so much raw emotion in Madison Square Garden that night, and it was as if, by becoming a target of a terrorist attack myself, I had somehow gained acceptance into the brotherhood of the brave people gathered there.

Apparently it didn't go unnoticed in Republican circles.

"That got our attention," the Republican source told me. "And it was a major factor in the campaign to come after you."

This was all a far cry from the promise Bush had made during his acceptance speech at the 2000 Republican National Convention, when he promised to "change the tone of Washington to one of civility and respect."

It had been one thing to watch the Republicans' relentless personal

194

attacks on Clinton, but now I was learning firsthand what it felt like to be a bull's-eye for these people. It also made me realize that the hate machine that had been constructed to diminish Clinton had not been dismantled after Bill Clinton left office. It had sat, idling, waiting for a new target at which to direct its vitriol.

We tried to respond by explaining the many things that the Senate had been able to accomplish under Democratic control. I went to the Senate floor and to the media dozens of times to discuss the remarkable amount of work the Senate was able to get done during my time as majority leader— and we had: a resolution giving the President authority and the resources he needed to find and fight those responsible for September 11; sweeping new anti-terrorism legislation; billions of dollars in aid to help New York and other affected areas rebuild and recover; emergency aid to keep the airlines in business and keep Americans flying. And those came on top of the Patients' Bill of Rights, legislation to lower the cost of prescription drugs, and major education reforms all passed by a Democratic Senate.

Those legislative accomplishments were formidable, and I will always look back on them with a great deal of pride. Still, the facts alone weren't enough to neutralize the continuing attacks.

One thing we didn't think to do was to ask that some objective study be done to determine to what degree President Bush and I agreed on the issues that came before the Senate. But it turns out that just such a study is published annually by *Congressional Quarterly* (*CQ*). According to *CQ*, I voted with the President 69 percent of the time in 2001 and 75 percent of the time in 2002. As a point of comparison, I voted with my own party 80 percent of the time in 2002. That study underscored just how much agreement there was between President Bush and me, how much common ground there is in Washington, and how ridiculous the obstructionist label really is. After all, those numbers were roughly similar to those of South Dakota's Republican congressman, John Thune, who supported the President 82 percent of the time but made his support for President Bush the centerpiece of his campaign against Tim Johnson.

Of course, the best way to defuse criticism is to show that you're able to laugh it off. Months before, I had been invited to be the Democratic speaker at the Gridiron Club Dinner. The Gridiron Club's annual white-tie dinner and show draws publishers, editors, and journalists from around the country to mingle with the Washington press elite and laugh with (and

sometimes at) the politicians they write about. The evening is full of musical skits about elected officials and current events and is highlighted by
keynote speeches delivered by one Democrat and one Republican. Usually,
the president then caps off the night with a speech of his own.

Speaking at the Gridiron is a rite of passage for national politicians. In
Washington, being funny is serious business, and the Gridiron can be an
extremely helpful forum to change public perceptions. For example, in
1982, Nancy Reagan, who had been battered by the press for gifts of
designer clothes, got onstage and sang "Second Hand Rose," effectively
defusing the issue.

In 1994, the famously stiff Al Gore mocked himself by being pushed onstage via hand truck. And in 1999, John McCain entered flanked by a
color guard, wearing easily 150 combat medals, to deny that his sole claim
to a presidential campaign was his status as a war hero—while of course
reminding everyone of his war hero status throughout the evening. While
the evening is technically "off the record," the details of a well-received
gridiron speech often leak out—and most of the speakers wouldn't want
it any other way. I accepted the Gridiron's invitation, and as the
"Democratic speaker" I would be sharing the long head table with both
the President and the Vice President.

In fact, as I spoke, President Bush would be sitting directly to my left. I
decided that the beginning of my speech would be a good vehicle for
addressing the "obstructionist" label.

As I walked up to the microphone, I cleared my throat and looked
around nervously at 550 of the most influential people in Washington. Then
I began speaking as if I were at my first Alcoholics Anonymous meeting:

"Hi,"—followed by a long pause.

"My name is Tom, and I'm an obstructionist."

Some people were already getting the joke and responded, "Hi, Tom."

I continued, "This is my first meeting. I haven't obstructed anything in
the last twenty-four hours. Well, actually . . . just a couple of minutes ago,
the President asked me to pass . . . the salt."

At this point, I stopped and looked at President Bush ruefully. "I
wanted to. I *tried* to. I just can't bring myself to pass *anything.*

"I guess I started obstructing when I was growing up in rural South
Dakota . . . or as the rest of the country thinks of it: a secret undisclosed
location. . . .

"As a young boy, I wanted to help the family out . . . so I'd sit in front of the farm trying to sell lemonade to passing cars.

"It was just five cents a cup—plus tax.

"But no one would stop.

"As car after car sped by . . . I vowed . . . then and there . . . if ever I was fortunate enough to attain a position of power . . . I would let nothing pass.

"But it turned out that I liked stopping things. I really liked it. . . . And I was good at it. In fact, I just kept getting better.

"In my time, I've stopped budget cuts. I've stopped tax breaks.

"When my hair started to turn gray . . . I put a stop to that, too.

"So I admit, I have a problem. And I'm not surprised that people have tried to demonize me for it. People . . . and also Tom DeLay.

"This demon label might be starting to stick. In a recent ad, I was compared to Saddam Hussein . . . and *he* was offended."

The evening was a hit. The next day's *Washington Post* had a cartoon of me refusing to pass the salt to President Bush. President Bush, for his part, got up to speak and said, "I can't believe I hugged that guy."

While the evening was fun, the truth is that the entire concept of "obstructionism" simply makes no sense to me. In a healthy democracy such as ours, it is not only the right, but it is the *duty* of the "opposition party" to fight for what it believes in. You hope to end up with principled compromise, to find common ground. But sometimes there is sacred ground, and that's when you agree to disagree. It is out of the process and discipline of reasoned and rigorous debate that strong and sound legislation and policy are shaped. Such debate is at the heart of the system of government created by our Founding Fathers.

Without it, we are left with a leadership that literally dictates what the government and the people must and will do. It's what I like to call the "noise of democracy," and to silence it—to silence the voices of opposition in a democratic society, wherever those voices may come from, whether they rise from the media, or from individuals or groups of citizen protesters, or, yes, from the membership of Congress, is to inhibit the freedom that gives strength to a democracy and is to invite something in the way of autocracy.

I know as well as anyone that politics is a full-contact sport, but there is a significant difference between rough-and-tumble intellectual debate over policies and ideas and the kind of personal "attack" politics we have seen from the Republican right wing during the past decade. These attacks are destructive, and they are aimed at inhibiting the very openness of opinion and freedom of speech upon which our democracy is based.

Laced throughout these salvos directed at me that December was the inference that, in this time of war, with our nation's security at stake, my opposition to any aspect of the President's agenda—domestic or foreign—was unpatriotic. Of course, this was not the first time in our nation's history that such charges have been made at such times. The *Wall Street Journal* pointed this out in an editorial addressing that Christmas season's Republican assault on me. The column quoted former Senate Republican leader Robert Taft, whose own patriotism was questioned when he opposed much of President Franklin Roosevelt's domestic agenda during World War II. "Criticism in a time of war," said Taft in his own defense, "is essential to the maintenance of any kind of democratic government."

Certainly the Republican Party leadership shared Taft's view during Bill Clinton's presidency. But by December of 2001, the Republican leadership had evidently made a tactical decision to feature "the patriotism card" right through the 2002 midterm elections as a means of both promoting their policy agenda and pursuing their political objectives.

With timing that could not have been more ironic—just as we were debating the merits of the President's plan to retroactively repeal the alternative minimum tax for large corporations—the news broke that one of the largest of those corporations was preparing to make the biggest bankruptcy filing in American history. Word was leaking out that the Houston-based Enron Corporation, one of the world's leading energy-trading companies, had concealed billions of dollars of debt through a shell game of false accounting, collusion among its top executives, and outright lying to its investors, including more than twenty thousand of its own employees, whose retirement savings were entirely dependent on the value of Enron stock.

With a similar scandal involving WorldCom breaking immediately after Enron and the sheer magnitude of the misstated earnings, legitimate questions began to emerge about the financial system itself. Was it all the inevitable aftermath of irrational exuberance and a market run greedily amok, or were there systemic problems—gaps in the structure of oversight and regulation—that had become so apparent, they could only encourage excesses and outright fraud?

Never before in America's history had we seen corporate corruption of the magnitude that began to emerge at this time. The Teapot Dome scandals that preceded the Great Depression were nothing compared to the breadth and depth of collusion and lying that began to reveal itself that December 2001 and would continue to shake the public's faith in corporate America.

In subsequent months, the lineup of cheating executives and scandal-plagued corporations grew steadily longer. By the time this wave of revelations, confessions, and, in some cases, arrests crested late that summer of 2002, the stock market would lose more than $5 trillion in capitalization—more than one-third of Wall Street's total capitalization. Not all of those losses were directly attributable to these scandals, but markets run on confidence, and these scandals undermined that confidence mightily. The integrity of America's financial markets depends on the accuracy and accessability of financial information. Without it, there can be no market efficiency because investors will lack the confidence to risk their capital. The nation's trust and faith in this system were shattered by the revelations that began to emerge that winter of 2001, and they remain severely damaged today.

But trust and faith weren't all that was shattered. Out in South Dakota, I met a number of people who worked for a company called Northern Natural Gas. In 1985, in a series of transactions, Northern Natural Gas was acquired by Enron, and the people who worked there ended up with much of their retirement savings in Enron stock. When Enron went bankrupt, one of those workers sent me a letter saying that he and his wife had worked together at Northern Natural Gas for a combined fifty-five years before retiring in June 2001. Now their retirement savings had almost entirely disappeared. He wrote that he and his wife had both gone back to work, feeling lucky to even have jobs, and happy to have had one year off, because he now believed that they would *never* be able to retire.

This damage is what my colleague Paul Sarbanes attempted to address and, as much as possible, to heal, with his introduction of legislation in early 2002 to impose higher standards of corporate governance, more rigorous responsibilities on corporate executives, and a new regulatory structure that would oversee corporate audits to ensure that financial information is both accurate and available in the future. In short, the Sarbanes bill, as virtually everyone acknowledged after its passage, was the most significant addition since the 1930s to our structure of rules enforcing standards of corporate accountability. It began the vital process of bringing the deregulatory pendulum back from the extreme point it had reached in the 1990s toward the reasonable center.

A critical focus of the Sarbanes bill was strengthening the Securities and Exchange Commission (SEC), the federal agency charged with overseeing compliance with U.S. securities law. I had long felt that the SEC had grown too cozy with the industries it regulated. When President Bush came to office, he appointed an accounting industry lawyer named Harvey Pitt to head the organization. As scandal after scandal unfolded, it became clear that the President could not have picked a worse man for the job. Harvey Pitt made his philosophy clear when he said that he wanted to build a "kinder, gentler" SEC. He opposed—sometimes subtly, sometimes overtly—reforms that would require more accountability from America's companies. As the Enron and WorldCom scandals unfolded, he seemed more interested in promoting legislation that would upgrade his position as chairman of the SEC to cabinet secretary status than in preventing future Enrons. If the SEC was a toothless tiger, Harvey Pitt was the man making sure it stayed that way.

I think it's important to point out here that the Sarbanes bill is a perfect example of how the Democratic Party's response to such an issue contrasts so markedly with that of the Republicans. I was—and still am—deeply troubled by the extent of the market manipulations and accounting schemes devised by some in the energy and technology sectors and by the extremely close and questionable connections among many of those industries' executives and our nation's leaders, including both the current President and Vice President.

There was much discussion among our Democratic leadership about how to respond to these revelations when they began breaking in the winter of 2001. Yes, we were outraged at the double standard evident in the treatment of Bush's and Cheney's ties to the accounting scandals by Republicans as opposed to the investigations they relentlessly pursued with the Clintons and Whitewater. We were also angry at the administration's refusal to cooperate with any investigation whatsoever into these ties and their determination to resist every effort to find out exactly what had happened here. And we were both disappointed and puzzled by the media's unwillingness to pursue this story and get to the bottom of these questions on their own—questions that remain largely unanswered to this day.

There were those among our own leadership who urged that we vilify Bush and Cheney, just as the Republicans had done to Clinton. But rather than take this route, which I have no doubt the Republicans would have chosen had the shoe been on the other foot, we decided to take the high road. Our approach was to set a different tone and a higher standard by holding hearings to pursue the facts that could form the basis of a policy solution—the Sarbanes bill—rather than going for the political jugular and trying to embarrass the administration, as the Republicans had done with Clinton.

The stepped-up attacks on me envisioned by Frank Luntz and choreographed by Republican operatives that began in late 2001 continued into 2003. They widened in scope as Linda was drawn into the fray with the planting and watering of magazine and newspaper stories about her ties to the airline industry and the suggestion that those ties cast shadows on my own legislative and political decisions.

The nation's capital is replete with examples of "Washington power couples"—individuals with separate careers influential in their own right. Bob and Elizabeth Dole, Jeff and Anne Bingaman, Chris and Rebecca Cox, Byron and Kim Dorgan, and Mitch McConnell and Elaine Chao are just a few who come immediately to mind. It is regrettable that in American society, too many women see their own accomplishments, as formidable as they may be, diminished by the fact that they are married to successful men. And now Frank Luntz's memo had sown the seeds of a new strain of this phenonomen that took root in stories that questioned Linda's credentials and our ethics simultaneously.

Linda is an influential aviation lobbyist. But her influence doesn't come from me. Aviation is in her blood. Her father was an aircraft mechanic, and her uncle built one of the first airstrips in Oklahoma. In college, she worked for the Federal Aviation Administration (FAA) as a weather observer at a flight station. At the age of twenty-three she attempted to start a new commuter airline based in Kansas City. That effort led to a job at the Civil Aeronautics Board, where she rose to become the first woman to head their Office of Congressional and Consumer Affairs.

After a stint in the private sector, Linda went back to work for the FAA, where she served first as deputy administrator, then as acting administrator—becoming the first woman to hold the number one position there. Throughout the years, Linda has been recognized for her many contributions to aviation and aviation policy. The latest occurred this year when she was presented with the annual Amelia Earhart Pioneering Achievement Award. When she moved into the private sector, the ethics rules she imposed on her activities were tougher than any that Congress has yet come up with—she still refuses to lobby anyone in the Senate. And the *Washington Post* once called for all lawmakers to institute the "Daschle Rule."

Drowning out discussion of everything else, however—overshadowing the news of corporate corruption, of the ailing economy, of my own purported conflicts of interest with my wife's career—were the drumbeats of war. If there was any doubt in the beginning, when the September 11 attacks occurred, it was clear by the turn of the New Year that the administration's paramount strategy was to keep the war against terrorism in the forefront of every American's mind and at the top of their list of concerns.

Karl Rove articulated this mind-set that January in a speech to the Republican National Committee in which he urged the assembled membership to politicize the war at every possible turn. Americans, he told the audience, "trust the Republicans to do a better job" of "protecting America." The flip side of that message, of course, is that the Democrats are not to be trusted to do this job well and, in fact, that they should be portrayed as doing quite the opposite. Tom Davis, head of the Republicans' House Campaign Committee at the time, actually accused our party of, as he put it, "giving aid and comfort to the enemy." This would not be the last time such language, questioning the very patriotism of Democrats, would be used. The President himself would eventually make the same outrageous assertion in the heat of the 2002 elections.

I was amazed at the audacity of this tactic.

But more amazing to me was the assertion that President Bush would make, in his State of the Union address that January, that Iraq, Iran, and North Korea constituted an "axis of evil." This phrase invoked memories of the World War II fascist "Axis" of Hitler's Germany, Mussolini's Italy, and Hirohito's Japan. While I had expressed concerns about the very real and serious threats posed by each of these nations individually, I certainly was not ready for the President to suggest they constituted an actual organized alliance against the United States, able to be lumped together as one problem that could presumably be solved with one solution. I was also surprised that with so much left undone in Afghanistan, the President appeared prepared to open three new fronts in the war on terrorism.

With an impressive display of force, bravery, and technological prowess, our troops had routed the Taliban. But the battle to secure the peace had not been nearly as successful—whether the administration would admit it or not.

Osama bin Laden and the Taliban leadership were still at large. Al-Qaeda was far from vanquished. And the Afghan people themselves were desperately in need of help to recover both from the brutalities they suffered under Taliban control and from the destruction that had taken place to rid them of that rule. Those people now faced a vacuum of leadership, with a shaky pastiche of factional tribesmen hastily cobbled together to try to fill this void. All of these things, if left unaddressed, could combine to make Afghanistan the one thing we sent troops there to guarantee it would never be again—a haven for terrorists. I had visited Afghanistan earlier in January 2002 as part of a larger trip to Central Asia. Our delegation of five senators flew in on a military C-130 aircraft, landing at Bagram Air Force Base about thirty miles from Kabul. The base and its 9,800-foot runway had originally been built by the Soviets, then was controlled by the Taliban, and now was ours, although there was still isolated combat and our troops were at risk from roving bands of Taliban still at large.

We got off the plane, and a number of Humvees and armored Suburbans pulled up. We were greeted by the military leadership from the base as well as Ambassador Ryan Crocker, the ranking American diplomat in Afghanistan.

Bagram wasn't a base as most of us have come to picture American bases, though. It was essentially a tent city, with virtually no infrastructure, no amenities, and not even a mess hall. The troops we met there were living in spartan conditions. Until recently, they had been eating MREs—meals ready to eat—three times a day. By the time we arrived, they were getting one hot meal a day, and that was considered a luxury. The windows in the air traffic control tower were blown out, and the airfield was strewn with the rusted-out hulls of Soviet aircraft and helicopters.

Earlier, in Uzbekistan I had met an Army private from a little town in South Dakota called Midland. He didn't look as though he could be much older than twenty-one or twenty-two. He volunteered to be a part of Operation Enduring Freedom after he finished a tour of duty in Bosnia. He could have gone home, but he said he wanted to go to Afghanistan because of the importance of the mission. When I met him, he had gone nearly two years without leave. I saw incredible dedication like that in the faces of American servicemen and -women throughout this troubled region: at Bagram Air Base, with the Tenth Mountain Division at a makeshift base in Uzbekistan, and with our Air Force personnel setting up a new U.S. air base in Kyrgyzstan.

I remember, as the sun came up the morning we arrived, how lovely the mountains surrounding Kabul looked, aglow in a soft purple-red haze. It was a striking contrast to the blast-charred remains of weapons and military equipment all around us—the burned shells of tanks, the bombed-out remains of buildings. I remember thinking that the devastation on the ground was so at odds with the beauty in the horizon. Shortly after our arrival, we began meeting Afghan citizens, people who had lost limbs from land mines or bullets or bombs.

We had an appointment to meet with President Hamid Karzai and other Afghan leaders that day. To get to the meeting, we were loaded into a caravan of armored vehicles. The highway was so blown out that the thirty-mile trip took more than an hour. As we rolled toward our destination, we passed groups of Afghan children who would motion toward us, then put their fingers up to their mouths—they wanted food. There is something about children that is universal, something we feel when we see them suffering that is unlike the suffering we see in any other way.

The deprivation we saw as we moved through the city that day—the rubble, the lack of anything like sanitation or electricity or water, the battered metal and wooden containers that families had fashioned into homes by the sides of the streets—made me wonder how anyone could possibly live like this. I looked out at teenagers and was struck by the realization that in their whole lives they had known nothing but conflict. Many were born during a Soviet invasion and then lived through a Soviet occupation, a decade of civil war, and the harsh rule of the Taliban. Now, after decades of conflict and oppression, they had pinned their hopes on liberation at the hands of the United States, whatever that might bring.

Television images, as riveting as they are, cannot capture the depth of suffering or sense of despair seen firsthand by our own troops or by the aid and humanitarian workers who followed them into Afghanistan. The experience is heart-wrenching and raises to a new level one's appreciation for the importance of any post-war reconstruction effort.

The meeting with Karzai was held in the presidential palace, in a large, spacious room filled with dozens of ministers, each of whom represented a region or tribe from all across Afghanistan. Everyone was wearing heavy winter coats, and they were dressed in an array of costumes of every imaginable color and fabric. With no communications infrastructure in the nation to speak of, the only way for these men to communicate with one another was to travel here and to gather in person, which they had done. Some had taken days to make the journey to Kabul. Each of them faced the same problem that President Karzai faced. They were now tasked with running a government, but they had no buildings to house their ministries, no computers or desks at which to work, and no money to run programs.

President Karzai presided, and he surprised me with his upbeat demeanor and command of the English language. He explained during a break in the formal meeting that he had a brother who ran a restaurant in Chicago (at which Senator Durbin, one of the members of our delegation, had recently dined) and another brother who lived in Baltimore. So America and its language were far from foreign to him.

His message to the gathering, as well as to us, was simple and direct. We need money and security, he said. We need money to open our stores and begin functioning as a society again. And then we need security so that they can stay open.

Prior to my trip, schoolchildren in South Dakota had gathered up more than one thousand pounds of clothing and toys for Afghan children. It was a beautiful gesture on their part. I had planned to visit an Afghan school to deliver the clothes and toys, but the security situation in Kabul was so tenuous that we were allowed to visit only the presidential palace and the new U.S. embassy.

Luckily, I was able to find Abdullah Wardak, the Afghan minister of

Chpt. 8 (cont.)
LIKE NO OTHER TIME / 205

205

orphans, widows, disabled, and martyrs. Tears filled the minister's eyes when he opened the boxes. "I'm supposed to take care of the orphans in my country—but I have nothing to give them," he said. "Thank you for giving me something to give them." Still, it was clear that the needs of this shattered country were far greater than boxes of clothing, and meeting those needs, not to mention rebuilding this society and culture, was going to be hard—just as hard as it was to find bin Laden, or to pinpoint the heart of al-Qaeda, or to identify victory against this new kind of enemy.

That's why I was so heartened to hear President Bush give a speech to the Virginia Military Institute in which he called for something akin to a "Marshall plan" for Afghanistan. The first opportunity for the President to make good on that promise was his 2003 budget request. I remember Pat Leahy coming up to me on the Senate floor after seeing President Bush's budget request. The subcommittee he chaired would be responsible for providing the rebuilding funds the President requested. Pat was absolutely flabbergasted. He informed me that the President had requested nothing for stabilizing and rebuilding or providing humanitarian aid to Afghanistan. Nothing.

Despite this clearly unfinished business in Afghanistan, we began to hear voices—within the administration and elsewhere—about the need to forcefully confront Saddam Hussein. While I agreed that we needed to go after Saddam, I also felt that we needed to remain focused on the main, imminent threats.

So, late that February, at one of my regular press briefings, I asked about the status of the war on terror, given that we hadn't yet fulfilled President Bush's pledge to catch Osama bin Laden—the man directly responsible for the deaths of almost three thousand Americans—or brought to justice the other people directly responsible for the attacks of September 11. I expressed my concern that President Bush seemed to be expanding the war on terrorism without a clear direction, while so much was still left undone in Afghanistan.

These were very careful, relatively mild words, expressing pretty reasonable concerns. But that's not how the administration and the Republican leadership took it. To even question the status and direction of this war was interpreted by the administration and the Republican leadership as near treason.

Trent Lott leaped on my words, telling the press, "How dare Senator

Daschle criticize President Bush while we are fighting our war on terrorism, especially when we have troops in the field? He should not be trying to divide our country while we are united." Tom DeLay was more succinct in his criticism, offering a one-word summation of my remarks: "Disgusting."

Ari Fleischer, speaking for the White House, made a thinly veiled swipe at my motives. "When it comes to the defense of the nation," he said, "the President surely hopes that nobody will vote to underfund our nation's defense needs. . . . Obviously, there's going to be politics involved," he added. "Some people may want to run for president one day."

My Senate colleagues were incensed by this reaction. Many of them approached me on the Senate floor to express their dismay at what they viewed to be a gross overreaction by Republicans. Several offered to respond, and some did.

"If they think they can get away with this," my friend Byron Dorgan said, "they will continue to do it and it will only get worse."

Little did I know at the time how prophetic his words would be.

Speculation that I might indeed run for president in 2004 led the Republican leadership in the South Dakota State Legislature to push through a bill that February prohibiting a South Dakota senator from running for president and for the Senate at the same time. This was so clearly directed at me and what people thought were my ambitions that I would later joke, "Boy, is Tim Johnson going to be mad!"

The truth is that while I had begun to consider both my reelection campaign and running for president, I never considered doing both simultaneously. Still, some detractors in South Dakota's highly Republican state legislature saw talk of a potential Daschle presidential campaign as an opportunity to undermine my political position in the state. Most South Dakotans I talked to just thought it was frivolous.

As America continued to focus on the war on terror, another struggle was quietly raging between the administration and the Senate—the struggle to dramatically reshape the faces and philosophy of the federal judiciary.

Mark Mellman, a Democratic pollster, has said, "We have never seen an issue that people are less concerned about than nominations to the federal bench. But," he added, "the core activists on both sides do care very deeply."

The truth is, everyone should care about the makeup of the federal judiciary. After all, Americans can vote out of office a representative who they feel is out of step with the mainstream, but federal judges, once confirmed by the Senate, serve for life. And the decisions they make can determine the interpretation—and even the constitutionality—of laws for years to come.

President Bush often talks about wanting to nominate judges who are "strict constructionists"—people who view the Constitution as a literal document not to be interpreted by the court to deal with changing situations. He has also said that he doesn't want judicial activists serving on the bench, that is, judges who use their position and their rulings to push for social change.

In practice, however, the right wing has long seen judicial appointments and *conservative* judicial activism as a way to achieve policy changes through the judiciary that they can't accomplish via Congress or the president, who are accountable to the people at the ballot box. As a result, we've seen the President nominate a number of people to the federal bench whose decisions and records demonstrate a willingness to roll back decades of progress on civil rights, women's rights, and workers' rights.

When Senator Jeffords switched parties, I made my position on judicial nominations clear: I told the President that I supported his right to nominate judges who share his views and that I was committed to making the process move more fairly and more quickly than it had when Bill Clinton was president and the Senate was under Republican control. But I was also clear that we would not abdicate our constitutional responsibility to offer advice and grant—or withhold—our consent.

On May 25, 2001, President Bush nominated a judge to the federal appeals court for whom I would be unable to provide my consent—a man from Mississippi named Charles Pickering.

Judge Pickering had served as Mississippi's Republican Party state chairman, as head of the Mississippi Baptist Convention, and as a federal district court judge. On the bench, he had been an opponent of a woman's right to choose, lawsuits regarding employment discrimination, and civil rights statutes. Judge Pickering was also a close personal friend of Trent Lott's.

Trent and I had a relationship, as leaders, where we would usually accommodate each other on issues of home state importance. This type of relationship exists in a lot of places in Congress—between leaders of opposing parties and between chairmen and ranking members of committees. As Trent put it, "There are times when you have to have something for your state, and there are times when I have to have something for mine." As leaders, we had to work together so frequently that we each had a "hot line" directly into the other's office, so we could quickly work out issues that arose.

At first, it looked as though Judge Pickering's nomination—despite his questionable record—was steaming toward confirmation, regardless of my feelings about him. Then it was discovered that Judge Pickering had misled the Judiciary Committee in 1990 during his confirmation hearing for the federal district court. He had been asked about his relationship with the Mississippi Sovereignty Commission—a segregation-era state spy agency. He claimed that he "never had any contact" with them. However, a memo directed to the commission stated that Pickering and two other state legislators asked the commission to investigate union activity that had resulted in a strike in Pickering's hometown.

Suddenly, the Pickering nomination was in doubt. It was soon discovered that Judge Pickering had also solicited letters of support from attorneys who appeared before him; this alone would have been ethically suspect, but it was further revealed that he had reviewed those letters before he sent them on to the Senate.

Also, and perhaps most damning to his prospects, Judge Pickering went to unusual lengths in an effort to reduce the prison sentence of a convicted cross burner—threatening to overturn the jury's verdict and going so far as to initiate an "ex parte" call to a high-ranking official at the Department of Justice to discuss the merits of the case, something that is prohibited under the Code of Judicial Conduct.

To me, Judge Pickering's nomination had become something larger than just an issue of home state importance to Trent. This was a nomination to the federal appeals court, and this man was clearly outside the mainstream.

At that point, I had served for eight months as majority leader. In that time, the Senate had confirmed forty-two of President Bush's judicial nominees—more than the number of judicial nominations confirmed in four of the six *years* Republicans controlled the Senate during the Clinton administration.

In addition to the record number of nominations confirmed, we had set a quick pace, reducing by two-thirds the average number of days between when a nominee is eligible for a Judiciary Committee hearing and when he or she is confirmed. Democrats did discuss these things despite the fact that during Republican control of the Senate, we were often appalled at the treatment that many of President Clinton's nominees received. Fifty-seven of his nominees *never* received a hearing before the Judiciary Committee; many more waited hundreds of days; and a number of nominees waited *years*. Secret "holds" were often used to delay and defeat nominees for political reasons. The effects of these practices were devastating not only to the nominee, but to the entire judicial system. For example, between 1999 and 2000, the number of judicial vacancies in America grew from 65 to 103, while at the same time, 32 judicial nominees *never* received a hearing. Senator Leahy and I worked hard to put an end to such a destructive and counterproductive process.

But Judge Pickering was different.

I had made it my usual practice, as leader, not to comment on the prospects for confirmation for judicial nominees until after the Judiciary Committee has had a chance to review and act on them. However, as Judge Pickering was nearing a vote in the Judiciary Committee, Trent Lott and I were invited to appear on *Meet the Press* together. The moderator, Tim Russert, anticipated how important this nominee was to Trent, and I knew that he'd ask me about it. My staff and I discussed whether—when the question about Pickering's prospects was asked—I should duck it and say I would wait for the committee's recommendation. But I knew that Russert would be too aggressive to let me get away with that, and the circumstances of this nominee were such that I pretty much knew he would be voted down in committee the following week. I decided I would answer the question openly. On March 3, Trent and I appeared on *Meet the Press*. As our interview neared an end, Russert said, "Before we go, there's a fellow named Charles Pickering who's been nominated by President Bush to the First Circuit Court of Appeals." Russert then quoted an Associated Press story in which Lott had said that Pickering was "going to get a vote and he's going to pass overwhelmingly, *or else.*" Russert then noted that the Judiciary Committee was likely to block the appointment. He then asked Lott to clarify his threat, "What happens *or else?*"

Trent replied, "Well, or else you'll look at what other alternatives you have, or else it'll probably contribute to a continuing deterioration of how we handle judicial nominations. First, I want to say, though, this has been a case of smear activity by outside groups. How they define this man is not the man I've known for over thirty years. This is a good man, well educated, has been a good judge. He has shown courage in the race area, and as a matter of fact, has been a uniter, not a divider, and it's a tragedy the way he has been treated, and he's not—"

Russert broke in, "He's not going to be confirmed, is he?"

Trent tried to put a good face on it. "Well, we don't know until the vote is taken, Tim. And there are some Democrats that now realize he has been mischaracterized, has been smeared, and they are concerned that, you know, perhaps some folks have tried to put them in a box that is not the right place to be."

Russert continued to press Trent. "If the Judiciary Committee votes against him, ten to nine, does it end there? Is it dead?"

Senator Lott answered, and Tim then turned to me. "Senator Daschle, if the committee votes ten to nine against, is the nomination dead?"

I responded with two words: "It is."

Trent and I managed to joke through the end of the interview. Tim noted that nearly as many people wanted to see me fight Trent as wanted to see Mike Tyson fight in Washington, and I joked about "no ear biting" between Trent and me, but the damage was done. Trent was stung, and he was angry.

The next week, in the Senate, Trent tried to follow through on his "or else." He essentially said, "That's it, we're shutting down the work of the Senate." In fact, Trent's actions had little impact on the overall workings of the Senate. He did, however, take the surprising action of blocking a $1.5 million appropriation to the Judiciary Committee that would have gone to investigating terrorism. His stated reason was that since the Judiciary Committee wasn't processing judges, it didn't need the money.

Trent also immediately placed a hold on the nomination of Jonathan Adelstein, a staff member of mine who had been nominated to be a commissioner of the Federal Communications Commission (FCC).

Trent's motives were thinly veiled. He felt that halting the nomination of someone close to me was partial payback for the fact that Judge Pickering's nomination wouldn't make it to the Senate floor. In public, he said that Jonathan was too young, although at thirty-nine he was a year older than the FCC's thirty-eight-year-old Republican chairman, Michael Powell.

Trent had come up to me on the floor and let me know how upset he was that I had hurt the chances of his nominee. He let others know that he couldn't believe I hadn't picked up the "hot line" to apologize, and he told the press that Pickering's rejection had "damaged" our relationship. I understood his frustration, but to me this wasn't an issue where I could accommodate him on a "home state" concern.

Ironically, his line-in-the-sand response also further stressed Trent's relationship with his caucus. Largely, our perception was that they didn't care about Pickering. If they were going to follow Trent into a major battle, our view was that they didn't want it to be one where they would have to rally to the support of someone who was fast becoming seen as an apologist for racist cross burners.

Soon thereafter, Trent began a habit, after his weekly caucus meetings, of coming out to talk to the press and announcing "his" legislative schedule for each week, even though, as minority leader, he had little official control over the schedule. I don't quite know what motivated him to do that, perhaps it was pressure from his caucus to appear to be battling, but the press seemed to be a bit baffled by it.

By June 2002, just as a year earlier, President's Bush's policies on both the domestic and foreign fronts were failing. The American economy was continuing to worsen, and it was clear that the downturn could not be blamed solely on the fallout from the September 11 attacks. Revelations of corporate malfeasance at the highest levels of American industry continued to emerge, as the twenty-fifth largest company in the nation, Mississippi-based telecom company WorldCom, revealed that month that it had overstated its profits by $3.8 billion—the largest accounting fraud in history (by the end of the year, that number would grow to more than $9 billion).

The images of the lavish mansions that WorldCom executives had built while hiding their company's massive losses didn't help the Bush administration's and Republican Party leadership's attempts to water down the Sarbanes bill. Phil Gramm fought tooth and nail to weaken the bill on the Senate side, and in the House, Michael Oxley of Ohio, the Republican chairman of the Committee on Financial Services, was among those most adamantly opposed to the legislation. Only when they realized they were fighting a losing battle did the Republicans turn 180 degrees, as they had done with aviation security, campaign finance reform, and so many other issues, and not only accepted a policy they had heretofore steadfastly opposed, but actually *embraced* it as their own. Oxley's name became affixed to Sarbanes's on the final version of the bill, and President Bush delivered a major speech expressing his outrage over this kind of corruption and emphasizing his commitment to coming down hard on corporate transgressors.

President Bush and his advisers had become skillful at reading public opinion and cutting their losses on politically popular issues. In the summer of 2002, Bush was poised to make the same sort of about-face he did on corporate accountability with homeland security legislation, which until that June he had refused even to consider. But before that—on the first day of that month—he delivered a commencement speech to the graduating cadets at West Point in which he previewed the so-called Bush doctrine—an unprecedented policy of preemptive strikes by the United States military against countries that our intelligence indicates *may* threaten the United States in the future. Prior to President Bush's statements, every president retained a right to act preemptively, but only in those cases where we faced a grave and imminent threat. In his speech, President Bush made clear that military preemption would now be his preferred approach. As Bush told the assembled cadets, "If we wait for threats to fully materialize, we will have waited too long."

While the American public was outraged over the lack of attention to corporate governance and unhappy with the failing economy, the Republicans' own consultants, with an eye on the November congressional elections, were counseling them to "change the subject and make it about the war." In retrospect, the West Point speech had put in place a framework that would allow the administration to do just that.

Whatever the motivation or merits, the President's decision to announce a policy of preemption also served to accomplish a political goal. After all, if the "war" we were fighting could be expanded at any time, in any direction the President chose, with no hard, clear definition of where it began or ended, then the administration could keep the American public's attention away from the developing problems that surrounded them right here at home.

chpt. 8 (cont)

213

There were so many transparent signals that June that the administration was gearing up for the coming elections. Andy Card said as much, when asked about the timing of so many of the President's shifts in positions that summer. Card answered by referring to a "new product" the Republicans would be "rolling out" in the fall—as if a new-model automobile would be coming off the assembly line.

The West Point speech signaled the President's determination to stake out an aggressive position in combating terrorism at its source. We did not yet know what he and his advisers were planning politically on the home front.

Before the September 11 attacks, Senator Lieberman, chairman of the Governmental Affairs Committee, had introduced legislation to reorganize the government to protect Americans against a new generation of threats. September 11 added new urgency to that work. Nonetheless, the administration continued to oppose Senator Lieberman's legislation in particular and the very idea of a governmental reorganization in general. To many Republicans, "homeland defense" had the smell of "expanded government."

In May, Senator Lieberman's bill to create a Department of Homeland Security was approved by the committee. Every Democrat voted for it. Not a single Republican voted for it, and many derided it as a worthless big-government solution. President Bush threatened—should it pass the Senate—to veto it.

The President's answer to the problem was to name one man—Governor Tom Ridge of Pennsylvania—to head a small office in the White House to coordinate domestic security efforts.

It quickly became evident that very few changes were being made by the government to address the many vulnerabilities that were exposed on September 11. The most visible things that came out of Governor Ridge's office were the "Homeland Security Advisory System"—the color-coded warning levels—and his recommendation that we use plastic and duct tape to protect ourselves from a terrorist attack. Both quickly became the subject of much national commentary. The idea that one color could adequately sum up the relative risk faced by 270 million people across an entire continent struck me as somewhat questionable, especially given the fact that the system was totally detached from any information about what people could do to prepare for or respond to an incident, other than the questionable practice of sealing oneself in a small room, or any information about how agencies would work together to protect the homeland. It's almost the equivalent of the federal government's top meteorologist issuing a daily forecast that characterizes the weather for the entire nation with a single word. Mother Nature doesn't work like that, and neither do terrorists.

Even as administration officials continued to deride the Lieberman plan publicly, they began hedging their bets privately. A small group of White House officials began meeting secretly to draft the President's plan for a Department of Homeland Security. Then, on June 6, 2002, President Bush delivered a nationally televised address announcing his plan to create a Homeland Security Department. This was five days after his West Point speech. While the Bush plan was fundamentally similar to the Lieberman plan, he inserted a controversial provision to reduce civil service protections for the employees who would be assigned to the new department. While there were other policy differences in the areas of intelligence sharing and funding oversight, I have no doubt those could have been quickly and easily overcome. Absent this "civil service" provision and the hard-line position the President took on it, I believe that Congress could have passed a homeland defense bill quickly and nearly unanimously—just as we had done with so much other legislation related to the September 11 tragedy.

But the administration wanted and chose a political fight, and the bill bogged down as they rejected effort after effort to find a workable compromise. For example, John Breaux, Lincoln Chafee, and Ben Nelson offered a series of compromises that moved progressively closer to the President's position and would have commanded the support of a majority of the Senate, but each was dismissed out of hand. As a result, we headed into election season without a bill, and Republicans used it to full political advantage, suggesting that Democrats would place their allegiance to "organized labor" ahead of their responsibility to the safety of the American people.

In Georgia, Saxby Chambliss called Max Cleland—a bronze and silver star medalist who had lost three limbs to a grenade explosion in Vietnam—unpatriotic for his position on this issue. One of his campaign commercials showed a picture of Osama bin Laden and said, ominously, that Max had "voted against homeland security eleven times." Never mind that Max hadn't been voting against anything. He had been voting for our bill. In fact, he'd voted for the department in the Governmental Affairs Committee at a time when both Chambliss and Bush vigorously opposed it.

After the election, we came back in a lame-duck session to wrap up unfinished business. Not content with having politicized this important piece of legislation and undermined long-standing civil service protections implemented in the early 1900s to end the infamous "spoils system" in federal employment, House Republicans saw that they now had an opportunity to use it as a vehicle to reward their supporters. They hastily rewrote the homeland security bill and then left town, saying effectively to the Senate, "Take it or leave it."

As we read through this bill—which had now ballooned by hundreds of pages—we found that they had added a number of special-interest kickbacks. For example, they gave the secretary of homeland security virtually unlimited authority to shield companies from lawsuits simply by designating their products as "anti-terrorism technologies." It gutted a critical part of the aviation security bill we had passed by providing special immunity for private companies that perform passenger and baggage screening at airports.

It also spent tens of millions of dollars on a university-based homeland security research center, which didn't sound like such a bad idea, except that instead of allowing universities to compete and establishing the center at the university with the best proposal, it was written in such a way that only one university—one university in all of America—would be eligible: Texas A&M.

It also had changes that allowed the secretary of homeland security to close advisory committee meetings to the public—even meetings on nonsensitive matters. This change would deny the American people their right to know much of what their government was doing in the name of "homeland security." It would also deny people much of the information they might need to hold accountable private companies that threaten public health.

Finally, and most egregiously, the bill gave liability protection to Eli Lilly and other makers of thimerosal, the mercury-based vaccine preservative that some have associated with autism in children. There was such an outcry about the Eli Lilly exception that one group offered a reward to anyone with knowledge of who actually put it in the bill. No one came forward.

These additions were so outrageous that Senator Arlen Specter, a Republican, called what the House Republicans had done "legislative blackmail." It was disgusting, and, now out of power and with the House adjourned for the year, the only thing we could do was get the House and the administration to pledge they'd come back in January 2003 and revisit the worst aspects of it. They promised they would. On many of these issues, they still haven't.

Also vital to any effort to protect America from future attacks was a clear understanding of the breakdowns that allowed the September 11 attacks to happen in the first place. Within weeks of September 11, Senator Bob Torricelli stood up in one of our weekly Democratic caucus meetings to report that he had gone home to New Jersey to meet with family members of the September 11 victims. He told us what they had told him—that mothers had come up to him and said that their children were afraid to go to school, to leave home, to let their surviving parent out of their sight. One mother told Bob that she wanted to be able to tell her children that this was never going to happen again—something she'd be incapable of doing until we learned what failures took place leading up to September 11.

The families deserved answers, Torricelli said, and we in the Senate needed those answers as well. He implored the caucus to insist that the White House and our Republican colleagues drop their opposition to the establishment of an independent commission to investigate the events that led up to September 11.

Such a commission would not be unprecedented. Directly after the attacks on Pearl Harbor, Congress quickly convened a special Pearl Harbor commission, with President Roosevelt's approval.

But this White House made it clear that it had no desire to have such a commission—essentially the same response they had when we proposed a Department of Homeland Security.

But Senator Torricelli wasn't alone in calling for an investigation. He was joined by Senator McCain. As the idea of a September 11 investigation picked up steam, I was sitting in my office being interviewed by Howard

Fineman of *Newsweek* magazine when I received a highly unusual call from Vice President Cheney.

The last time I had gotten a call from the Vice President was Friday, July 20. At the time, we were working on the fiscal year (FY) 2001 supplemental appropriations bill for the military. Cheney called to say that they needed the Senate to pass the final bill that day if at all possible. If we didn't get it passed, he told me, the military pay raises it called for would be deferred and certain training exercises would have to be canceled. Unfortunately, I had already announced to all senators that there would be no further roll call votes on Friday. I told Vice President Cheney that I would do my best to convince my colleagues to pass this major piece of legislation without a recorded vote. I quickly picked up the phone and called a number of senators, twisting their arms to allow us to pass the bill by consent, which we were able to do later that day. Given the urgency the Vice President had expressed, I expected the bill would be signed by the President as soon as it arrived at the White House. Instead, the President held it for four days (no training exercises that I know of were called off) and took the bill with him to Kosovo, where he signed it in front of a cheering throng of troops, saying, "I promised America that help is on the way for the men and women who wear our uniform."

Needless to say, that episode undermined my trust in Dick Cheney.

This time, when I picked up the phone, the Vice President was cordial but direct. He didn't want this investigation to happen. He told me that the leaders of the war on terror—especially the FBI and CIA—were too busy to go back through their records or to "waste time" preparing for testimony in front of committees. It would be a drain on resources, he said. In his message there was an implied threat: If you keep pushing for this, we're going to say that you're interfering with the war effort.

The Vice President's hard-line approach did not sell with the public. The families and a bipartisan group from Congress continued to press their case. Eventually, Congressman Tim Roemer got legislation creating the commission included, as an amendment, in the FY 2003 intelligence authorization bill in the House. In the Senate, we adopted it on the homeland security bill.

At this point, the administration realized that it could no longer explain why it opposed an honest, objective assessment of what had happened on September 11 and why. So it switched gears once again and, while publicly supporting the commission, turned its attention to limiting its independence and ability to get access to all of the facts.

We felt that to really get to the bottom of our intelligence failures, the commission should be truly independent. We proposed that the panel be equally divided between Republicans and Democrats. We also felt that its members should choose their chairman and that any five members could vote to issue subpoenas. That was a little too much independence for the White House, which insisted that the President pick the commission chairman and that six members be required to sign off on any subpoena the commission wished to issue, which assured that the White House could block any subpoena through its Republican appointments on the commission.

The commission cleared Congress on November 15, 2002, and the President signed it into law two weeks later. Not surprisingly, the commission has had a tough time getting up and running. It has been hamstrung by a lack of money, space, and, most important, access to information. Still, it was a moment of pride for me when the commission convened its first meeting—with the families of the September 11 victims. I have hope that despite the contentious process that led to the commission's creation, our nation—and those families—will get the answers we deserve.

A tumultuous month of June continued with the discovery early on in Lafayette Park, just across from the White House, of a computer disk containing two PowerPoint presentations on the Republicans' strategy for the upcoming 2002 elections. The disk was apparently dropped by a member of the White House staff on the way back from a meeting of political operatives at the Hay-Adams hotel. In an "only in Washington" coincidence, it was picked up by the girlfriend of a Democratic Senate staffer, who gave it to her boyfriend, who gave it to his boss, until it found its way into the hands of the Democratic National Committee.

What they saw on that disk jolted Democratic strategists.

The disk's contents were written by Ken Mehlman, the White House's political director, and—no surprise here—Karl Rove. Among its points was the explicit statement of the Republicans' intent to "focus on war" as the linchpin of their campaign strategy for that fall.

When I first saw this presentation, with its heading, "One Party Will

Chpt. 8 (cont)

219.

Make History," I thought, Just look at this. This is as revealing as anything we're ever going to see. Talk about getting inside the White House's political head. This disk provided an incredible window into the White House strategy to maximize the value of war for political purposes.

A number of Democratic operatives tried to shop the disk around to reporters, but only one saw fit to write about it—Ed Henry, a reporter for *Roll Call.* He put the full PowerPoint presentation up on *Roll Call's* website and analyzed it. Only then did other newspapers follow suit. Then, after a brief flurry of interest, the story died. It had no "legs."

I was incredulous that the press could skim past a story like this, letting it evaporate with so little notice, just as I was amazed that they would swallow Bush's about-face on the homeland security issue. The White House strategy on homeland defense was to embrace the bill as its own, blame Democrats for blocking the bill for political reasons, and allow Republican candidates to charge their opponents with jeopardizing the safety of the country to curry favor with their political benefactor—organized labor. And the White House disk clearly laid out the predicate for that strategy.

By August 2002, as we prepared for that month's traditional congressional recess, the political landscape looked similar to that of one year earlier. Bush's domestic policies were floundering, especially on the economic front, where the stock market continued to plunge, corporate corruption continued to be exposed, and unemployment was growing at an alarming pace. More than two million Americans had lost their jobs since Bush had become president, a disturbing fact that could not be explained away by the shock of September 11. Osama bin Laden had not been found; al-Qaeda had been battered but was clearly not broken; and the question of what to do next about the terrorist threat was unanswered.

With the elections of 2002 approaching, the Republicans and the President were on the defensive. It was clear to them—and to us—that if this election became a referendum on the President's domestic policies, it was going to be a bad year for Republicans. Karl Rove himself had been saying as much all year long, both in public speeches and on the disk that was found in Lafayette Park. His message was that the Republican Party had to make this election about the war.

Meanwhile, Senate and House campaigns across the country were already swinging into high gear as Congress recessed in early August and members returned home, many of them to defend their own seats. I wasn't up for reelection that November, but my colleague Tim Johnson was, and his opponent, handpicked by the Republican leadership, was a popular three-term congressman, John Thune. Thune had intended to run for governor that fall, but after a private dinner at the White House with President Bush and many conversations with Karl Rove, Thune had been convinced to enter the race for the Senate.

As November drew near, with so many crises demanding his attention at home and abroad, President Bush began spending his time and energy campaigning across the country with unprecedented intensity. From that August through election day, the President crisscrossed the nation, making stump speeches and fund-raising appearances for Republican candidates from coast to coast. It seemed as if he were running for office himself, and in a sense he was. If Bush could help the Republicans take control of the Senate, he would remove the last obstacle that stood between them and across-the-board power in Washington.

That obstacle was our Democratic majority in the Senate. As the leader of the opposition party, I had spent the better part of the past year as the focal point for Republican attacks. Now, transparently, Bush himself joined the attack. The media frequently reported that Bush's involvement in this particular Senate race—the South Dakota race—was personal, with the target being not just Tim Johnson, but also me. By the time that election campaign of 2002 was finished, President Bush would make five visits to South Dakota in a year and a half.

Actually, in terms of the one domestic issue that mattered most to South Dakotans that August, George Bush apparently cared not a whit. That issue was drought relief.

Rainfall in the Midwest that summer had been an astonishing 80 percent below normal—a full 30 percent less than what fell during the worst Dust Bowl years of the Great Depression. Cornstalks that typically stood at least ten feet high in the fields by that time of year were dry, shriveled dwarfs no more than three feet tall.

It wasn't just South Dakota that was suffering, either, but the entire Midwest. With such devastation added to the myriad other challenges facing our nation's farmers—and with consumers bound to end up paying the price in higher costs for lower crop yields at the grocery store—my

Senate colleagues proposed that the federal government step in and provide drought relief to these farmers. We decided that $5 billion would be the right amount to compensate producers for economic losses caused by a natural disaster—an amount comparable to what the government had done for flood victims in Texas and hurricane victims in Florida.

President Bush's response was to say that the government could not afford to spend that kind of money. In fact, he said the government would spend *nothing* on this emergency. Saying he was not about to increase a federal deficit that was largely of his own creation, Bush decided that any money the farmers needed would have to come out of existing farm programs, which were not established to deal with emergency situations such as drought.

At this time, all Americans were of course absorbed with strengthening our national security and combating terrorism. But on the home front, for South Dakotans, this issue of drought relief was a priority. These drought-stricken families needed our help, purely and simply. But the President and the Republican-controlled House were stopping it.

Naturally, when President Bush made a visit to Mount Rushmore that August 15, the audience expected him to address those concerns. Instead, however, he chose to use the setting as a photogenic backdrop for a speech about combating terrorism.

At Mount Rushmore, it seemed the Bush team's primary concern was to position the President so that the carved stone faces of Lincoln, Washington, Jefferson, and Roosevelt would appear behind him as he spoke.

Rather than address the issue of these farmers' crops dying in the fields along with their hopes for the future, Bush chose to speak on behalf of John Thune, using the same rhetoric that framed the President's message wherever he went. He might as well have been speaking in Alaska that day. Or Florida. It didn't matter. Bush's purposes—the big picture for his political team—transcended such trivial concerns as the welfare of some farmers and ranchers in South Dakota.

The audience at Mount Rushmore recognized this, as did many South Dakotans who weren't there that day. In the end, I think the President's insensitivity to the effect the drought was having on real people's lives, and what South Dakotans felt that said about his commitment to our state, is in part what cost John Thune the election. Thune's message to South

Dakota was, "Elect me, and I will have the ear of the President himself." Yet on the issue that mattered most to South Dakotans, having the President's ear didn't seem to matter. The President was against drought relief.

I think most pundits agreed that on Bush's other four visits to South Dakota during that campaign season, he was effective in helping John Thune. But in this case, that August morning, the President hurt his candidate more than he helped.

As that month of August drew toward a close and Congress prepared to reconvene after the Labor Day weekend, our prospects for the coming election—our opportunity to keep control of the Senate and possibly even regain control of the House—looked good, just as it had a year earlier.

Late in July, a group of Democratic senators gathered in Nantucket with some of our consultants and pollsters to talk about the prospects for that fall's elections. The optimism that infected this particular gathering was very high—too high, I have to say, for my comfort. I've always been cautious about being too overconfident about anything. I tend to minimize expectations, and not to take anything for granted.

So, naturally, I winced a little when I heard some of these consultants, along with several of my colleagues, predicting that by the time the smoke cleared from this particular election, we would hold fifty-four or fifty-five seats in the Senate and that we could realistically look at taking back the majority in the House as well. As I listened to these encouraging predictions, I remember thinking, I hope they're right.

Also in July, I gathered the Democratic national security leaders in the Senate—Carl Levin, chairman of the Armed Services Committee, Bob Graham, chairman of the Intelligence Committee, and Joe Biden, chairman of the Foreign Relations committee. We discussed how we could contribute to the debate that was now brewing about Iraq. In an effort to address the many questions on the minds of senators and the American people, the chairmen agreed to conduct hearings, schedule briefings, and explore other questions surrounding this issue.

Senator Biden's hearings, in particular, raised a number of troubling concerns—including what should happen in a post-Saddam Iraq. As Americans heard more about the questions and costs associated with a war in Iraq, their concerns grew. The largest black eye administered to the Bush administration's war in the Iraq talk came in August from Brent Scowcroft, who had served as the national security adviser for President Bush's father. In a *Wall Street Journal* op-ed he wrote, "An attack on Iraq at this time would seriously jeopardize, if not destroy, the global counter-terrorist campaign we have undertaken." A majority of Americans agreed with Scowcroft. And then, just as had happened a year earlier with the attacks of September 11, the landscape suddenly, quite swiftly, changed. Speaking to the Veterans of Foreign Wars (VFW), Vice President Cheney outlined the possibility that "Saddam will acquire nuclear weapons fairly soon," thereby activating the Bush doctrine announced at West Point that previous June.

CHENEY SAYS PERIL OF A NUCLEAR IRAQ JUSTIFIES ATTACK. That was the front page headline of the August 27 *New York Times,* the morning after Cheney delivered that speech to the VFW. Telling the group he had "no doubt" that Saddam Hussein was preparing to use weapons of mass destruction against the United States, the Vice President declared that the United States needed to strike first. "The risks of inaction," he declared, "are far greater than the risks of action." Those who might disagree, he said, were victims of "wishful thinking or willful blindness." Cheney's speech mentioned conferring with other allies about such action, but it quite clearly indicated that the United States was prepared to act without their involvement or support.

I was in Kenya at the time, witnessing the devastation wrought by AIDS in Africa. My foreign policy adviser, Denis McDonough, had found and printed the speech for me. I read it as we bounced around the streets of Nairobi. I finished it, put it down, turned to Denis, and said, "It looks like we're going to war."

End of Chpt. 8

goes to pg. 266 = 42 pp

Election 2002

O<small>UR SENATE DEMOCRATIC CAUCUS'S</small> expectations about the 2002 election, going into the August recess of that year, were high for several reasons, not least of which was the fact that we had no member retiring. Some had thought about it. Paul Wellstone had made a pledge when he was elected in 1990 that he would serve no more than two terms. We had talked on several occasions on the Senate floor and in my office about his decision regarding a third term in the Senate. Paul was torn about his pledge. Upon arriving in the Senate in 1990, he hadn't anticipated how long it takes to accomplish one's legislative goals. Nor had he ever dreamed of the horror of September 11 and its aftermath and the role he felt he had in helping America meet its new challenges in a way that was consistent with maintaining a free and open society. Most important, he felt strongly about his role in standing up to the Bush administration on behalf of his people in Minnesota. He felt that his role had become more important than ever before, and that became a major motivation for him in making his decision to run for a third term.

Dick Durbin also considered leaving the Senate. Many people in Illinois encouraged Dick to run for governor in 2002, and he gave it a great deal of thought. As we discussed it, many of us expressed the hope that he would stay in the Senate. Dick is incredibly articulate and accomplished, and I urged him to stay in the Senate not only so we could take advantage of his considerable skills, but also so he could continue to build on his impressive record. I am very grateful that he has.

We also were excited about the fact that we had more women running for Senate that fall than at any time in history. Besides incumbents Mary

Landrieu in Louisiana and Jean Carnahan in Missouri, we had Susan Parker in Alabama, Lois Weinberg in Kentucky, Joyce Corcoran in Wyoming, Gloria Tristani in New Mexico, Chellie Pingree in Maine, and Jeanne Shaheen in New Hampshire. And the Democratic Senatorial Campaign Committee was chaired by Senator Patty Murray, the first woman ever to hold that position.

I asked Patty to chair the DSCC because she deserved it. I also believed it was time that a woman be appointed to that position. Despite the outcome of the elections, Patty did a phenomenal job recruiting candidates, raising money, and providing technical campaign assistance to our candidates. No one could have done better.

At the same time, as our slate of Senate candidates was taking shape, the Republicans, with Bill Frist heading their campaign committee, had been preparing theirs. In Minnesota, they persuaded a former Democrat named Norm Coleman, who was planning to run for governor, to challenge Paul Wellstone instead. In my own state of South Dakota, the White House was also successful, as I noted earlier, with another Republican planning to run for governor—Congressman John Thune—convincing him to take on my Senate colleague Tim Johnson.

This was just the beginning of what would become an unprecedented involvement by a United States president in an off-year election. From the beginning of September right through to election day, George Bush crisscrossed the country a dizzying number of times, stumping for Republican candidates in every key state where a Senate or House seat was contested. Before that campaign season was over, Bush would visit Georgia—where Max Cleland was locked in an extremely tight race against a congressman named Saxby Chambliss—six times. He would visit South Dakota five times.

Never had a president put his political credibility—and his political capital—on the line so completely. To us his objective was obvious. He wanted to nationalize the 2002 elections and, given his popularity, create the longest possible coattails for Republican candidates even though he was not on the ballot. Those coattails are produced by energizing one's political base, persuading undecided voters, and then getting your voters to the polls on election day.

It is a big roll of the presidential dice. If the president's candidate wins the election in those states in which he has campaigned, he gets the credit. If the candidate loses, so does the president.

The more states in which one puts his name on the line on behalf of a candidate, the greater the risk. This President's determination to appear in so many states in the 2002 elections was a clear indication that he was going to be a participant, not a spectator, in this election. It would be, in many ways, a referendum on the first two years of his presidency.

A number of people who had friends or contacts high in the White House reported to me that they had been told George Bush had made winning the Senate election in South Dakota his number one political priority—to beat me, at least by proxy, in my own backyard. That thought energized everyone involved in Tim's campaign, not that we needed any more motivation to campaign as hard as we did.

Not since Calvin Coolidge spent three months in the Black Hills in 1927 had a president spent so much time in South Dakota as did President Bush in the last election cycle. We joked that with one more visit to South Dakota, the President would have been eligible for an in-state hunting license.

But President Bush's interest in South Dakota wasn't a laughing matter, and Tim's race was a tight one. In his first couple of visits, President Bush scheduled a public event in addition to his political ones. The first time he toured our public health clinic in Sioux Falls. The second time he visited an ethanol plant nearby. The third included that trip to Mount Rushmore. On each occasion, he invited Tim and me to attend the public events, and we did.

It was odd being at those events. The President was respectful of us, and we were respectful of him. In his public remarks, he walked a tightrope, not attacking Tim personally but talking about the need to elect a Senate that supported him and his agenda. At the end of each event, Tim and I would shake hands with the President and then go to the cameras, where we would walk the same tightrope, being respectful of the President while talking about local South Dakota issues and the larger need for checks and balances in Washington.

I spoke of the hope that Jim Jeffords had shared with me upon leaving the Republican Party—that he, and *we*, could make a difference. And I reminded everyone that contrary to what they were hearing about obstruction, we had made a difference, both in what we had accomplished in the Senate during the 107th Congress—like the flurry of post–September 11 legislation, the Patients' Bill of Rights, the No Child Left Behind bill, the campaign finance reform bill, election reform, and a comprehensive trade bill, to mention just a few—and in what we *hadn't* allowed to happen.

The legislation we had not allowed to pass was, in many ways, just as important to the vast majority of Americans as the legislation we had been able to push through. We didn't confirm judges who were so far to the right that their ideology would affect their objectivity. We didn't allow the President to reduce the standards for arsenic in water, or give a $250 million tax break to Enron, or allow our airport security to be left in the hands of the lowest bidder.

When most people think of the phrase *checks and balances,* they think of the separate branches of government—the presidency, Congress, federal and state governments, the judiciary, and so forth. But the phrase also pinpoints exactly what our duty in the Senate had been during the bulk of the 107th Congress, which was to check and to balance, wherever we thought it necessary, the legislative intentions of the Republican Party and of the Republican White House. The Republicans pursued the same goal—through decidedly different means—during the Clinton presidency.

The Republicans' strategy in the 2002 elections—with the President as their chief spokesman—was to emphasize national security. As it said on that dropped disk: "focus on war."

That was no surprise. In spite of the fact that the economy was floundering, polls showed that Americans were feeling deeply insecure—and justifiably so. Republicans began talking about virtually every issue in terms of security and patriotism, of danger and defense—even the issue of judicial appointments. The White House talked about its work to make America more secure, but when it came to politics, they focused virtually all of their campaign rhetoric on America's insecurity. In veiled terms, they were saying that the security of our country would be determined by the outcome of the November elections.

That was the Republicans' message in the autumn of 2002. It continues to be their message today. And if the economy continues on its present course, I suspect it will be their message in 2004. And so far this strategy has worked well—in no small part because of the finely tuned message delivery system the Republicans have created, amplified by the bully pulpit they've got with George Bush in the White House. Trying to get your own message across in the face of such a machine is often like shouting into a hurricane—your voice is drowned out by the gale-force winds around you.

But that's all hindsight at this point. At *that* time, going into the 2002 election season, we were more than merely optimistic. We were confident—confident that our message was strong; confident that the American people would see that the current Republican leadership was leading the nation down a dangerous path; confident that our position on every issue would improve and strengthen our nation, both at home and abroad; and confident that the majority of Americans agreed with us. Our challenge was to articulate these convictions in a message that would resonate with the voters.

As soon as we returned from that August recess, we knew there were two key national legislative issues that we had to take care of in the following six weeks if we were going to be able to leave Washington by the middle of October and continue our campaigns for the coming election. Those two issues were the creation of a Department of Homeland Security and, after the Enron and WorldCom scandals, reform of our pension systems to provide greater protections to retirees.

The drought issue in South Dakota that I discussed earlier also needed urgent attention.

As we neared the end of the legislative session, the pressure to provide some relief mounted. The situation continued to worsen in South Dakota and parts of surrounding states. To bring attention to our efforts, we kept a daily count of how long it had been since the effort began. By the beginning of October, we were at 230 days and counting. Drought aid was fast becoming the most significant political issue in the South Dakota Senate race.

In addition, we had to consider many of the remaining appropriations bills that have to be passed each year by October 1, the beginning of the new fiscal year. These bills fund all the activities of the federal government with the exception of Social Security and Medicare, which are funded automatically.

To accommodate this schedule, we began a legislative procedure called "dual tracking" by which the Senate can work on two pieces of legislation simultaneously—dealing with one, say, in the morning and part of the afternoon and picking up the other later in the day and into the evening.

With all our determination to push these bills through as quickly as possible, beginning with the Departments of Homeland Security and Defense appropriations, it immediately became apparent that the Republicans did not share our sense of urgency. Quite the contrary. No sooner did those bills reach the Senate floor than the Republicans began to filibuster them.

And no sooner did the filibusters begin than we had to set everything aside to deal with a new issue put before us—a resolution to give the President war-making powers to deal with the threats posed by Iraq.

Actually, the fact that we found ourselves dealing with an Iraq resolution was a bit of a surprise. Throughout the summer, Democrats—and even some Republicans—had been urging the President to come to Congress to discuss how to deal with Saddam Hussein and Iraq. We called for these discussions because it was clear that dealing with Iraq could mean a military intervention and that the most successful military interventions are those that have the informed consent of the American people. We felt that a full and thorough congressional debate and a vote on a statutory authorization would be the single best proxy for the American public's voice and vote.

Disappointingly, White House staff repeatedly told reporters that the President had no intention of coming to Congress with such a resolution, and the White House counsel, Alberto Gonzales, went so far as to provide an opinion that the President did not need the approval of Congress to attack Iraq. So it was a surprise when I, along with the other congressional leaders, met with the President just after Labor Day, and he told us that he wanted Congress to pass a resolution authorizing the use of force in Iraq within sixty days.

Both the nature and the urgency of this resolution were surprising. From a military standpoint, we didn't have the necessary forces in the region to carry out such quick action. What's more, the President had publicly repeated several times—and had actually written to me in a letter he handed me that morning—that he had not made up his mind on how best to confront Saddam Hussein.

At first blush, it seemed odd that the President would want immediate discussion on a resolution giving him the authority to use force in Iraq when he maintained that he hadn't decided whether force would be necessary at all. However, you didn't have to be a mathematician to calculate that the timeline the President had prescribed would leave us debating a war in Iraq right before the election—the exact debate that Republican political documents had told us they wanted to have. And there was a third surprise. That morning, the President told us he would use his previously scheduled speech to the United Nation's General Assembly in New York to seek UN and international support for our efforts in Iraq.

From my service in the Air Force and through my service in Congress, I've become increasingly awed by our military prowess. At the same time, I've come to believe that our power is used most effectively to achieve our policy objectives when we act in concert with our allies. That is not because I feel we don't have the military capability to deal with threats like Iraq alone—we clearly do. It is also not because I believe we do not have the right—or the obligation—to act without the approval of other nations when our security is at risk—we do and we must. And it is not because I think that the United Nations is the answer to our problems—too many times it has proven that it is not.

It is because I've realized that so many threats we face—like the war on terror—require the help of nations that we simply shouldn't be alienating, especially if we don't have to. The administration, however, seemed to believe that since we *can* do everything on our own, we *should* do everything on our own. That was the point Vice President Cheney made clear in his August speeches on Iraq.

That morning, the President appeared to have reversed course.

As we began discussing Iraq, two things were clear at the outset. One, there was universal contempt for Saddam Hussein and his repressive regime. Even the one senator who was regularly singled out by the White House as not sufficiently supportive of the war in Iraq—Robert C. Byrd— had this to say about Saddam Hussein: "I think Saddam Hussein is lower than a snake's belly myself. I wouldn't shed any tear if anything happened to him."

Two, there was a recognition that, for the first time in American history, the President was seeking congressional approval to use military force against a country based not on what it had done, but on what we assessed it may do.

The debate in the Senate boiled down to an assessment of the imminence of the threat to U.S. interests and a discussion of the conditions under which Congress should give this or any president unprecedented authority to preemptively strike another country. Since we were also considering this resolution at a time when we were deep in the war on terrorism—with troops in Afghanistan, the Philippines, Georgia, Yemen, Colombia, and elsewhere—Democrats voiced the concern that in the end, American soldiers might be assuming all the risk and that American taxpayers might ultimately assume the entire burden not only for the war, but also for the inevitable postwar reconstruction.

Some in our caucus, like Joe Lieberman, Evan Bayh, and Zell Miller, agreed with the administration that the threat was so grave that we needed to act fast to confront Saddam militarily, even if acting fast meant that we would be acting largely alone. Others, including our Foreign Relations Committee chairman Joe Biden, John Kerry, and myself argued that while Saddam posed a threat, the threat was not so imminent that we did not have the time to build a coalition like the one George H. W. Bush and Jim Baker built in 1991—when nearly twenty countries contributed more than two hundred thousand ground troops and our friends and allies covered 90 percent of the costs. We also believed that assembling such a coalition offered the best chances for convincing Saddam that he should peacefully accede to international demands. Should military force became unavoidable, we all felt that a broad coalition offered the best prospects for military success while reducing the risk to our troops and the burden on our taxpayers.

A subset of our caucus, led by Senator Levin, chairman of the Armed Services Committee, and Senator Byrd, chairman of the Appropriations Committee, wanted to require the President to get UN approval before any attack on Iraq was launched to ensure that if we took action, we would be acting with the support of the international community. As the month of September wore on, we called meeting after meeting to discuss the most profound responsibility granted to Congress in the Constitution: whether to grant the President the authority to put America's young men and women in harm's way.

Each member of the caucus brought personal perspective to the debate. For example, Tim Johnson would make his decision not only as a public servant, but as a parent—his son Brooks was serving in the 101st Airborne, which had returned from Kandahar, Afghanistan, earlier that year, and was likely to be deployed to the Persian Gulf should hostilities with Iraq become inevitable.

From Max Cleland in Georgia to Tim Johnson in South Dakota, the decision of whether or not to go to war was a very difficult one to make—collectively, personally, and politically. I remember Paul Wellstone standing up in one of our caucus meetings during the debate. In characteristic fashion, Paul argued passionately against the unilateral use of U.S. force without prior UN approval and declared that his vote was more important than his election. Accordingly, he told us that he had every intention of speaking out against the war in Iraq and looked forward to the opportunity to explain his vote in every town in the state of Minnesota. Choked with emotion, he said, "And if that means the end of my Senate career," he said, "so be it."

The debates within the caucus were both emotional and sobering. We all recognized that what we were about to do would impact the lives of hundreds of thousands of U.S. troops and their families and loved ones. We also recognized that for the first time in American history, we were considering war against a country based on what we feared it might do, not on what it had done.

That demanded we take a hard look at the nature of the threat posed by Saddam's weapons of mass destruction (WMD). In an effort to rally the American people and the world to its side, the administration laid out in statement after statement—building on Vice President Cheney's assertions in August—that Saddam Hussein not only likely possessed chemical and biological weapons, but that he also either already possessed nuclear weapons or was soon to have them. At the same time, administration representatives argued that Hussein was working hand in glove with al-Qaeda and could conceivably give or sell these awful weapons to al-Qaeda or other terrorist groups.

So in addition to the heavy responsibility of putting our young men and women in harm's way, we recognized that we were putting America's credibility on the line. The President was asking Congress and the rest of the world to join us in this unprecedented effort based largely on his administration's interpretation of our intelligence community's assessment of Saddam's weapons of mass destruction and his links to terrorism.

Although the President said he had not made up his mind on options for Iraq, there was a growing belief that he had already decided to use force and that he and his administration had seized on weapons of mass destruction as the easiest means to rationalize this decision for the American people and the world. Adding to this skepticism was the Bush administration's September 20 release of its national security strategy. The annual document, required by Congress since 1986, was the Bush administration's first comprehensive strategic statement of its national security priorities and how it believed those priorities could best be advanced.

The most striking element of the document was the administration's decision to replace deterrence, a doctrine applied by Democratic and Republican presidents for more than five decades, with the threat of pre-emptive military action. While previous Republican and Democratic presidents retained preemption as one option among many to be exercised only when other options had been exhausted, the administration seemed to be suggesting that preemption had become a first—even the only— option. Its central thesis is summarized in one paragraph:

> While the United States will constantly strive to enlist the support of the international community, we will not hesitate to act alone, if necessary, to exercise our right of self-defense by acting pre-emptively. . . .

Of course, to even consider acting preemptively against a threat, you need to be confident of what that threat is. Already there were troubling signs that we and the public were not being given a full and complete assessment of Saddam's WMD programs.

I had received countless briefings on this issue over the course of the previous decade, and I had become especially concerned about both Saddam's chemical and biological weapons programs and our inability to monitor them after Saddam kicked inspectors out of his country in 1998. But the administration, with its assertions about nuclear weapons and links to al-Qaeda, brought new urgency to the threat posed by Iraq. As Condoleezza Rice said on CNN on September 8, "The only time we may be 100 percent sure [that Saddam Hussein has weapons of mass destruction that can reach the United States] is when something lands on our territory. We don't want the smoking gun to be a mushroom cloud."

That's what the American people heard. But the categorical and definitive public statements were much more conditional in classified settings. These classified briefings were vitally important, and I urged my colleagues to treat the classified material we received with utmost care. I was amazed, however, at the administration's ability to quickly declassify and widely disseminate the information that was most supportive of its public case, like the CIA's white paper on Iraq's WMD released in October, while documents questioning those conclusions remained hidden from public view.

This disconcerting pattern of behavior was not lost on the members of the Intelligence Committee. Led by Chairman Bob Graham, Dick Durbin, and Carl Levin, the committee worked tirelessly to get the full—and decidedly complex—picture before Congress and the American people. Contrary to the public assertions that Saddam was poised to use WMD, Senator Levin got the CIA to declassify its assessment that the likelihood of Saddam Hussein using WMD was actually "low."

So much was transpiring so quickly in that month of September that we hardly had time to catch our breath. Even as the debate on the Iraq resolution was reaching its climax, the same kind of heated debate over the homeland security bill was reaching critical mass as well.

Again, what seemed to get lost in the heat of that battle is how *opposed* the Republicans and the White House had been to any kind of Department of Homeland Security until the summer, even going so far as to vote unanimously against this idea in committee the previous July. Interestingly, their attitude seemed to change precisely when questions began to be raised in the media about what the White House knew about terrorist activity before September 11 and the momentum for an investigation of that subject began to build.

Some senators in our caucus were convinced that the Bush White House was once again determined to "change the subject," drawing attention away from what they knew, or should have known, about terrorist plans prior to September 11 by putting their own version of a homeland security bill on the table.

The Republicans essentially took the Lieberman bill, which set in motion the most massive overhaul of the federal bureaucracy in over sixty years, and removed many basic civil service protections designed to ensure that government jobs would be filled competitively rather than by political patronage, and unveiled this package as a new initiative.

As this Republican version of the homeland security bill was drafted, the employees of this new agency would have virtually no rights. They could be reassigned, reorganized, restructured, or removed with absolutely no recourse. On this and a number of other issues—including funding, the one area over which Congress has constitutional authority—the president would have almost total autonomy. The President framed this legislation as essential to protecting the American people from terrorist attack. And he insisted that in the interests of "national security," the employees in the Department of Homeland Security would have to be stripped of labor protections.

With this bill, the stage was set for a major confrontation between the two parties. And this confrontation posed a serious political risk for Senate Democrats. If we supported the proposal, for the first time in more than a century since the civil service reforms had been enacted in response to the notorious "spoils system," tens of thousands of federal workers would lose vital protections in the workplace. If we fought it, the Republicans could point their fingers at the "obstructionist" Democrats, who they would suggest view organized labor as more important then national security. The Republican argument ignored the reality that many of these same workers were the *heroes* of September 11.

Protection of federal workers' rights was the primary difference between the two bills. And that debate, unfortunately for Democrats, *did* draw itself out through the election. While we had the support of an overwhelming number of Democratic senators, we were never able to break the Republican filibuster of our bill. The price they demanded for ending the debate was to pass the administration's proposal, verbatim, and this, we felt, was too high a price to pay.

Negotiations continued in an effort to resolve the impasse. Ben Nelson, Lincoln Chafee, and John Breaux explored bipartisan compromise solutions and even offered amendments in an effort to bring both sides together. Democrats moved a great distance toward the administration's position in an effort to resolve the matter, but the Republicans were in no mood to compromise. They sensed a political victory.

The debate became even more contentious and political as the election drew near.

Assertions were made and repeated that Democrats simply did not care as much for our national security as we did for the protection of government employee unions. The charges and countercharges generated some of the highest political tension of the entire legislative session.

Late that September, President Bush appeared at a Republican rally in New Jersey and told his audience that the Senate, under Democratic leadership, was "not interested in the security of the American people." When I read the President's words in the paper the next morning, I got very angry. Having read the comments once, I put the paper down, to pick it up only moments later and read them again. The more I read, the more livid I got.

My anger continued to mount a couple of hours later, when I arrived at the office.

I asked the staff if they had seen the comments. Most of them had. What they hadn't seen, a few of them told me later, was me this angry. Our regularly scheduled leadership meeting was the first thing on my schedule.

I read the comments to members of the Democratic leadership, and they, too, were shocked that the President of the United States would make such an assertion. I said that I was going to go to the Senate floor to respond, and several of my colleagues cautioned me to think carefully about my response and try to contain my anger. My staff strongly urged me to hold off a couple of minutes so they could at least put together some talking points for me—but I didn't want talking points. I wanted nothing less than an apology from the President. Many of my fellow senators came to the floor in a show of support as I approached my desk in the front row on the left side of the center aisle. I hadn't given specific thought to what I was going to say when I arrived at my desk. I began by calmly reiterating the President's assertion that we were not interested in the security of the American people. Then, looking at my Democratic colleagues, who included not just Max Cleland, but also Daniel Inouye, who lost his right arm as an Army officer fighting in Italy in World War II, I grew angry again and I said—no, I guess I began shouting—"You tell Senator Inouye he's not interested in the security of the American people! You tell those who fought in Vietnam and in World War II they're not interested in the security of the American people!" Still fuming, I ripped off my glasses.

"This is outrageous, *outrageous!*" I continued. "We ought not to politicize the rhetoric about war and life and death.

"This has got to end, Mr. President," I said.

But it didn't.

The immediate response from the White House was predictable and "on message." True to its doctrine of framing every issue in terms of security and defense, Bush spokesman Ari Fleischer declared, "Now is a time for everybody to take a deep breath, to stop finger-pointing and to work well together to protect our national security and homeland defense." Trent Lott stepped up and told reporters how "deeply saddened" he was by the "tenor and tone" of my comments. "Who is the enemy here?" he asked. "The President of the United States or Saddam Hussein?"

Others, however, felt my words as a rallying cry—a cathartic moment for Democrats who felt that they had not only the right, but the obligation to debate these issues and didn't appreciate having their patriotism called into question.

Looking back, I have no regrets about calling attention to what was an irresponsible, divisive, and reckless statement. Something had to be said. As Senate Democratic leader, it was my responsibility to say it. And for a while, it may have made some difference in the tone and general demeanor of the debate that followed.

At the same time all this was transpiring, yet another crisis presented itself on the morning of Monday, September 30. I was in New York, having breakfast at the Regency Hotel and preparing for a series of meetings that day, when the phone rang. Bob Torricelli, our senior senator from New Jersey, was on the other end of the line.

"Tom," he said, getting straight to the point, "I've decided to announce my retirement and my decision not to continue my campaign for reelection. I want to do it today. I just don't want to take it anymore."

Bob was up for reelection that November and was locked in an intense campaign with a well-funded Republican challenger backed by President Bush. He had been taking a relentless pounding both from his opponent, a businessman named Douglas Forrester, and from the press over the question of improprieties involving gifts and illegal campaign contributions allegedly given to Bob by a New Jersey businessman named David Chang. Following an intensive investigation, the U.S. attorney had declined to prosecute Senator Torricelli, but the Senate Ethics Committee did severely admonish Bob in July, concluding that the circumstances of his involvement with Mr. Chang raised at least an appearance of impropriety. For my part, I had been troubled when these allegations first surfaced, and I had talked to Bob several times about them over the course of that summer. Each time he told me, "Tom, there is nothing to these accusations. I promise you that they are not true."

Bob and I had worked closely together during his time in the Senate ever since I had appointed him to lead the Democratic Senatorial Campaign Committee. He was aggressive, tough, smart, and an eloquent speaker. He had worked very hard on behalf of the caucus, first as our vice chair and then as chairman of the DSCC. Bob had earned the respect of the caucus and Senate leadership for his work and his success, and he had found new passion in helping the many New Jerseyans who had lost loved ones on September 11. He told me he was innocent, and I believed him.

As Bob's reelection race heated up, things got more complicated. The effect of the Ethics Committee decision in July still lingered, and Forrester's campaign, which was based almost completely on this issue, continued to repeat the allegations against Bob.

Just a week earlier, Bob had asked me if I would come to New Jersey and give a speech to a rally for him in Trenton, and I had agreed. It was a good rally. The audience, largely members of the Communications Workers of America, was very enthusiastic. But I could sense a feeling among the people putting it together—Bob's staff, the volunteers, everyone working so hard for the Torricelli campaign—that things were not where they wanted them to be. It's hard to put a finger on such a feeling—it's almost like a sixth sense that comes from having gone through so many political campaigns—but I could just feel a bad vibe about the direction of the race.

Then, that last weekend of September, I came to New York again—for a Democratic Senate Campaign Committee event. No sooner did I arrive than the news broke that David Chang had given an interview in which he listed specific times, dates, and locations of meetings he had had with Bob Torricelli. Even though Mr. Chang's credibility had been severely undermined, this report was repeated over and over on television, print, and radio news throughout the entire weekend.

I gave Bob a call and told him to tough it out, to hang in there. He was both angered and deeply hurt that Chang's accusations were generating such a level of attention and sensationalism.

That Sunday evening, at the New York reception preceding the DSCC event, the coverage was the topic of much of the conversation. Among those who attended was Bob's former Democratic Senate colleague Frank Lautenberg. Frank had retired just two years earlier, having served in the Senate eighteen years and risen to chair the Senate Budget Committee and the Appropriations Subcommittee on Transportation. He told me that night that he was already restless in retirement and would be willing to fill the vacancy should one develop in the Senate race in New Jersey. I responded by saying that it appeared Bob was going to do what many of us had urged him to do—tough it out.

It was widely known and even reported that Frank and Bob had a contentious relationship throughout the time they served together in the Senate. Unfortunately, that is not uncommon among members of the same Senate delegation, even among those of the same party. That realization has always made me especially grateful for the close personal and working relationship I have had with my colleague from South Dakota, Tim Johnson.

I had just assured Frank the night before that I felt reasonably confident Bob was staying in the race. I was not ready for Bob's call on the following Monday morning, telling me that he was pulling out with hardly a month left until election day.

Later that morning, in the backseat of a car traveling through the streets of New York on my way to my first appointment, I phoned Bob and encouraged him to think carefully about his decision and its ramifications—for him, his state, and our party.

"We don't even know if you have the *option* of getting out. Do you know what the laws are for replacing somebody at this point?" I asked.

He said that he didn't. Neither did I.

He agreed to hold off on any formal announcement. We talked several more times during the course of that day, with our political staffs researching the situation and what our options might be. We hadn't been prepared for this. We had no contingency plan. Bob had ridden out tough political situations many times before. He is such a strong campaigner and fund-raiser, *and* he has great organizational abilities. *And* he was facing what we thought was such a relatively weak opponent that we figured, even with this issue beating its wings around him, he'd be able to eke out a vic-

cht. 9 (cont)

241.

tory. But that final Chang interview, playing over and over and over again, tipped the scales.

By that Monday afternoon, it became clear that it was indeed possible for Bob to pull out of the race, but replacing him would almost certainly be challenged by the Republicans. The issue would most likely have to be decided by the New Jersey State Supreme Court.

Bob had made his decision. He called a press conference and announced he was stepping down from the campaign and would retire from the Senate at the end of the legislative session.

It was an emotional address. That Monday afternoon, speaking in front of friends and supporters, fellow political leaders, and the press, Bob spoke at some length about his career, his aspirations, and his decision to retire. Fighting back tears at times, Bob bared his soul in his own characteristic fashion: eloquent yet defiant.

As soon as Bob's announcement was made, I called Jon Corzine, Bob's New Jersey Senate colleague (and the current chair of the Democratic Senatorial Campaign Committee). It would be the first of many conversations I would have with Jon and the governor of New Jersey, Jim McGreevey, in the coming days.

Almost immediately, the Republicans argued that it was unconstitutional for Bob to resign and for the party to seek a replacement. Arguments in the press and before the court focused on process issues, emphasizing how difficult it would be to reprint ballots and insisting that the technical deadline for naming a new candidate had passed. Democrats argued that the law should be interpreted to protect the voters' right to be given a meaningful choice between candidates. Given that Bob was no longer a candidate, it was difficult to argue that forcing his name to remain on the ballot would provide the people with a legitimate choice.

Fortunately, the New Jersey Supreme Court, with virtually every one of its justices appointed by a Republican governor, sided with the argument of Democrats. The court ruled unanimously that New Jersey law allowed the party to choose a candidate to replace Bob on the ballot. Republicans sought to have the U.S. Supreme Court stay the New Jersey opinion, but the Supreme Court refused, assuring that New Jersey Democrats would be able to name a new candidate.

Congressman Bob Menendez, the highest-ranking Hispanic member of

Congress, was mentioned prominently. So was Frank Pallone, another respected House member from New Jersey. I also talked to Bill Bradley about returning to public life. He appreciated the calls he had received from many friends and admirers but was not interested in a second political career. In addition, a number of state political leaders were considered.

As the deliberations continued through the week, Frank Lautenberg called me on several occasions, offering to be helpful and reminding me of his interest in reentering public life.

Frank had been an extraordinarily successful businessman before running for the Senate. He had founded his own company and was well-known for his generous philanthropy. Elected to the Senate in 1982, Frank had served three terms before retiring voluntarily in 2000.

As the conversations with those under consideration continued, we realized we needed someone who could hit the ground running, someone who had experience as a candidate. Frank fit that bill, and he was also an experienced legislator, in contrast with the neophyte Forrester.

Ultimately, Governor McGreevey made the decision: Frank would be our candidate. As each of us called him to share the news, you could feel the enthusiasm in his voice. He was ready and more than willing. He may have been a Senate retiree, but he sounded like a man who was running for the first time.

"Let's go to work. We're going to win this thing. I promise you that!" he shouted into the telephone.

At the same time all *this* was happening, at the beginning of October, both the homeland security bill and the Iraq resolution remained unresolved. Public opinion polls showed that the economy and jobs were once again the number one concern for the majority of American voters. The stock market was continuing to plunge, the Nasdaq had hit a six-year low, unemployment was climbing steadily, and the federal budget had swung from a projected surplus of $5.5 trillion in 2001 to a projected $2 trillion deficit over ten years in 2002.

The Republicans were determined to keep the focus on war. For our part, we knew that even if we weren't able to settle the homeland security issue, it was imperative that Congress be heard on the conflict with Iraq.

Already Republicans were laying the predicate for the charge that Democratic senators, up for reelection, were resisting the President's call to arms against Iraq. Paul Wellstone's opponent in Minnesota, Norm Coleman, whose first entry into politics as a student in the 1960s was to protest the Vietnam War, assailed Paul for having what Coleman called "the worst record in the United States Senate" on the military. Back home in South Dakota, John Thune used images of Saddam Hussein to attack Tim Johnson for his vote eleven years earlier against the use-of-force resolution requested by George Bush's father before the first Gulf War.

As for the resolution to authorize the use of force in Iraq, our staffs were negotiating quite intensely with the President's people to hammer out some kind of agreement. But we weren't making much headway. Our primary concerns were fourfold.

First, we wanted assurance that any potential war in Iraq would not detract from the war on terror and our efforts to bring to justice those responsible for September 11.

Second, we wanted a commitment that the United States would have the support of a broad coalition of friends and allies in the war effort.

Third, we felt that the administration should focus its efforts less on regime change and preemption and more on Iraq's failure to live up to its international obligation to disarm its weapons of mass destruction.

Fourth, we felt it was important to remind the President that his responsibility to work with Congress did not end after Congress gave him the authorization to use force. We wanted continuing consultation from the President and assurance that the presidential team was planning for a post-Saddam Iraq. I felt that ongoing consultation with Congress was particularly important because I still had lingering doubts about the imminence of the threat posed by Saddam Hussein.

I had hoped to follow the template we had used to successfully negotiate the war on terrorism resolution about a year earlier. In that instance, the White House submitted an initial proposal that raised concerns on both sides of the aisle. The bipartisan leadership from the House and Senate sat down with the White House and successfully negotiated a final resolution that enjoyed the unanimous support of the Senate and the near unanimous support of the House.

Knowing how well the process had worked just a year earlier, I was not too concerned when the administration submitted an overly broad Iraq resolution that raised concerns from Republican and Democratic members.

We succeeded in making some changes to some of the most egregious aspects of the resolution. For example, a reference in the President's proposal that would have provided him authority to use force "to restore peace and security in the region" was struck. Such language would have given the President—or any future president—blanket authority to put U.S. forces in harm's way at any time and anywhere in the Middle East.

The administration was also persuaded to acknowledge its responsibility to report to Congress and the American people on its post-Saddam plans. But on our other bipartisan concerns, it quickly became clear that the administration would not meet us even halfway.

As a result, I tried to work with a bipartisan group of centrist senators—including Joe Biden, a Democrat, and Republican senators Dick Lugar and Chuck Hagel, who had just conducted months of hearings in the Foreign Relations Committee on U.S. efforts in Iraq.

They had crafted an alternative resolution that would have allowed us to build a larger coalition in Congress and the international community by making clear that our principal concern in Iraq was insisting that Saddam Hussein live up to his obligations under the fifteen United Nations security resolutions. The bipartisan alternative also required the administration to level with the American people about our efforts in Iraq—both before and after the war—and ensured a more robust role for Congress in the decision-making process.

But the President and his key officials, National Security Adviser Condoleezza Rice, Secretary of State Colin Powell, and Secretary of Defense Donald Rumsfeld, lobbied hard for his position. Beginning late in the day on September 30, they put through a flurry of phone calls to Biden and Lugar and Dick Gephardt as well. The President invited Dick Lugar over to the White House the next morning for a personal conference with Powell and Rice. While intense administration lobbying on such an important priority is to be expected, I was taken aback by the administration's treatment of Senator Lugar, a foreign policy expert admired by Republicans and Democrats alike. Clearly the administration was not prepared to brook any dissent on its approach from either party.

By the end of that day—or, more precisely, that evening, as the negotiations wore on until close to midnight—the President had melted away most of the bipartisan coalition that had been working on an alternative bill. He had also solidified the support of Joe Lieberman and the rest of the wing of our caucus who had been most supportive of the President's resolution from the beginning.

The following morning, October 2, our leadership met at the White House for another breakfast with the President. After that discussion, Dick Gephardt announced to the press gathered out on the White House driveway that a deal had been sealed. I had felt that we were really close to a Biden-Lugar-Hagel compromise and that their compromise reflected the uncertainty that Democrats, and more than a few Republicans, were feeling about this resolution. However, the President's intense lobbying of wavering Republican senators, combined with Dick's announcement, took the wind out of those sails.

Dick felt that what the White House was offering was "as good as we're going to get"—and he may have been right. I canceled my daily press conference in order to confer with Senator Biden and others, but it was becoming clear to all of us that there was no longer any chance for the bipartisan compromise resolution.

That afternoon, in a Rose Garden ceremony hastily pulled together by the White House staff, the President, flanked by Gephardt and Lieberman, announced that an agreement on the Iraq resolution had been reached. Trent Lott and Dennis Hastert were there, too, of course.

Once the President had melted away the bipartisan alternative, the Senate was left with two legislative options. One was to support the President's resolution as modified by our negotiations. The other was to support a resolution offered by Senator Levin that would have given the President the authority to use force only after the UN Security Council had passed a resolution expressing its support for such an action.

I chose option one and went to the Senate floor to explain why. I talked about the significant issues we were confronting—war and peace, the appropriate response to a murderous dictator, and whether we should authorize the preemptive use of American military power.

I talked about the improvements we were able to make to the administration's original proposal and Saddam Hussein's horrific record of violating UN resolutions, killing his own people, and seeking deadly weapons. I expressed my concern about the unilateral path the President first chose to take and commended President Bush for recognizing that, under the Constitution, Congress must be involved in decisions that send our young men and women into harm's way.

And then I had to announce how I would vote.

> For me, the deciding factor is my belief that a united Congress will help the President unite the world. And by uniting the world, we can increase the world's chances of succeeding in this effort, and reduce both the risks and the costs that America may have to bear.

I would support our President—but I was clear that I was giving him my support in the hope that he would use it to gain the world's support. I went on to voice my expectation that he would take five key steps before he made his final decision on using force in Iraq.

I continued:

> First and foremost, the President needs to be honest with the American people—not only about the benefits of action against Iraq, but also about the risks and the costs of such action. We are no longer talking about driving Saddam Hussein back to within his borders. We are talking about driving him from power. That is a much more difficult and complicated goal.
>
> A story in this past Sunday's *Philadelphia Inquirer* suggests that top officials in the administration "have exaggerated the degree of allied support for a war in Iraq." The story goes on to say that others in the administration "are rankled by what they charge is a tendency" by some in the administration "to gloss over the unpleasant realities" of a potential war with Iraq.
>
> A report in yesterday's *Washington Post* suggests that "an increasing number of intelligence officials, including former and current intelligence agency employees—are concerned the agency is tailoring its public stance to fit the administration's views."
>
> I do not know whether these reports are accurate. We do know from our own national experience, however, that public support

for military action can evaporate quickly if the American people come to believe they have not been given all of the facts. If that should happen, no resolution Congress might pass will be able to unify our nation. The American people expect, and success demands, that they be told both the benefits and the risks involved in any action against Iraq.

Second: We need to make it clear to the world that the reason we would use force in Iraq is to remove Saddam Hussein's weapons of mass destruction. I would prefer that this goal had been made explicit in this resolution. However, it is clear from this debate that Saddam's weapons of mass destruction are the principal threat to the United States—and the only threat that would justify the use of United States military force against Iraq. It is the threat that the President cited repeatedly in his speech to the American people Monday night. It may also be the only threat that can rally the world to support our efforts. Therefore, we expect, and success demands, that the administration not lose sight of this essential mission.

Third: We need to prepare for what might happen in Iraq after Saddam Hussein. "Regime change" is an easy expression for a difficult job. One thing we have learned from our action in Afghanistan is that it is easier to topple illegitimate regimes than it is to build legitimate democracies. We will need to do much better in post-Saddam Iraq than the administration has done so far in post-Taliban Afghanistan.

Iraq is riven by religious and ethnic differences and demoralized by a repressive government and crushing poverty. It has no experience with democracy. History tells us that it is not enough merely to hope that well-intentioned leaders will rise to fill the void that the departure of Saddam Hussein would leave. We must help create the conditions under which such a leader can arise and govern.

Unless we want to risk seeing Iraq go from bad to worse, we must help the Iraqi people rebuild their political and economic institutions after Saddam. That could take many years, and many billions of dollars—which is another reason we must build a global coalition. The American people expect, and success demands, that we plan for stability, and for economic and political progress in Iraq after Saddam.

Fourth: We need to minimize the chances that any action we may take in Iraq will destabilize the region. Throughout the Persian Gulf, there are extremists who would like nothing more than to transform a confrontation with Iraq into a wider war between the Arab world and Israel, or the Arab world and the West.

What happens if—by acting in Iraq—we undermine the government in Jordan, a critical ally and a strategic buffer between Iraq and Israel? What happens if we destabilize Pakistan and empower Islamic fundamentalists? Unlike Iraq, Pakistan already has nuclear weapons—and the means to deliver them. What happens if that arsenal falls into the hands of al-Qaeda or other extremists?

We can tell the Arab world that this is not a fight between their nations and ours. But a far better way to maintain stability in the Gulf is to demonstrate that—by building a global coalition to confront Saddam. That is why the administration must make every reasonable effort to secure a UN resolution, just as we did in 1991. With UN support, we can count a number of Arab countries as full allies. Without UN support, we can't even count on their airspace. We expect, and success demands, that any action we take in Iraq make the region more stable, not less.

Fifth and finally: We cannot allow a war in Iraq to jeopardize the war on terrorism. We are fighting terrorist organizations with global networks, we need partners around the globe. Some— including the chairman of the President's own Foreign Intelligence Advisory Board—doubt whether we can count on this continued cooperation in the war on terror if we go to war against Iraq.

I do not know if that is true. I do know, however, that the military, intelligence, and political cooperation we receive from nations throughout the world is critical to the war on terrorism. Saddam Hussein may yet target America. Al-Qaeda already has.

The American people expect, and our national security

demands, that the administration make plans to ensure that any action we take in Iraq does not distract or detract from the war on terror. If they fail to do so, any victory we win in Iraq would come at a terrible cost.

I closed my remarks by saying that the resolution represented a beginning and not an end and that I hoped the President would respond to my five concerns in the days ahead.

The only thing of which I was certain, I added, was that our men and women would be up to whatever was asked of them. I also knew that some of those men and women would be South Dakotans. A willingness to serve is a tradition that runs through South Dakota. In World War II, 68,000 South Dakotans enrolled in the armed services. Of these, 2,200 never came home—a greater percentage of World War II *deaths* than any other state. Those who *did* make it home passed on that same sense of loyalty and duty to their sons and daughters, who served in Vietnam at one of the highest rates in the nation.

As I gave the President my vote and my trust, I thought of all these things. Now, as I look back on those words, they appear to me to present a realistic assessment of the situation the Senate faced that day, as well as sound counsel about the challenges ahead. Since the Balkan Wars, we've learned that post-conflict presence is as dangerous and challenging for our armed forces as the conflicts themselves. We owe it to our troops and their families to work as hard at winning the peace as at winning the war.

With that vote on the Iraq resolution, legislative business in Congress effectively ended until after the November elections. The homeland security bill was still unresolved, and politics was clearly in the air. Making an analogy that stretched the bounds of imagination, Dick Armey compared the Senate's failure to pass the homeland security measure with the al-Qaeda network's ability to survive the U.S. assault on Afghanistan. "Al-Qaeda doesn't have a Senate," Armey told reporters. "Al-Qaeda doesn't have a Senator Daschle who has another focus. Al-Qaeda has a clear focus."

Congress officially recessed October 12. By then, President Bush had announced his plans to sweep through nearly two dozen states in the coming three weeks in order to bolster Republican congressional and gubernatorial candidates in close races. Before this barnstorming tour even began, Bush had already traveled to fifty-seven cities that year for political purposes. By comparison, President Clinton made forty-seven such trips in all of 1994—another midterm election year—and fifty-three in all of 1998.

Certainly, every president is also the leader of his political party, but this "all politics, all the time" seemed out of character with the times. At a time when we had so many serious issues to debate, I called on the President to "show the American people that you are more concerned about *their* jobs than you are about Republican jobs."

Meanwhile, knowing that a one-seat swing could once again change the entire complexion of the Senate, we—and the Republicans—were looking at nine races that would fall into the "too close to call" category: North Carolina, where Republican Elizabeth Dole was facing Erskine Bowles for the seat vacated by Jesse Helms's retirement; New Hampshire, where John Sununu defeated incumbent Republican senator Bob Smith in a primary and now faced Governor Jeanne Shaheen for Smith's vacated seat; Colorado, where Republican Wayne Allard was fighting to hold his seat against Tom Strickland in a rematch of their 1996 Senate contest; Missouri, where Jean Carnahan was facing former Republican congressman and gubernatorial candidate Jim Talent; Texas, where Phil Gramm's retirement set the stage for a race between that state's Republican attorney general, John Cornyn, and the former mayor of Dallas, Ron Kirk; Arkansas, where Republican incumbent Tim Hutchinson was challenged by that state's attorney general, Mark Pryor, whose father, David, had been a U.S. senator for eighteen years; Louisiana, where our incumbent, Mary Landrieu, was involved in a race against three Republican challengers, against whom she would have to win 50 percent of the vote to avoid a subsequent runoff election; Minnesota, where Paul Wellstone was facing Norm Coleman; and, of course, South Dakota, where Tim Johnson was up against the Bush-bolstered challenge of John Thune.

Late that month—Friday, October 25—as the campaigns entered their stretch run, I was in Gregory, a community of about a thousand people in south-central South Dakota. I'd just finished speaking to a student assembly—first- through twelfth-graders—at the Gregory school and decided to stop at the Stukel corner café, on Main Street, before taking the long drive to the Crow Creek Indian Reservation, where I was scheduled to speak that afternoon.

My day would end that evening in Springfield, a beautiful little town in the southeastern corner of the state. From there, I was planning to fly to Minnesota the next morning to take part in the wedding of one of my goddaughters in St. Paul. Her father, my uncle, Alvin Abeln, had passed away, and she'd asked if I'd give her away at the wedding.

Since I was going to be in St. Paul already, I had called Paul Wellstone and told him I'd love to campaign with him while I was there, if he'd like. "Oh, that would be great," he said. "Let's do it." So we'd set up some events for that Sunday, October 27.

I'd just finished going around to the tables in Stukel's, shaking hands and saying hello, and was sitting with a fellow named Kenny Miner. Kenny and his wife, Doris, have been close friends of mine for over twenty years. They host my annual pheasant hunt virtually every year in October, just after pheasant-hunting season opens. Their hospitality has become so well-known among my friends who join me on the hunt that their famous brunch has become nearly as popular as the hunt itself.

We had just taken a seat when a waitress came out of the kitchen and said there was a phone call for me from someone on my staff. She said it was urgent.

I didn't even know my staff knew where I was, other than somewhere in Gregory. It's almost impossible to use cell phone service in many parts of South Dakota because they're so remote. But in a small community like this, a caller can track you down pretty fast through a land line. They just dial anyone in town and ask, "Where's Senator Daschle?"

"Oh, he's at the café," someone will answer. And that's that.

I went back to the kitchen and was handed the phone. Jay Carson, my press secretary, was on the line from Sioux Falls.

"Tom," he said, "I have some bad news. We were just informed that Paul Wellstone and his wife, Sheila, were in an airplane that went down this morning in Minnesota. You're supposed to call the secretary of transportation right away. Here's the number."

I remember being numb, feeling nothing—not yet—as I dialed Norm Mineta's number. Norm confirmed that Paul and Sheila, along with their thirty-three-year-old daughter, Marcia, three campaign aides, and two pilots, had been in a twin-engine turboprop aircraft that had crashed that morning in freezing rain in a forest near Eveleth, Minnesota. There were no survivors.

I hung up, still numb, turned to my security detail, and said, "I can't believe what I just heard. Paul and Sheila Wellstone were just killed in a plane crash."

Even as I write those words now, almost a year later, it's still gut-wrenching, still so hard to believe. I remember being essentially in a daze as I went back out and shared the news with Kenny Miner. We ate quietly and reminisced about Paul. We talked about his passion, his energy, his devotion to public service. We talked about his diminutive physical stature and his boundless spirit. I remember Kenny saying, "It's not the size of the man in the fight, but the size of the fight in the man that counts." By that measure, we both agreed, Paul Wellstone was a giant.

I then left to drive on to Crow Creek, where some of my staff would be waiting to talk about what to do next. It's not a long way from Gregory to Crow Creek—about sixty miles. But there's a lot of beautiful, open prairie. A lot of time to think.

I had so many thoughts during that drive on that gray afternoon. I just couldn't believe Paul was dead. It's a tragedy for anyone to die under such circumstances, so suddenly, before his time—Paul was only fifty-eight years old. It's such a loss for everyone who knew Paul and Sheila, who loved them. But for Paul Wellstone to be gone this way was beyond stunning.

If there was ever a man who exuded sheer, heart-beating, passionate, youthful, roll-up-your-sleeves-and-grab-it-by-the-throat *life*, it was Paul Wellstone. I was lucky to know Paul not just as a colleague, but as a close personal friend. I'd been to his home in St. Paul. We'd shared so many things during our years together, personally and professionally.

Paul suffered many physical ailments. I was very concerned about them and his tendency to minimize his pain and the consequences of inattention to these problems. I would ask about them frequently. In part, they were the result of his many years of wrestling in high school and college. Paul was actually inducted into the National Wrestling Hall of Fame.

But in part, in recent years, they also stemmed from his newly diagnosed multiple sclerosis. His back, in particular, caused him severe pain. I remember one unusual Saturday morning session in the Senate. Paul had just risen to give one of his passionate speeches when a piercing pain emanating from his back shot through his body.

It was so severe that he was forced to end his speech, leave his Senate desk, and lie down on a sofa in the cloakroom. As he writhed on the sofa, Dr. John Eisold, the Capitol physician, was called to examine him.

After the exam, it was Dr. Eisold's opinion that Paul should enter the hospital immediately. But as much as Paul fought for others to have access to hospitals, he had a strong dislike of them himself. Besides, Sheila had already left for Minnesota, and he told me that he would not go to the hospital without her.

I will never forget that morning. As he lay there in pain, he was determined to get up and get back into the debate on the Senate floor. Finally, we convinced him to forgo the debate. Since he couldn't walk or even sit up, we arranged for a private aircraft to fly him to Sheila's care in Minnesota.

I think Linda and I are very, very close, but when I watched Paul and Sheila together, I saw a couple who were as close as two people could possibly be. That was one of my first thoughts as I was making that drive to Crow Creek. I thought about the fact that it was a blessing, in a way, that Sheila had died along with Paul, because, frankly, I'm not sure either of them could have survived the loss of the other. Life would seem just too unbearable.

At one point early on during that drive, my cell phone service connected and a call came through from my son, Nathan. He was calling from the office of the law firm that he had just joined a month earlier.

The connection was terrible. I could hardly make out his words. We were cut off a couple of times, but he kept calling back, and we were able to talk a little bit. He asked how I was doing. He'd heard the news and he wanted to make sure I was all right.

That's where it all broke through. I'd kept the grief inside up until then, but this was my son talking to me, my own flesh and blood, and now it just let itself out. I broke down and cried—cried as I hadn't done in I don't know how long.

I've driven over a lot of long, lonely stretches of South Dakota, but that day was the longest, loneliest drive I think I've ever had. It was chilly. Late

October. No sun, just a blanket of gray clouds overhead, with rough, rocky hillsides rolling off to each side of the highway. That barrenness is actually quite beautiful in its own harsh way, but I wasn't feeling much beauty that particular day. I was scoured out.

At one point, I looked off into the distance and saw a bald eagle sitting on the leafless branch of a tree. The eagle is a powerful symbol in the Sioux culture, and it's not that common a sight anymore, not even in such remote parts of this historically Indian land.

I remember being struck enough by the sight of that eagle that I pointed it out to my security detail. We didn't make much more of it at the time than that it was a rare, beautiful thing to see. It would not be until four days later, at Paul's memorial service, when his son David closed his heart-wrenching remarks with the story of seeing an eagle drifting above his dad's crash site, that I was jolted by the powerful sense of meaning in this moment, of some kind of connection to Paul.

It was also during that drive that feelings began to wash through me about the waves of bad fortune coming at us on the political front, one after the other. In the closing days of the campaign, Tim Johnson would have to contend with two more visits to South Dakota by President Bush, as well as solo campaign stops by Rudy Giuliani, several cabinet secretaries, and the First Lady. We were still regrouping in New Jersey after the replacement of Bob Torricelli by Frank Lautenberg. And now, with barely a week until election day, we were supposed to find someone to replace Paul Wellstone.

With all that had already happened, that was the first time I thought, This election is just not meant to be.

It was early afternoon when I got to Crow Creek. A crowd of about seven hundred people was waiting in the auditorium there. This was a big event for the community, one that had been organized for months. The plan was for me to speak and then change into running gear for a ceremonial jog with the community.

Michelle Singer, who handles Indian Affairs issues for me, took me aside as soon as I arrived and said, "We don't have to do this. We can just cancel it all." I told her no, it was okay. Everyone was there. I needed to go ahead.

Before I did, though, I got on the phone with my staff in Washington and we briefly discussed Paul's death and what that meant in terms of the Minnesota election. I'd thought about it during the drive, whether Paul's name would stay on the ballot, as Mel Carnahan's had in Missouri, or whether a replacement candidate would have to be found.

I had thought about Walter Mondale as the obvious first choice, having no idea what the law required in circumstances like this or if Fritz might be willing or even available. I did know that Fritz, who had served in the Senate from 1964 to 1976, had often stated publicly that those years were by far the happiest years of his political life. He was practicing law now, at age seventy-four, far from retired. I had a strong hunch that Paul's family and his staff would also want Fritz to step in. But I wasn't certain about any of this. I had so many questions, with so few answers and so little time to find those answers.

It turned out that my staff had been thinking along the same lines as I had. They told me they were in the process of checking on Minnesota's state law concerning this situation. Everyone agreed that if Paul was to be replaced, it ought to be by Fritz Mondale—as long, of course, as Paul's family and staff felt the same way. My staff felt it was important that I call Fritz immediately, so I did. I was able to reach him in Minneapolis. We spoke for just a few minutes.

We talked about what we knew of the circumstances surrounding Paul's death. We also talked about how incredible it was that we were even having the conversation. And how much Paul and Sheila meant to both of us.

It was then that I raised the question of whether he would consider picking up the campaign to fill in for Paul. I said that I didn't want an answer then. I wanted him to think about it, and I wanted to give him another call later that night when I would be in my motel room.

We agreed to talk later, although Fritz was reluctant to talk about it at all until he had spoken to the Wellstone family and some time had passed.

The speech I gave that afternoon was one of the most difficult of my career. The audience was composed largely of reservation schoolchildren, many of whom were already aware of the news about Paul. I could barely control my emotions, referring to what had just happened that morning, and I could see that their feelings were just as strong. There were a lot of tears that afternoon, a lot of empathy.

I talked about Billy Mills, the Native American Olympian, and about a young South Dakota Sioux girl named SuAnne Big Crow, who had been a star basketball player in high school and had died in a tragic automobile accident.

The connection between these Indian athletes and Paul Wellstone was natural—a role model for the young, a person who followed his passion, who committed his life to what he believed in, and now, so shockingly, a person whose life had been cut short much too soon.

The connection I felt with that audience of Indian children that afternoon was amazing, the sense of loss they allowed me to share with them by feeling that same loss themselves. Here were these people whose needs are so great, giving me what *I* needed so much at that moment, which was the gift of their empathy. There's no way to describe what that generosity of spirit meant to me.

So I finished my talk. Then the kids came up and surrounded me, hugging me with smiles and with tears. Afterward we took that ceremonial run, and then I changed and got back in the car for the drive to Chamberlain, a town right on the Missouri River, south of Crow Creek. From there we flew on to Springfield, where I'd be spending the night.

When I got to Springfield that evening, I checked into the Wagon Wheel Motel, a little place with just six rooms or so, the kind of motel people would stay at on cross-country drives back in the sixties, before interstates and franchise chains began putting mom-and-pop places out of business. Of course, the owners were there and wanted my stay to be as comfortable as possible, especially given the circumstances.

I pulled myself up onto the room's small kitchen counter and immediately began making phone calls. By then my staff had learned that we had four days to find a replacement for Paul, according to Minnesota law. It was imperative now that I get through to Fritz as soon as I could. I began dialing several numbers I'd been given, and after a few tries, I was able to reach him.

I had been talking to several of my colleagues since I arrived in Crow Creek. One of those calls was with Ted Kennedy. Ted related a conversation he had had with David McCullough, the noted historian, about John Adams and his son, John Quincy. McCullough noted that throughout their lives, the two Adamses served their country in many capacities. In all their years, neither had ever turned down a request to serve, yet again, in public life. According to Ted, McCullough reasoned that this fact was a significant part of the basis for the Adamses' greatness—their willingness to serve, especially in times of adversity.

When I reached Fritz, I repeated the story Ted had told me. I argued that this could also be said of Fritz Mondale. Now, his party and his state needed him again. And I sincerely hoped he would consider becoming a candidate.

Fritz repeated his desire to give it some time so that everyone could stay focused on Paul's loss, the upcoming funerals, and the family survivors. He also reiterated that he would be talking to Paul's family the following day and that their views on the matter would carry great weight.

The next morning—Saturday, October 26—I flew to Minnesota for my goddaughter Denise's wedding. I was able to set aside the feelings of grief I had over Paul's death in order to share in the joy of Denise's marriage. I gave her away at the ceremony, was able to say a few words at the wedding dinner, and then went back to my hotel in St. Paul to get on the phone with my staff in Washington and in Sioux Falls.

Arrangements had been made by then for me to visit the Wellstone campaign headquarters the next morning. I hadn't yet spoken to Fritz again.

First thing the following morning, Sunday, I spoke to Paul's sons, David and Mark, on the phone. I called them from my hotel room. They were on their way to the crash site.

The conversations didn't last long. The quality of the phone line was not very good. I told them how deeply saddened we were and how much I loved their father. I said that I knew I was speaking for every member of the Senate in expressing heartfelt condolences to them and their family.

We agreed to talk later about funeral arrangements and all of the political questions we were now forced to face. They reported that they already had had a good conversation with Walter Mondale. We hung up, agreeing to talk again soon.

Then I went over to Wellstone headquarters. There must have been about forty of Paul's staff and volunteers there when I arrived. Many of them were still crying. Most looked as though they hadn't slept since Friday. I said just a few short words. I'd brought with me a poem a very dear friend of mine used when he lost his daughter. Its words have always been so beautiful to me. And I thought they reflected exactly the message I wanted to impart to Paul's staff.

> *Do not stand at my grave and weep. I am not there. I do not sleep.*
> *I am the thousands of winds that blow . . . the glint of diamonds in the snow.*
> *I am the sunlight on ripened grain. I am the gentle autumn rain.*
> *When you awaken in the morning hush, I am the swift uplifting rush.*
> *Of quiet birds circled flight, I am the soft star that shines at night.*
> *So do not stand at my grave and cry. I am not there. I did not die.*

When I was done, we all hugged. Then I went into a small back room with Paul's campaign manager, Jeff Blodgett. We sat down and talked about Mondale stepping in and the Wellstone campaign's willingness to do all they could to make it happen. Then we turned to the subject of a memorial service.

I asked Jeff, "What kind of a service are you going to do? When are you thinking about doing it?"

"Well," he said, "we're not sure yet. We don't really have the specifics, but what we're thinking about is having a big sort of a Wellstonian event rather than a somber, subdued, church-focused, more traditional service."

We then discussed what kind of a campaign would make the most sense, given the extraordinary timing and circumstances here. Jesse Ventura was already talking about his prerogative, as Minnesota's governor, to immediately appoint a replacement for Paul. If Ventura did that, this individual would serve out the remainder of Paul's term through what was left of the 107th Congress after the election.

This was significant, because there would still be important issues to be resolved after the election but before new senators were sworn in, not the least of which was the homeland security legislation. If Paul, as a Democrat, was replaced by either a Republican or an independent—the likely choice of Ventura, who himself, of course, is an independent—then we would lose our one-seat Senate majority, which would massively affect the balance of power and the legislation that ensued in the coming "lame duck" session.

I didn't really know Jesse Ventura. I had met him a couple of times, once with Bob Kerrey in Bob's Senate office in Washington. Paul had little time for the governor. They had many public and private confrontations over the years both were in office. The thought of Ventura picking someone to replace Paul seemed such a bitter irony.

By the time I left the Wellstone headquarters that day, there was a throng of several dozen reporters and television cameras outside the building. I gave a brief impromptu press conference, then went to the airport to fly to St. Louis, where I was scheduled to join Jean Carnahan at a campaign event. I'd spoken to Jean since the crash, and her grief over Paul's death was compounded by the memory of Mel's plane crash two years earlier. She had canceled her entire schedule the previous day—Saturday. But now she was back at it, and our events—a rally in an African American neighborhood, followed by a big fund-raiser—were still on.

Early Monday morning, I flew out to Iowa for an appearance with Tom Harkin. Then, that afternoon, I flew back to Washington, where I learned that the Wellstone memorial service would be held the following evening, Tuesday, October 29, in St. Paul. I hadn't seen Linda since I'd left five days before. We always talk on the telephone at the beginning of every travel day and at the end of the day when I have arrived at my room.

So we had spent a good deal of time on the telephone talking about the accident, about Paul and Sheila, and about our many memories of when we were with them.

But Paul's death reminded me again of how fragile our lives are, how easy it is to leave home and take for granted that you will walk through the front door again, yet how the twists and turns of life sometimes bring death when you are least prepared for it, moved both of us to a long, emotional embrace as I walked through the door this time.

The following day, Linda and I boarded one of three military aircraft waiting at Andrews Air Force Base to carry roughly two dozen current and former senators, along with several spouses and staff, to St. Paul. My plane included Ted Kennedy, Pete Domenici, Arlen Specter, Jim Jeffords, Chris Dodd, Paul Sarbanes, and John Glenn. Along the way, my staff informed me that the memorial was going to be held at the University of Minnesota's Williams Arena, where the school's basketball team plays its home games.

"The Barn," as it's called, seats twenty thousand people, and I remember Jim Jeffords remarking that he had no doubt the place would be filled. Twenty thousand. I couldn't imagine that many people turning out on such short notice. How in the world, I thought, do you prepare logistically for something that large in just twenty-four hours? And how do you do it when everyone is so stricken with grief?

We arrived at the arena at 6:00 P.M., an hour and a half after the doors were opened to the public, and the gymnasium was indeed packed wall to wall and floor to rafters with mourners, many wearing the Wellstone color of green that Paul had painted his fabled campaign bus—the bus that was now parked outside the arena in the cold Minnesota night, in silent tribute to Paul. The crowd was anything but subdued. They were crying but smiling, cheering, and chanting as a rap singer onstage boomed her lyrics through the public address system. Just as Jeff Blodgett had predicted, this was a "Wellstonian" event.

The service wasn't set to begin for another half hour, so we were led to a large upstairs reception room crowded shoulder to shoulder with senators and congressmen past and present, Republican and Democratic, some of whom hadn't seen one another in years, many of whom had seen one another just a couple of weeks ago, but acknowledged that, under these circumstances, it *seemed* as if it had been years. There were a lot of tears in that room, along with a lot of hugging and greeting.

Bill and Hillary Clinton were both there, as were Tipper and Al Gore. I was particularly impressed that Trent and Tricia Lott were there, too. In fact, I said something about it to them when we were standing, waiting to be introduced to the crowd, as we walked into the large auditorium.

Trent said, "I'm here because Paul would have done the same for me."

Finally, about 7:15 P.M., we began filing down to the auditorium. By then an overflow crowd of thousands more had been directed to a nearby sports pavilion, where the event was broadcast live, and that venue, too, was filled to capacity. The crowd in the arena went crazy as a video screen suspended above the stage showed Bill and Hillary Clinton taking their seats, along with Al Gore and Ted and Vicki Kennedy. When Walter Mondale appeared, the place erupted with the loudest applause of the night. Moments later, Trent and Tricia descended to their seats and were showered with boos and catcalls from the crowd.

I felt very bad for Trent and Tricia. I think Paul Wellstone would have felt bad, too. He would not have abided the people responding that way—his people or anyone else's.

That was one of Paul's great strengths—he could disagree with someone without being disagreeable. If he'd had his way, the crowd would have cheered Trent Lott for coming to pay his respects to Paul. Trent actually took it quite well, smiling and waving in the face of the negative response, but I knew how he felt. I've been booed before, and I know that you try not to take it too seriously, you try not to take it personally, but it still stings.

Jesse Ventura, who was sitting two seats to my right—and who got a lukewarm greeting at best from the crowd—was visibly upset, really outraged at the cascade of booing for Trent. And I have to say, while I understand the emotion that fueled that response from the crowd, the booing was not in the spirit of Paul, and on this night it was inappropriate and wrong.

We all know what happened from that point on, how powerfully emotional the testimonies from Paul's colleagues, friends, and family were, how the political fervor of some of the speeches sounded as much like old-fashioned stem-winders as they did eulogies, how the crowd's numerous outbursts of cheering and foot stomping gave the event the feel of a campaign rally, how one of the speakers urged several Republicans in the audience to drop their party affiliation for the moment and work for Wellstone's reelection—or that of his replacement.

You'd have to be almost inhuman not to have been infected by the waves of pure, raw emotion sweeping through that arena that night. The people onstage, one after another, were pouring their hearts out, and the audience was pouring theirs back. In this day and age where so many political "events" are so controlled and staged that virtually nothing spontaneous or unscripted occurs, it was like an invigorating breath of fresh air to witness and feel such raw, genuine passion.

Tom Harkin's eulogy, in particular, was both powerful and memorable. He and Paul were very close friends. They had known each other for a long time. Paul's loss was particularly painful for Tom. And you could feel the raw emotion in his words that night.

It was, in a way, almost a laboratory experiment, a litmus test of how well the old-fashioned school of "yellow dog" Democrat liberalism would actually play in today's America. The speakers and the crowd let it all hang out that night in St. Paul, representing and appealing to the liberal "core," to that part of the "base" of our party who exulted in the spirit of the event.

But even as I felt the joy of that enthusiasm, I was uncomfortable with the blatant politicization that occurred, not to mention the booing. I knew it was natural, for this audience, in this place, under these circumstances, to unfurl the flag of their beliefs and to express them this way, to say, "Here's where we stand; here's who we are."

But I knew it could easily be seen as alienation, polarization, or sheer rudeness by others. And others were watching. I knew this spectacle was not going to help our cause—or Paul's—not with a national audience watching live on C-SPAN and with the nation's press corps there to record the event for their front-page stories the next morning.

I wasn't surprised to see Jesse Ventura stand up midway through the evening, lean over to speak to Ted Kennedy, and then walk—or, more accurately, stomp—out. He didn't acknowledge or say good-bye to anyone else around him. He was very upset, very exercised. Trent and Tricia left early as well, although their reason was practical—a pilot and plane were waiting to fly them back to Mississippi that night, and they had to get to the airport in time to take off.

By the time we had boarded our own plane back to D.C. late that evening, I was pretty certain that what had transpired that night was going to turn out badly for us. The passengers on that flight back included Al and Tipper Gore, Chris Dodd, Byron and Kim Dorgan, Barbara Mikulski, and Maria Cantwell.

At one point, Chris, Byron, and I were sitting together, talking about how anyone who knew Paul or his politics would understand and appreciate how his spirit was reflected in that evening's enthusiasm. But we knew how many people did not know Paul and did not share his politics, and we agreed that among those people—millions of them across America—we were going to pay a price for what had just happened.

"We may just have lost the Minnesota Senate race," Chris said.

"That may not be all," Byron replied.

And we did.

Jesse Ventura vented his wrath by following through before the election with the nomination of a replacement—a Minnesota independent named Dean Barkley—to fill Paul Wellstone's Senate seat for the duration of the calendar year, which meant we would lose our one-seat majority status for the remainder of the 107th Congress.

As for Trent, I called him first thing the next morning and apologized for the ill-treatment he had received.

"That's all right," Trent said. "I know how crowds sometimes can get carried away. Although I was a little taken aback by it all.

"I hope you know," he added, "we didn't leave because we were booed. Our pilots were bumping up against their time constraints and we had to get back for them."

But the greatest effect by far of that memorial service was an immediate plunge in the polls for Democratic candidates across the nation. Not only did Walter Mondale slip overnight from eight points up to ten points down in polls that were already being taken in Minnesota despite the fact that he had not yet officially announced his candidacy, but fully half the nation's registered voters said the service made them less likely to vote for a Democrat in the coming election.

In South Dakota, where Tim Johnson's people were going door-to-door all over the state, reports were coming back that more than a few South Dakotans were saying, "I am so outraged at what happened in Minnesota that I *was* going to vote for Tim, but now I'm going to vote Republican." And in Missouri, where Paul's death had evoked a warm feeling toward Jean Carnahan, his memorial service flipped that feeling 180 degrees.

It was the political equivalent of a terrible storm . . . a hurricane or a tornado.

The damage in its wake can be enough to dramatically change the political landscape and end political lives. I've been through some of them myself. They are devastating.

Our pollsters told us it is very rare that polling can change as dramatically as it did in just twenty-four hours in Minnesota. An eighteen-point shift in that short a period of time is almost unheard of.

But colleagues who watched it on television reported to me that they were not surprised. Like me, they were torn by the irony of it all. A tribute to Paul's life and political success develops unexpectedly into an event that triggered his campaign's ultimate failure.

I remember talking to Fritz Mondale in the afternoon the following day. He, too, was shocked at the rapid turn of events. He had already personally experienced the vitriol among many Minnesotans that morning.

"We don't have much time to turn it around," he said as he hung up the phone.

With less than a week now to go until the election, it was still impossible to tell whether we would emerge victors once November 5th came and the votes were all counted. We still had nine races too close to call, and the press was having just as hard a time making predictions. What concerned me were the distractions capturing the voters' attention—the brewing war with Iraq, the hunt for the "D.C. sniper," whose nightmarish twenty-three-day killing spree had just ended late that October. It was hard to get people to focus on prescription drug costs or the safety of Social Security or even the economy in the face of such sensational news.

Which was just fine by Republican strategists. As for the voters who *did* care about issues like health care or corporate reform, the Republicans were able to blur the lines between their stand on these issues and ours, so that it was hard for most voters to tell the difference. This perceived lack of a difference between the two parties was accentuated by the Republicans' ability to focus on two bedrock issues—the Bush tax cut and the Iraq resolution—and to point out how many Democrats had voted *with* the Republicans on these bills.

The press picked up on all of this and dutifully reported it. In the week prior to the election, editorials across the nation decried what they called the "homogenization" of American politics, the "dulling down" of the differences between the two parties, and the consequent "lack of interest" among the American voting public. More than one pundit opined that voters in this election had "a choice between beige and brown." What excitement there might be on election day, they predicted, would be a slew of cliff-hanger races between candidates who were pretty much alike.

How anyone could say that Saxby Chambliss was anything like Max Cleland, or that Walter Mondale was anything like Norm Coleman, was beyond me. But it was true that as election day neared, there was no telling how all this would shake out in the voting booths. For once I actually agreed with Newt Gingrich, when he was quoted in the November 3 issue of the *New York Times* as saying, "The correct analysis on the Sunday before this election is, 'Who knows?'"

Because so many races that November 5 were so close, and because our pollsters were still predicting favorable results right up to the end, I went into that election day feeling something I normally never allow myself to feel in such a situation—high expectations. My head was filled with notions of our party picking up a number of Senate seats by the time that day was done.

Even midway through that afternoon, as I camped with my staff in our hotel suite in Sioux Falls, fielding and making calls to our candidates all over the country, I was still optimistic. Jean Carnahan, who was trailing in the early Missouri returns when I spoke to her at lunch, assured me she was "going to pull a Harry Truman." In North Carolina, where Erskine Bowles and Elizabeth Dole were virtually deadlocked, voter turnout among African Americans was reported as being extremely high—"at presidential election levels," according to one network—which we thought boded well for Erskine.

In Minnesota, where Mondale and Coleman were running neck and neck, Jesse Ventura was virtually preempting election news coverage by doing a series of live television interviews with the networks, lashing out at both the Democrats and the Republicans for not including an independent candidate in the only televised debate between Mondale and Coleman. He was particularly upset with Mondale, whom he felt had set the terms of that debate. It was that exclusion that had prompted Ventura to interrupt the telecast of that debate by announcing that he had named Dean Barkley as an interim U.S. senator.

Late that afternoon, I conducted a conference call with staff members in South Dakota and back in Washington. By then, almost all the tightest races were beginning to tip in the Republicans' direction. I had just gotten off the phone with Max Cleland in Atlanta, where Max told me a massive rainstorm was sweeping through that area. This is never good news for Democrats, whose number of supporters among the poor and people with disabilities—people who would have particular trouble getting to the polls in such weather—is generally much higher than that for the Republicans.

We later learned that while we were able to turn out our vote at respectable levels in Georgia, we didn't come close to what the Republicans were able to do in most of rural Georgia as a result of their effort to politicize Governor Roy Barnes's efforts to change the state flag.

By the time the sun set, just past 6:00 P.M., the networks' first projected result was in—Mitch McConnell was reported the winner in Kentucky, beating Lois Weinberg. It wasn't pleasant to hear that news, but few people had realistically expected Lois to defeat an ensconced incumbent like McConnell. As the night drew on, however, and the returns on the other races continued to come in, I could feel my earlier optimism fading. Race after race was beginning to look like a Republican victory.

I don't think it was a coincidence that that evening's election coverage almost completely overshadowed what would have been major breaking news on any other day, as well as a major embarrassment for the Bush administration: Harvey Pitt had announced his resignation earlier that day as chairman of the SEC. What better way to bury an announcement like that than to make it on election day? And it was indeed buried—the readers of most of the nation's newspapers the next morning had to turn a few pages to find the news of Pitt stepping down. Almost all the front pages were devoted entirely to coverage of the election.

In a way, the Pitt story was a perfect reflection of this election. Just as the Republicans and the Bush administration had been able, during virtually the entirety of the 107th Congress, to divert the nation's attention from the hamstrung and ailing economy, one of the most visible symbols of that failed economy was able to orchestrate his own departure at a time when most of America's attention was drawn elsewhere.

By 10:00 P.M. I knew it was over. I went downstairs to face the music—I was scheduled for the next hour to do interviews with all three major networks plus FOX and CNN. As I made my way through the crowds still swelling the downstairs auditorium and hallways, I felt like the guest of honor at my own funeral. The heartfelt faithfulness of the people who stopped to shake my hand, to give me a hug, to tell me we were still going to somehow pull this thing out, was simply incredible. It meant so much to me in the face of the facts, which were now undeniable.

We had lost. While the margins of loss were small, the loss of the majority was big. And now it was time to face the music.

End of chpt. 9

Epilogue grest to fg. 276 = 10/4/3

I WAS RAISED CATHOLIC, and my Catholicism was a huge part of my life when I was a young man. I remember riding my bike to mass every morning before school—even in the dead of winter. It was so cold on some of those winter mornings in South Dakota that I'd have to stop along the way—at the Laundromat, at the drugstore—to warm my face and hands so that I could ride the next quarter-mile before turning numb again.

When I finally arrived at Sacred Heart Church, there was always something in the certainty of walking into the hush of that holy place and feeling the presence of something greater than myself—the sweep and scope of eternity—that was both comforting and, in the classic sense of the term, awesome. It still is.

For many people—not just for those in the clergy, but for the millions of men, women, and children who volunteer and serve others through faith-affiliated groups and activities—the church is a calling, a way of serving something beyond themselves, a way of helping others. For me, the one thing that conjures many of the same sensations as walking into a church is stepping onto the Senate floor to tackle the issue of the day. The majesty, the richness, the history, and sometimes the hush of the Senate chamber is akin to that of a sacred place. It is my secular temple.

Nearly a year has passed since that difficult election night in South Dakota, and as I look out from my Senate office, I see a world that is both fundamentally changed and fundamentally the same as it was on that cold November evening.

In Iraq, as virtually everyone expected, we won a complete and total military victory. The humanitarian and diplomatic aftermath, however, has become even more challenging, in its own ways, than the military battle. The weapons of mass destruction that were relied on so heavily as the justification for an invasion have yet to be found.

Al-Qaeda has reemerged with devastating bombings in Saudi Arabia and Morocco. Afghanistan is tilting dangerously toward chaos and disorder. In the Middle East, what we hoped would be a road map to peace is fraught with yet more terrorism, distrust, and violence.

Domestically, the economy continues to stagger despite the fact that we have passed yet another massive tax cut—the second in two years. The September 11 commission continues to find its investigation into the circumstances preceding those terrorist attacks slowed by the Bush administration's intransigence. And even as I write these words, the FBI has drained a pond in Maryland with the hope that it will yield clues as to who was responsible for the anthrax attacks on my office and others.

Politically, the Senate remains nearly as closely divided today—with a one-seat difference separating the two parties—as it was in the wake of the election of 2000. And both parties have one eye on the next elections one year away.

Still, there is no denying that the 2002 elections dealt the Democratic Party as a whole, and me individually, a staggering blow. A lot of people tried to console me, including, quite incredibly, some of my colleagues in our caucus who had been casualties of that election.

Max Cleland called after the election to tell me that it wasn't my fault. Not long after that, as if to underscore the fact that life does indeed carry on, Max, a lifelong bachelor, honored me by making me one of the first people he telephoned to share the news that he had gotten engaged to be married.

At our first caucus meeting shortly after the election, Robert Byrd surprised me by making a motion that I be reelected as Democratic leader by acclamation, and the caucus responded with their unanimous support. It was a truly gratifying moment for me, and I will always be grateful to Senator Byrd and the caucus for their confidence in me.

Nevertheless, I did feel our electoral losses acutely. In the Senate, as leader, when a colleague loses an election, the leader loses a comrade, a fellow foot soldier, and, in many cases, the assuring presence of a very close friend. Each of these losses settles in its own way, in its own time. There are moments now when I wish more than anything that we still had Paul Wellstone to speak with that unmistakable voice—a voice that was not afraid to stand by itself. Every time I realize that Paul isn't here, I feel the pain of his death anew.

But life does indeed go on, for a politician as for anyone else. Politicians are often described as being driven by ambition or competitiveness or a hunger for power or fame. I would describe myself as driven more by a restlessness to make a difference and the need for a challenge than anything else. When I've worked at something for a long time, the restlessness begins to stir and I start looking for ways to make more of a difference, in some new, different way.

When I look back on my life, there are a number of clear moments at which I had decisions to make. The first time was when I was in the Air Force and I had to decide whether or not to make a career of military service. The second time was when I decided to run for Congress. A third time was when I first decided to run for the Senate. A fourth was when I chose to run for leader, in 1994.

In the aftermath of the 2002 elections, I felt that same restlessness beginning to stir again. While I continued to take great pride and satisfaction in serving the people of South Dakota, being so centrally involved in the monumental chain of events that occurred during the 107th Congress underscored my appreciation of the power of the president to individually shape America's agenda and to advance or hinder the aspirations of millions of Americans in a way that no senator, not even a Senate leader, ever could. Now, for the first time in my career, I seriously considered seeking that position myself.

I chose to wait until after those elections to make my decision. I did so for a number of reasons. First, I knew that the campaign for the majority in the Senate would be my political priority in 2002. Second, because it was, I didn't want to be perceived as one who was simply, and perhaps not so subtly, campaigning for myself as I traveled the country and appeared on the talk shows. Finally, I felt that the results of the election might be a factor in my decision. A successful campaign to retain or build our majority in the Senate would propel me into a better position as a candidate for president. An unsuccessful one would not.

One of my earliest political memories growing up in South Dakota was putting up signs for John F. Kennedy during the 1960 election. For me, as for so many others, Kennedy embodied not only youth, vigor, and optimism about the future's possibilities, but the outlandish hope that a Catholic man could be elected president. Now, forty-two years later, I was considering that dream for myself. I began talking to as many people as I could for advice on what would be required of my family and me.

I talked to my colleague Tom Harkin, who told me that at age fifty-five

I was at just the right time in my life for a run—if I was much older, he said, I wouldn't have the energy for it. I talked to both Bill and Hillary Clinton. What Hillary said in a long conversation we had less than a month after the election really struck me. She told me that a presidential campaign is a "glorious adventure." "You can't imagine," she said, "how big and wide and incredible this country is. It's something you will experience in a way unlike any other on a presidential campaign."

Linda and I discussed the prospect of a presidential run with many of our closest friends and supporters from South Dakota and around the nation. I think it is accurate to say that most hoped that I would stay in the Senate and remain as the Democratic leader. All, however, pledged their enthusiastic support should I make the decision to run.

I also began talking to political operatives who had been involved in national campaigns before. Each warned me of the extraordinary effort that would be required to raise the necessary campaign resources to be successful. Their estimate was that a successful candidate this time would need to raise approximately $1 million a week. George Bush has already exceeded that mark.

They also reminded us that our public as well as our personal lives would assume a new level of public interest and be subject to greater media attention far beyond anything we had experienced so far.

I spent a lot of time talking to Linda about the personal cost of living in such a fishbowl environment. Lack of privacy is one of the downsides of political life, especially at this level. In part for this reason, Linda had expressed reluctance initially at the thought of my running for president. But to her great credit, she ultimately decided that if I decided to run, she would not only support my decision, but quit her job and work full-time to see that we were successful. Her willingness to do so was a gift I will always treasure.

Our children, too, were very supportive, saying they would embrace whatever course I chose. Kelly and her husband, Eric Chader, were becoming very engaged in the many issues that had to be addressed early on. Nathan and his wife, Jill, also spent an increasing amount of time thinking through and talking about how the campaign might be run. And Lindsay, our youngest daughter, fresh out of college, was ready to sign up and devote much of her effort to mobilizing college campuses—something she correctly argues needs greater emphasis if we are to encourage young adults to participate in the democratic process.

On December 21, I convened a meeting of senior staff to continue discussing the possibility of running for president. I said that I thought I started with a 10 percent chance of winning, but that those odds, along with circumstances, would likely change remarkably, and in unforeseen ways, during a campaign and that they would absolutely be different by the time of the election itself.

I pointed out my track record of facing long odds and working doubly hard to defeat them. I talked about the "pain being worth the gain," in terms of the price Linda and the rest of my family would pay with the loss of their privacy. Their willingness to stand in the spotlight of public attention and endure pressure of an unimaginable magnitude to give me an opportunity to make a difference for our nation is a sacrifice only someone who has experienced that reality can appreciate.

My staff's greatest concern, it turned out—more than the daunting logistical or financial or organizational challenges that lay ahead—was whether my family and I truly appreciated and were prepared for the virtual hand-to-hand combat that a modern presidential campaign entails. It gets tough. At times it can get ugly. And, as John McCain saw, it can get highly personal. But I firmly believe that it is not necessary to compromise one's integrity or convictions to run for president.

I emerged from that meeting both sobered and exhilarated. The response from my staff was overwhelmingly encouraging. They scolded me for estimating my chances of winning as only 10 percent. They counseled me to forget decision trees and mathematical formulas and to go with my gut, with my instincts.

A week later, in the week between the Christmas and New Year's holidays, I called another senior staff meeting. Linda was there as well. I looked at all of them gathered around the conference table and I welcomed them to what could be the first meeting of the "Daschle for President" campaign. I thanked Pete Rouse by name. Pete has been my chief of staff for eighteen years, but we have known each other much longer than that—since the mid-1970s, when we were Senate staffers together for Jim Abourezk. Without Pete's counsel, I said, I wouldn't have been in a place to even consider running for president, and I wanted him to know that I recognized that.

I then turned to Linda and said, "And this girl here . . . " That's when the magnitude of the sacrifice she was willing to make—the scope of the undertaking we were both considering—hit me fully, and I choked up.

I then said a few words about what I thought we could accomplish for South Dakota and America if I ran and won. The room was suffused with a sense of possibility. The mood of the meeting then shifted from enthusiastic to pedestrian as we began to discuss how I would announce my intention to run. I was very clear that this campaign would be based in South Dakota, not Washington.

I was not about to concede South Dakota. South Dakota is home to me. It is a huge part of who I am and how I view the world, and I intended to make South Dakota's values a big part of my campaign. We decided that I would go to South Dakota to spend a few days talking to longtime friends and supporters and feeling them out before making a final decision.

It was a very gratifying experience. Friends from all over the state gathered in the homes of other friends to talk about the prospect of my running for president. Many of the same concerns that I had heard earlier from friends and political advisers were concerns I heard again at home.

I responded that I knew a presidential campaign would be uphill. But I reminded them that I have faced uphill battles before, including my first election to the House of Representatives, my first statewide election against the other congressman when we were redistricted to one seat, my first Senate race against a popular incumbent, and my leadership race in 1994.

I said I believed this country needed new strength. It was a strength that only greater emphasis on education, health, children, and the economy could provide. It would be the call for new strength that would define a Daschle presidential candidacy.

I had thought a lot about that. On many days, as I pondered this decision, I thought about how much more I could do for my state as president. I thought of the opportunities that I would have to address the unique needs of rural states like ours. I thought of the message I would bring to the nation about agriculture, rural health care, education, and our rural economy. And I shared those thoughts with my South Dakota friends.

By the end of that week, I was prepared to enter the race to become the forty-fourth president of the United States. By the end of that meeting, we had decided that I would go to South Dakota to spend a few days talking to long-time friends and supporters and feeling them out before making my final decision.

I got back to Washington Monday night and was immediately besieged by calls about how we were going to start the new congressional work *"anathema"* →

period. I was inundated by requests from members of my caucus for meetings and return phone calls.

My colleagues' concerns ranged from the national—"What is our legislative agenda when we return?"—to the personal—"I want a different committee assignment." I've always said that one of the reasons I've been able to serve as leader of a fractious Democratic caucus that truly spans the ideological spectrum is that I've never given any of my colleagues reason to question my motives. They know I am there to serve South Dakota and the nation, and to look out for their best interests. As I talked to a number of them individually about running for president, I began to see that some felt that, as both a leader and a candidate, I was making decisions based on my own future rather than on their best interests. Those sentiments were anathema to my philosophy of Senate leadership.

I was greatly concerned about this development. While I had foreseen some conflict, it troubled me deeply that it was emerging so quickly. I hadn't thought that my effectiveness as leader in the Senate would be compromised by a run for the presidency. In fact, some of my friends and staff had argued that it would be *enhanced*. I thought for a while about ways to quell such talk.

For my part, I had some real concerns about my ability to lead the caucus and run for president simultaneously. Dick Gephardt and I had discussed this very question. He had decided that it would be too hard to do both and resigned as leader to run full-time for president. Already I saw that leading my caucus in a new Senate that had an aggressive and extremely empowered Republican majority would be a significant undertaking. Important issues were going to be decided in the new, 108th Congress—the future of Medicare and Social Security, America's role in the world, the war on terror, the future of public education, and access to and the cost of health care. As the reality of the Senate resuming its work began to set in, I thought more about those issues and about the critical role *this* Senate would play in shaping them.

And that Monday night, the more I thought about giving up my South Dakota Senate seat, the more I began to realize that I wasn't ready to give up on being South Dakota's senator—or a Senate Democratic leader—and that the tremendously important decisions that would be made between now and November 2004, both in South Dakota and in the country, were ones in which I wanted very much to play a part.

Though a run for the presidency beckoned, I felt that I was needed right here, right now, and it was looking as though a choice had to be made. What had felt so right while I was talking to my staff and to South Dakotans began to feel wrong as I talked to my colleagues and as I sat in my study at night in total solitude.

The inner turmoil I felt over this decision was excruciating. I had trouble sleeping at night. Finally, late on the evening of Monday, January 6, the night before the 108th Congress was to convene, after yet another round of weighing all the arguments, I made one of the biggest decisions of my political career. I would not run.

I went into our bedroom to talk to Linda, who was already sleeping. I woke her and said, "Sweetheart, I just don't think I'm ready to do this yet. I've decided that I want to make my decision public tomorrow." She was startled and challenged me to determine if I was sure that this was what I wanted to do. I reaffirmed to her that it was.

I called Pete Rouse. I told him the same thing and asked if we could meet immediately in the morning to discuss our strategy for announcing the decision. He sounded somewhat surprised. But, characteristically, he went into "organization mode" and began to list the actions we needed to consider first thing in the morning.

The next morning, my senior staff was in our office's conference room, debating ways to drum up support among our caucus for me to stay on as leader while making a run for the presidency, when Pete walked in on their conversation.

"We're solving that problem right now," he said. Then he turned around and left, closing the door behind him.

The staff was nonplussed. They had no idea what was going on. I had just arrived, and Pete joined me in my Capitol office. Sitting beneath a Gilbert Stuart portrait of George Washington, we discussed what needed to be done to announce my decision.

Ten minutes later, Pete returned to his meeting with the staff.

"We're pulling the plug," he announced.

"On what?" said my counsel, Mark Childress. "On staying as leader?"

"No," answered Pete. "On running."

The room was completely silent. Shock would probably be the best word to describe what my staff felt at that moment. Imagine prepping a team for a championship ball game, drawing the game plan, going through every play, preparing, achieving the mind-set of total commitment, and then, minutes before game time, as the players gather in the locker room, ready to take the field, walking in and telling them the game's off. That's probably what this felt like.

As much as a surprise as it may have been to my family, friends, and staff, I felt a quiet peace inside for the first time in weeks. I hoped that I could transmit that internal peace to each of the people I cared about. While I knew that I had to find a way to try to do so, I also knew that they would be confident of the correctness of the decision if I exuded confidence in it myself.

We drafted a statement, and I then held a brief press conference. Everyone was extremely gracious about my decision, and I was gratified to receive calls from my colleagues considering their own presidential candidacies who said they were relieved not to have me in the race.

As I watch my incredibly capable colleagues who are now running for president, I have no regrets about my own decision. Nor do I have any doubt that any number of them could win the election. If the two years of the 107th Congress taught us anything, it was that there is no way to predict what unimaginable events lie just around the corner—events of such magnitude that they completely reshape the landscape of our lives.

As for me, I've gone back to work in the 108th Congress. We are continuing to deal with issues that will shape the face of America for generations to come, and I find that deeply rewarding. I also look forward to those trips through South Dakota that I take alone, with no schedule and no staff, where I talk with our people about the issues affecting their everyday lives.

I have to say that I often sit in my office and reflect on all that happened between the election of 2000 and the election of 2002, and I realize that it is unlikely the events of those two years will ever be repeated. In many ways, that's a good thing.

When a newly elected member first arrives in the Senate, he or she is given a number that correlates with that person's place in the line of all senators who have ever served in this chamber since the Senate was created. There have been 1,875. Robert Morris and William Maclay of Pennsylvania are considered to be numbers 1 and 2, because Pennsylvania was the first state to actually elect its senators. The first group of twelve senators arrived at the same time: April 6, 1789. When I first arrived, I was both amazed and delighted at the significance of the number I was given: 1,776, the year the American colonies declared their independence from Britain.

I think historians who have the luxury of time and perspective will look back and see *these* as revolutionary times. As a nation, we are making monumental decisions about our very identity as a society and role on this planet—decisions that will affect our citizens and the entire world for many years to come.

Will we use our incredible might as a force just for vengeance and protection against those who seek our destruction, or will we also use it as a force for progress in the world?

Will we define strength solely in terms of sheer military might, or will we recognize that true strength embraces the qualities of wisdom, compassion, tolerance, and cooperation, not just among ourselves, but with our neighbors throughout the world?

Will we honor the uniquely American ideal that we make our nation better for each successive generation, or will we forfeit the promise of our future for the rewards of the moment?

Everything we do in the Senate in the coming days, weeks, and months will, in ways large and small, help lead us toward an answer to those questions.

On my last day as majority leader, November 22, 2002, I sat in my historic leadership office just across the hall from the Senate floor, with the drawer from my Senate floor desk in front of me. Dick Baker, the Senate historian, had removed the Plexiglas from its bottom, revealing the carved signatures of the men who had sat at that desk before me. Joe Robinson, Lyndon Johnson, Mike Mansfield, George Mitchell. It was time for me to sign my name alongside theirs: "Thomas Daschle, 2001–2002."

As I did so, I was careful to leave a little room beside those dates should I have the privilege of being majority leader again. After all, if those two years taught me one thing, it is that nothing is predictable. And I can say nothing with more certainty than those years—and all that happened during them—were, indeed, like no other time.

End of Epilogue

Acknowledgments ⟩ *goes to p. 279*

The writing of this book has been every bit as enjoyable an experience as I hoped it would be. No one deserves more of my gratitude for getting to this point than my wife, Linda, who has been the source of my strength, determination, and many of my ideas. Her role here is a metaphor for her role in the rest of my life. As with everything I do, she listened, advised, tolerated, and humored me from beginning to end.

I must also thank and acknowledge my mother and the rest of my special family—Kelly, Eric, Nathan, Jill, and Lindsay—for their love and encouragement over the course of this project, just as they have provided it so generously over all the years of my public life. Whatever success I have enjoyed is due in large measure to them. As one of my invaluable editors, the results of Kelly's wise advice can be seen on virtually every page. I also want to mention my grandchildren Henry and Ava, who may be too young to know it, but who provide me with continuing inspiration to do the work I do.

Of course, this book may not have been written at all were it not for the extraordinary ideas, direction, and writing of my partner in this project, Michael D'Orso. Choosing to work with Mike was one of the best decisions I made. Long before I met him, I was one of his biggest fans, having had the good fortune to read many of his earlier books. Working with Mike has been a remarkable learning experience and a sheer joy. We have gone from being writing partners to friends. It is a friendship that I treasure.

Another friend whose early support and assistance was vital is Bob Barnett. I don't know how he decides whose projects he chooses to support, given the scores of now-famous authors who have come to him for help. But I am indebted to him for choosing mine as one, and for his incredibly helpful guidance and advice from the early stages of this project through to its publication. It just wouldn't have happened without him.

I also want to thank David Black for his help in creating the opportunity for Mike and me to begin our work together. I am most grateful to him.

I owe a big debt of gratitude to my editor, Doug Pepper, whose insights, judgment, and professionalism have made *Like No Other Time* as good as it can be and have made the writing of it an experience that I will always remember fondly. That can also be said of Steve Ross, the publisher of Crown, who ably guided me through the creation, publishing, and marketing of this book.

Jeff Nussbaum has been invaluable to me as well. As a very gifted speechwriter, Jeff has helped me shape my words in speeches for some time. I have now learned that he is just as able to help shape the written words of a book. I have been very fortunate to have the benefit of Jeff's friendship and his genius, and I can only hope that it continues for a long time to come.

There is one person for whom I am particularly grateful, not only because of his tremendous help with this project, but because of the extraordinary partner that he has been to me for twenty years in our work in public service. Pete Rouse, my chief of staff and very special friend, is someone I have turned to at every critical juncture in my career, from running for the Senate to running for Democratic leader to considering my candidacy for president to, in recent months, putting together a campaign for re-election to the Senate. It should be no surprise that I turned to Pete for his wisdom and advice with this project as well. His remarkably good judgment and keen eye in guiding me through these pages were absolutely invaluable.

I happen to think that I have the very best staff on Capitol Hill. Their willingness to take their own time to help accurately reconstruct these two years proves it to me once more. I want to thank each of them for their loyalty, work, and continued dedication to public service. Laura Petrou, my administrative assistant, is a fabulous editor and was particularly helpful in assembling our account of the anthrax attack. Special recognition and thanks must also go to Amber Danter, Michele Ballantyne, Jay Carson, Mark Childress, Randy DeValk, Daniel Franklin, Nancy Erickson, Kelly Fado, Grant Leslie, Denis McDonough, Tim Mitrovich, Marty Paone, Mark Patterson, Dan Pfeiffer, Molly Rowley, Darcell Savage, Ranit Schmelzer, Michelle Singer, and Jeri Thomson.

Al Lenhardt, Dr. John Eisold, Dr. Greg Martin, Richard Rupert, Dick Baker, and Don Ritchie were so very helpful throughout the research for this book. I am deeply grateful to them for their patience, their help, and their memories.

I also want to thank Deputy Chief James Rohan and Public Information Officer Jessica Gissubel of the Capitol Police, as well as Mike DiSilvestro of the Office of Senate Security, for helping to ensure that my descriptions of the Senate's security apparatus as it dealt with unprecedented challenges are accurate.

And I would like to mention the photographers who contributed their work to this book—Mike Albans, P. F. Bentley, Stephen Crowley, Val Hoeppner, Justin Lane, C. Stephen Payne, Callie Shell, and Vyto Starinskas. Many of the images in this book have never been seen publicly before, and I'm grateful that these artists have allowed me to share them here.

Obviously this book could not have been written at all had I not had the good fortune to be elected by the wonderful people of my state of South Dakota. I am deeply grateful to them and I thank them for having confidence in me and for sending me to the United States House of Representatives and the United States Senate in seven elections over the past twenty-five years.

I also wish to thank my colleagues in the United States Senate. I especially thank the members of my Senate Democratic caucus for giving me the privilege of being their leader these past nine years. They have been the best years of my life.

Finally, I wish to thank Deborah Lattimore and her team of crack transcribers, who turned hours of conversation between Michael D'Orso and me into words we could work with in writing each page of this book.

Teddy Roosevelt was right. He once said, "Far and away the best prize that life offers is the chance to work hard at work worth doing." Throughout my life I have always felt that my family, my staff, and I have worked hard on many things. That is true of this book as well. The hard work that went into it, on so many people's part, has been a gift, and I hope the conclusion will be that it was truly work worth doing.

End of acknowledgments

Index goes to pg. 292... = 12 pgs...

-A-

-A-

About the Author

TOM DASCHLE was born in Aberdeen, South Dakota, where he grew up as the eldest of four brothers. He became the first person in his family to graduate from college when he earned a degree from South Dakota State University in 1969. Following college, Daschle enlisted in the Air Force and served as an intelligence officer. In 1978, South Dakotans elected him to the United States House of Representatives and eight years later sent him to the U.S. Senate. In 1994, Daschle's colleagues elected him Senate Democratic leader, marking the quickest ascent to the post since that of Lyndon Johnson. Vermont senator Jim Jeffords's historic departure from the Republican Party in 2001 made Daschle the majority leader of the Senate. He returned to his position of minority leader following the 2002 elections, when Republicans regained control of the Senate. He is married to Linda Hall Daschle and has three children and two grandchildren.